Lion
For A Day

The Life and Times of War
Hero and Olympic Medallist
Anton Hegarty

Malcolm McCausland

authorHOUSE®

AuthorHouse™ UK
1663 Liberty Drive
Bloomington, IN 47403 USA
www.authorhouse.co.uk
Phone: UK TFN: 0800 0148641 (Toll Free inside the UK)
*   UK Local: 02036 956322 (+44 20 3695 6322 from outside the UK)*

© 2020 Malcolm McCausland. All rights reserved.

Front Cover painting by John B Vallely

No part of this book may be reproduced, stored in a retrieval system, or transmitted by any means without the written permission of the author.

Published by AuthorHouse 09/18/2020

ISBN: 978-1-7283-5672-3 (sc)
ISBN: 978-1-7283-5671-6 (e)

Print information available on the last page.

Any people depicted in stock imagery provided by Getty Images are models, and such images are being used for illustrative purposes only. Certain stock imagery © Getty Images.

This book is printed on acid-free paper.

Because of the dynamic nature of the Internet, any web addresses or links contained in this book may have changed since publication and may no longer be valid. The views expressed in this work are solely those of the author and do not necessarily reflect the views of the publisher, and the publisher hereby disclaims any responsibility for them.

For Ryan

INTRODUCTION

To be forgotten is to die twice.
—Paul Ricoeur

I have been involved in athletics all my life as an athlete, coach, official and for the past 20 years as correspondent of *The Irish News* in Belfast.

It came as some surprise to me about a decade or so ago when I learned that an athlete who came from the city, in which I have lived half my life, had won an Olympic medal but I had not heard of him.

Furthermore, he was not included in the official list of Irishmen who had competed in the Olympic Games from 1896 until the then present day. Thankfully that omission has been put right but little is known of the life and times of Anton Hegarty even by relations in his native city, much less in the wider world.

Through extensive research, both by myself and my brother Adrian McCausland, we have been able to retrace the steps of a remarkable man who lived through the turbulent upheavals of the early twentieth century.

He was born in a poor quarter of Londonderry, more familiarly known as Derry in some circles, a seaport in the northwest of Ireland. It was a city with a history of conflict that arguably exists right down to the present time. He was born into a Catholic family which meant he started life disadvantaged in terms of social status, educational opportunities and employment possibilities.

A Protestant minority had ruled the City for centuries with Catholics regarded as second class citizens. Most of the businesses in the Londonderry were owned by Protestants who favoured their co-religionists when it came to handing out jobs.

To escape a lifetime of employment, he joined the British army in his teenage years like many other young Catholics. In doing so he was following in the footsteps of thousands of Irishmen who served with distinction in Irish regiments such as the Inniskilling Fusiliers, the Connaught Rangers and Munster Fusiliers.

However, with the approach of the First World War and the Easter Rising, attitudes among the Catholic population changed and instead of receiving a hero's welcome on their return from the killing fields of France and Gallipoli, they were given a cold shoulder by family and friends.

I have written this book including chapters to contemporise events for the reader alongside what would have been Anton's personal recollections of his experiences. These hopefully throw more light on matters currently in focus such as the role of the British in India.

In this I have relied heavily on a contemporary account of serving in the British army in India described by Richard Holmes in his book *Sahib* and *Old Soldier Sahib* by Frank Richards. More contemporary accounts such as *India* by John Keay, *Empire* by Jeremy Paxman and the excellent Inglorious *Empire by Shashi Tharoor* educated me further.

In relation to Gallipoli, no book came near Alan Moorehead's eponymous account that dealt in detail with lead up to and execution of possibly the most foolhardy episode in British military history. Unfortunately, it was poor soldiers like Anton and not the politicians back in London who had to suffer the consequences of what proved to be a debacle.

The people at the Inniskillings Fusiliers' museum were more than helpful in providing details of Anton's involvement in France during WW1. He was sent home twice with shellshock which in today's terms would be described as Post Traumatic Stress Disorder (PTSD). This was common at the time and diagnosed as neurasthenia, but medics were at a loss how to treat it.

That meant that men came home with the condition untreated. Many self-medicated on alcohol but significant numbers suicided years later for no reason apparent at the time. There is no evidence that Anton suffered long term damage with his running maybe contributing to the healing process.

He then got caught up in an internecine war between Catholics and Protestants on his return to Derry after WW1. Living in the Catholic quarter, he would have had to take sides no matter how much he wished to stay on the side-line.

It was probably for this reason, he seems to have packed his bags at the end of June 1920 and left for England. The fact that the shipyard was about to be run down no doubt contributed to his decision.

How he met his sweetheart, Gertie, was a difficult question to answer for my brother and myself. Finally, finally we resolved that it could only have happened when the Inniskillings were billeted out in Rugby. That meant they corresponded for over five years before they were married.

The 1920 Olympics were an interesting backcloth to his greatest moment in athletics. The characters he would have met and run against in Antwerp are still legendary in the sport.

I must thank Noel Hegarty, Anton's great nephew, and Michael O'Dwyer for their input at the start of my long journey to uncovering this story. More recently thanks are due to Hugo Hegarty for introducing me to Anton's nephew, Willie Hegarty, who is well into his nineties but can still tell a story or two.

Finally, I must express my gratitude to Adrian, not just for the research, but for his valued feedback and suggestions at every point of writing this book.

Malcolm McCausland

CHAPTER 1

THE ARRIVAL

Maybe this isn't home, nor ever was—maybe home is where I have to go tonight. Home is the place where when you go there, you have to finally face the thing in the dark.

—Stephen King

Figure 1: Nailors Row at the turn of the 20th century. The street is no more, demolished and cleared away as part of urban regeneration. The photo shows the plinth of Walker's Column which was blown up by Republicans in 1973 : Photo: Unkown

Anthony Francis Hegarty arrived in this world on 14 December 1892 at 36 Nailors Row, Londonderry, a street that hugged Derry's historic walls and faced down a steep slope into the Bogside district. It was almost completely demolished as part of an urban regeneration of the area some years ago. A small part adjoining Bishop Gate still remains and has been used recently on several occasions as a filming location for the Channel 4 series *Derry Girls*.

It comprised a poor level of housing, with landlords charging exorbitant rents and usually more than one family occupying each dwelling. The street was so-called because that was where the nails came from for the now-defunct shipbuilding industry in the city.

Anton was the tenth of twelve children born to John Hegarty and his wife, Isabella (née O'Neill), of whom four died in childhood. The couple had married in St Columba's Church Long Tower, a Catholic chapel in the city, on 16 May 1878. John was described as a "butler of City Hotel, Derry," while Bella was a factory girl of the nearby Fountain Street, which was regarded as a Protestant enclave by the Nationalist community into which John had been born. Anton's paternal grandfather, James Hegarty, had been a saddler, and John O'Neill, his maternal grandfather, a cooper.

John and Bella's first child, Mary Ann, was born on 28 February 1879 at 30 Fountain Street, where the couple was presumably lodging with Isabella's parents. With rented accommodation being in such short supply and relatively expensive, many young couples were forced to do this. James

(1880–1885; bronchitis), John (b. 1882), David (b. 1883), Ellen (1884–1885; measles and tuberculosis), Margaret (1886–1887; measles and bronchitis), Joseph (b. 1887), William (b. 1888), and Catherine (b. 1890) arrived in fairly regular intervals until it was Anton's turn in 1892. Hugh (1895) and Margaret Josephine, who died in infancy from unspecified causes, came a little later in 1896.

Derry had been rebuilt in the eighteenth century and prosperous merchants occupied its fine Georgian houses in places, such as Clarendon Street, Lawrence Hill, and Crawford Square. Many of these still survive today. However, the Hegarty family lived in fairly cramped and squalid conditions, a common feature in the city at the time.

Overcrowding, whilst not confined to the Catholic community, was endemic, as was the poor standard of the housing in terms of lacking both running water and sanitation. This led to all sorts of health problems, not least bronchitis, asthma, and other respiratory diseases. In many instances, what would have appeared initially to be an innocuous chest infection brought about by cold and damp conditions rapidly developed into pneumonia, which in an age before antibiotics, often proved fatal.

Some shipbuilding had been carried out in Derry since the eighteenth century despite the lack of adequate slipways or indeed a dry dock, but the industry reached new heights when Captain William Coppin took over the shipyard and started to build sailing vessels for the Atlantic crossing and steamers for cross-channel businesses.

In 1843, a public holiday was declared to launch the *Great Northern*, the largest screw-propulsion vessel of its kind yet built anywhere in the world. However, its anticipated sale to the government never materialised and Coppin had to sell it off in London at a huge loss. Undeterred, he returned to Derry and set about building a similar ship but suffered the misfortune of the ship burning when ready to be launched.

This second setback forced Coppin out of the shipbuilding business, and it was not until 1882 that the industry was resuscitated in Derry by W.F. Biggar, who opened his Foyle Shipyard in Pennyburn. The yard built twenty-six sailing vessels and six steamers in the ten years up to 1892 and was eventually taken over by Swan Hunter in 1912. It continued to flourish in a modest fashion but closed in the 1920s, was briefly resuscitated during World War II, and disappeared once again in peacetime.

Many skilled workers were brought over from Scotland, and the shipyard employed over four hundred people when Anton came into the world. Streets named Glasgow Terrace, Argyle Street, and Argyle Terrace are all situated close by to Nailors Row and bear evidence of the influx of Scots, while the district is still known to this day as the Scotch Quarter.

During the eighteenth and nineteenth centuries, Derry became an important departure port for emigrants heading to America and Canada in search of new lives. Many towns, particularly in New England, were named Derry or Londonderry. In New Hampshire, the towns of those names, which were founded by Ulster-Scots settlers, lie on opposite sides of Interstate 93, only a few miles apart. Together they constitute a large part of Rockingham County.

The local papers in Derry, at the time of Anton's birth, were full of advertisements for sea passages to many cities in North America, offering a better life to those brave enough, or in many cases desperate enough, to make the journey.

The shipping trade was intricately linked to emigration, and Derry's location made it an important final stop-off point to the United States and Canada. Initially, at the end of the eighteenth century, it was largely Ulster-Scots from the Presbyterian churches who made the exodus westward. From the mid-1840s onwards, the flow of emigrants increased and was mainly made up of Catholics fleeing to the New World to escape the Great Famine, which followed the failure of the potato crop over several years. Derry merchants were quick to take advantage of the situation. They bought Canadian-built ships and carried outward-bound emigrants to places like St John and New Brunswick in Canada, making the return journey with cargoes of timber.

During the winter, some of these ships would go to Charleston, Savannah, and New Orleans, where they would load up with cotton destined for Liverpool and the Lancashire spinning mills. Having traversed the Atlantic in treacherous winter storms, they were then ready for the lucrative annual wave of springtime emigrations. Later, the trade expanded to cities on the eastern seaboard, particularly Philadelphia. One company, J. & J.L. Cooke, sent eight ships from Londonderry port in the spring of 1847 with a grand total of 1,197 passengers on board. Travel by rail and ferry was also widely offered to just about any town or city "across the water" in Britain.

Odds were heavily in favour of a young man like Anton following the path taken by so many Derry men and women at that time. Certainly, he could not have imagined just where his travels would take him in the first three decades of his life.

Meantime, he had arrived in a violent society, if that week's contemporary proceedings at the Winter Assizes of the Crown Court in Belfast are anything to go by. His Lordship, Justice Gibson, heard four cases for the county of Londonderry, including one where a man called James McGeown was accused of murdering his wife while, as he claimed, under the influence of alcohol. She had died of erysipelas, a skin infection, sometime after injuries had been inflicted on her by McGeown.

Another concerned a man called John Boyle, who had also allegedly killed his wife. Again, it was said to be under the influence of drink. Boyle was found guilty, and Judge Gibson appointed the place of execution to be the Derry Prison. The date of the hanging was set for Friday, 6 January 1893, just days after Anton's baptism.

There were obviously religious tensions at the time. An example is of a man named McSwiggin, whose original charge of manslaughter was subsequently reduced by the Crown to assault. The allegation against him was that, while driving a jaunting car, a light, two-wheeled, horse-drawn vehicle used in Ireland at the time, he jumped down from the vehicle to accost a young man who was seemingly standing innocently by the side of the road with his sister. McSwiggin accused the youth of being the son of an Orangeman and proceeded to beat him about the head and body. The boy did not appear to suffer any serious injury and went back to school at Foyle College but died six weeks later. The medical evidence was not conclusive as to whether the beating was the cause of his death. For that reason, the authorities did not proceed with the manslaughter charge.

There were also many instances of cattle rustling, which seemed to be particularly rife at the time.

Sectarian tension was also evident on the local political stage. Many Protestants and Catholics saw the Derry parliamentary constituency as the most critical in Ulster. Both sides had developed advanced political machines to maximise their respective votes in advance of the 1886 General Election, which saw Nationalists take the seat by a narrow margin.

The opposing factions continued to be controlled by traditional influences. In the case of the Protestants, it was the aristocratic Hamilton family, with the Earl of Abercorn at its head, while the clergy were firmly in charge of the Catholic and Nationalist community. Their hold had been strengthened by the demise of Charles Stewart Parnell from national politics. Parnell had been born into a powerful Anglo Irish, Protestant, landowning family but was a forceful proponent of land reform.

He had founded the Irish National Land League in 1879 and became leader of the Home Rule League, operating independently of the Liberals. He won influence by his astute political nous and adroit use of parliamentary procedure. Parnell was imprisoned in Kilmainham Gaol in 1882 but released when he renounced violent extra-parliamentary action. The same year, he reformed the Home Rule League as the Irish Parliamentary Party, which he controlled minutely as Britain's first disciplined democratic party.

It held the balance of power in the hung Parliament of 1885, forcing the English prime minister, William Gladstone, to pass the first Home Rule Act in 1886. Parnell's reputation reached its zenith in 1889–90 when letters published in *The Times* linking him to the Phoenix Park killings of 1882 were shown to have been forged.

Unfortunately for the advocates of home rule, his Irish Parliamentary Party split in 1890 after the discovery by the general public of Parnell's adulterous love affair with a married woman, Katie O'Shea. She was an Englishwoman of aristocratic background, and her ten-year affair with Parnell led to his very messy divorce before the couple could marry. When the affair became public knowledge, many English Liberals refused to work with Parnell, and it prompted strong opposition from Catholic bishops for obvious moral reasons. Regarded as one of the greatest parliamentarians, Parnell headed a small minority faction until his death in 1891 at just 45 years of age. Many believe that, but for his affair, he could have delivered home rule for Ireland without a drop of blood being shed.

Unionists won back the parliamentary seat in Derry in 1892, only to lose it again three years later. That same year, the local corporation took a decision that was to hugely affect the city right up to the present day. After losing the parliamentary seat in 1895, there was fear that Parliament might intervene to reform the undemocratic form of local government in the city. Against a background of Nationalist disarray at Westminster, the Unionist-backed Londonderry Improvement Bill was passed, which ensured that power would remain in the hands of the minority Protestant community.

This became known as a "gerrymander," a tactic named after Elbridge Gerry, governor of Massachusetts in 1812, who contrived to ensure a majority in a district of an area in Boston by boundary manipulation. When shown on the map, the resulting voting district was compared to the shape of a mythological salamander—with gerrymander being the merger of his name and the word salamander. Gerry's contrivance ensured his Democratic-Republican party took the Essex South senatorial district.

Another decision taken at the time also has echoes right down to the present day in Derry. The support for Parnell by the Gaelic Athletic Association (GAA) after the Kitty O'Shea affair prompted the Catholic clergy in the city to change their sporting allegiance. Priests began to encourage their working-class male congregations to play soccer, and soon a professional team was formed. The club, formed as St Columb's Hall in 1890, changed its name to St Columb's Hall Celtic in 1893 and to Derry Celtic six years later. The club played at Celtic Park, which is now the Derry GAA stadium, from 1894 to 1900, before moving down the Lone Moor Road to the Brandywell from 1900 until the club was voted out of the Irish League in 1913.

As St Columb's Hall Celtic, the club reached the Irish Cup final in the 1897–98 season only to lose 2–0 to Linfield. The club entered the Irish League for the first time in 1900–01 but had a tough baptism, finishing its first season without a single win. Things improved in the next few seasons, with the club picking up its first win in the 1901–02 season and finishing in sixth place. This improved to fifth the following year, which along with the 1909–10 season was to prove its highest ever placing.

In 1913, the club was voted out of the Irish League and never again played senior soccer. Earlier, St Columb's Court Football Club from Derry was a founder member of the County Derry Football Association and joined the Irish Football Association in 1888. The team wore red shirts and played in the Irish League for one season in 1901–02 when it finished bottom but reached the semi-finals of the Irish Cup on three occasions.

Derry Olympic Football Club was another soccer team from Derry which had membership of the Irish League. It finished tenth in the only season it competed, 1892–93, but withdrew from the league at the end of that season. The city was to be without a professional team until 1929, when Derry City Football Club was formed and admitted into the Irish League.

Such was the influence of the clergy that the Derry newspapers at the time did not contain a single report of a GAA match, while the sports columns were filled with soccer at all levels. Since that time, Derry has been firmly a soccer city, and it was this background of playing "association football" in the street that enabled Anton to later to gain a place in the regimental team and to continue playing at a good local level until well into his 30s.

Local soccer in Derry could be a rough and even violent game. The local newspapers reported a match between St Columb's Court and Rosemount, who played out a friendly at the Brandywell. The contemporary report states that the weather was very severe, with spectators having the "unique sight of football by moonlight and in a snowstorm." The fact that the match was a "friendly" seemed lost on the participants, with the referee, Mr Huffington, being kept very busy. The correspondent was of the opinion that McNulty, of Rosemount, played "an exceedingly nasty game," adding "if he does not drop his present tactics, he will have them stopped for him and that very summarily." McNulty's roughhouse approach did not seem to produce the desired result for him, with St Columb's Court running out 2–0 winners.

Anton Hegarty would not have been aware that far away from Derry a movement was being formed that would arguably lead to one of the defining moments of his life. Small-scale sporting festivals had taken place in Europe throughout the nineteenth century, with many of these named after the ancient Olympic Games.

The 1870 Olympics at the Panathenaic stadium in Athens attracted a crowd of 30,000 people. This gave French teacher and historian Pierre de Coubertin the inspiration to establish a multinational and multisport event open to both males and females. De Coubertin wrote an article in *La Revue Athletique* which highlighted the games that took place each year in Much Wenlock, a rural market town in Shropshire, where the local physician, William Penny Brookes, had founded the Wenlock Olympian Games in 1850. The Wenlock festival included a number of sports, including cricket and football.

De Coubertin was almost certainly aware of the Tailteann Games in Ireland, which had been held during the last fortnight of July each year and were claimed to go back to 1600 BC. Some sources suggested the even earlier date of 1829 BC, but promotional literature for the Gaelic Athletic Association's revival of the games in 1924 claimed a later date of their foundation in 632 BC. There is evidence that the games were held between the sixth and ninth centuries right up AD 1171, when they petered out after the Norman invasion.

The Tailteann Games included many of the events now included in the modern Olympics, such as the long jump, high jump, and spear (javelin) throwing as well as running, hurling, and boxing. They also included cultural competitions, such as singing, dancing, and storytelling along with crafts competitions for artisan tradesmen. Certainly, De Coubertin included this type of activity in the initial games, suggesting he was influenced by the Irish festival.

LION FOR A DAY

Certainly, he had visited Ireland during the 1880s, by which time both the Gaelic Athletic Association and the Irish Amateur Athletics Association had been formed. He formally invited both bodies to send representatives to the meeting he proposed to organise in Paris "for the purpose of studying the question of Amateurism."

It is not known what the response of the GAA was, but IAAA honorary secretary, Edward J. (Ned) Walsh, responded in the affirmative, suggesting at least one but possibly two representatives of the association may attend. On 18 June 1894, at the Sorbonne in Paris, De Coubertin presented his plans to representatives of sporting bodies and societies from eleven countries, including two from the IAAA, though none from the GAA. The Irish attendees were Dan Bulger and Jim Magee, and their presence made the International Olympic Committee aware of the existence of the IAAA and of Irish athletics.

Following his proposal's acceptance by the congress, a date for the first modern Olympic Games was chosen. While it would have been attractive in conjunction with 1900 Universal Exposition of Paris, a six-year waiting period concerned the congress in that public interest may wane during such a long period. In the end, it was decided to hold the inaugural Games in 1896, with Athens the venue.

Athletics had the highest international profile of the sports hosted in Athens, with twelve events down for decision. A total of sixty-four athletes, all men and from ten nations, competed, and a total of twenty-five medals—twelve silver for winners, thirteen bronze for runner-up, but none for third—were awarded. All of the events except the marathon were held in the Panathinaiko Stadium, which was also the finishing point for the marathon.

The eleven-strong USA team dominated, taking nine of the twelve titles. No world records were set, in no small way as a consequence of the tight bends on the track which made fast times in the running events virtually impossible. The race that attracted the most attention was the marathon, based on the legendary exploits of Greek hero Pheidippides, who had completed a two-day run to seek Spartan help in defence of Athens against the invading Persians. The battle had taken place at Marathon, some 40 kilometres from Athens, and Pheidippides then ran back to Athens to convey news of the Greek victory only to drop dead on completion of his journey.

The home crowds had been disappointed not to see a Greek winner in the athletics stadium but were delighted that a Greek runner, Spiridon Louis, a water carrier from Maroussi, had taken the lead in the marathon. On arrival at the stadium, he was met by the Greek crown prince, who accompanied him on his final victory lap. It was the last race ever undertaken by Louis, but his victory ensured he would die a national hero.

Neither the IAAA nor the GAA sent representatives to first Games in Athens, and there was little contemporary press coverage of the Olympics in the Irish press, with the newspapers relying on fairly dry and fleshless reports from the Press Association and Reuters. The successes of one Irish-born and two Irish Americans went unnoticed. John

Pius Boland, of the Boland's Bakery family, was the winner of both singles and doubles tennis competitions. Boland attended at the invitation of a Greek friend and fellow archaeology enthusiast, Konstantinos Manos. Despite not even being close to Ireland's best tennis player, he won the doubles with a German 800-metre runner called Friedrich Traun, before beating a Greek, Dionysios Kasdaglis, in the singles. Ironically, it had been on the suggestion of Kasdaglis that Boland had entered the tennis competitions.

The presentation ceremony triggered a question of identity that was to rear its head from that time forward. Boland was not a staunch Irish Nationalist and was representing Great Britain at the Games. He described himself as English in his own diary on a number of occasions and seemed comfortable in the company of the other English competitors, which admittedly included the Australian Edwin Flack, winner of the 800 metres and 1,500 metres. Nevertheless, when they ran up the Austrian (they mistakenly thought Traun was from Austria) flag and the Union Jack, Boland objected and asked for an Irish flag, which he explained was a golden harp on a green background. When the officials could not locate an Irish flag, Boland was not too concerned, saying, "Never mind. The Union Jack will do to be going on with; but maybe you'd better just have a flag ready with J. P. Boland on it …"

Technically, Boland was British, as any other Irish person was in 1896, but the question of identity would be one that would feature throughout Anton Hegarty's life, resulting in two bloody conflicts in his native land during the first quarter of the twentieth century. It would not end there either, rumbling on in one manner or another right down to the present. The dichotomy of being Irish in Britain and British in Ireland would be something Anton would have to deal with in the future, and it would be 1924 before the green, white, and orange flag would be legitimately flown at an Olympic Games and Irish athletes competed as Ireland.

Boland was just one of just three competitors with strong Irish links who competed in Athens. Both of the others represented the USA, with Thomas Burke having the honour of winning the first ever race, his 100-metre heat, at the Olympics, while James Brendan Connolly lifted the first title decided, winning the hop, step, and jump and also finishing third in the long jump.

The casual nature of the competition was illustrated by Connolly, whose parents came from the Aran Islands, being allowed to take two hops and a jump. Connolly is supposed to have shouted, "Here's for the honour of County Galway!" before taking his winning leap.

Burke won the 100-metre and the 400-metre titles. He was the only reigning American champion to take part in the Athens athletics competitions. His exact Irish connections have never been confirmed, despite extensive research, and his victories were seen back in his native Boston as successes for Boston College and the city as opposed to American triumphs.

CHAPTER 2

GROWING UP
IN DERRY

*Growing up is never straightforward.
There are moments when everything
is fine, and other moments where you
realise that there are certain memories
that you'll never get back, and certain
people that are going to change, and
the hardest part is knowing that there's
nothing you can do except watch them.*

—Alden Nowlan

I remember my childhood as being tough but full of happy memories. It certainly prepared me well for what was to follow in my life. Our street was a single row of houses facing the ancient walls of Derry. Walker's Column, erected in memory of George Walker, who had been governor of the city during the siege, dominated the view.

We used to have races to the base of the column and back to the top of the street at Butchers Gate. Later, we moved to Donegal Place, right in the heart of the Bogside and fitted snugly between Celtic Park and the Brandywell. When I was only 4, we had an addition to the family when my little sister Maggie was born to complete our family. But unfortunately, she did not live that long. Hugh arrived the following year to complete the clan which now comprised eight of us: six boys and two girls.

I recall us being content and well-fed, despite enduring what were, on reflection, relatively hard times, with high rates of unemployment, poor housing, and a religious tension that I only realised later was ever-present. As a child, you do not notice these things, and my earliest memories were of playing with my brothers and sisters as well as the other children in the street. Most of our games involved running and jumping, and it was from these I probably developed football skills and athletic ability, which shaped most of my life.

When I was 5, it was my turn to join the short trek down Bishop Street and turn left for the Christian Brothers School. It was an even shorter journey after we moved to the Brandywell area. The school had been founded by a Brother Larkin in 1854 and had an initial roll of 290 boys. This number continued to grow until there were well over four hundred by the time I started.

A strict and, at times, brutal regime was applied by the brothers, and any sign of slowness or disobedience was met with the dreaded strap. We were beaten for the most trivial of reasons, and some of the brothers seemed to take pleasure in handing out pain for the least excuse, using a leather strap with a strip of lead sewn up the middle to give it rigidity.

Most carried this tucked into the belt, securing their black cassock like a clerical-collared, gunslinger in the Wild West.

I was relatively quick to learn, but as I was considered one of the best footballers, I avoided the harshest of punishments meted out by the brothers. Although they could be cruel at times, a few of the brothers had a great love of sport, particularly athletics and Gaelic games, which went against the tide in a city obsessed with association football.

They often related to us things that were going on in the sporting world, opening us up to a whole new vista on life. Brother O'Connell spoke highly of men like Michael Cusack and Maurice Davin, who he said had founded the Gaelic Athletic Association and would never be forgotten as long as there was a Gael alive in Ireland.

He would be disparaging about soccer, saying it was an "English invention," and sometimes would spend a whole class telling us about great Irish athletes. He related tales about people like Peter O'Connor, who had won gold and silver medals at the Olympics and who had shinned up a pole to put an Irish flag at the top of it during the presentation ceremony.

He had a particular admiration for O'Connor because he had grown up in the same Wicklow village. I do not think they ever met because the brother had left home before O'Connor had moved there from Cumberland where he was born. One boy foolishly suggested that that made O'Connor English, which got him six of the best from

Brother O'Connell, who was not generally given to dishing out on-the-spot punishments.

I remember two events that seemed to enthral the brother at the time and have stayed in my memory to this day. One of these was a race from Belfast to Lurgan, the "Go as You Please" as it was called. This took place in 1907, when I was not yet 15 and was in my final year at the CBS. I had watched sports at the Brandywell stadium and had always been in awe of the athletes and had even run in a few underage races at local sports. These were generally over 100 yards or less, and I never managed to feature at the front.

The brother said that the public's imagination was captured by the huge prizes of cash and material goods offered for the winner as well as the leader at intermediate points of what was originally to be 24 and three quarters of a mile route. To avoid the hills between Dromore and Lurgan, a detour through Waringstown was added, bringing the distance up to 26 and a half miles.

According to him, over one hundred prizes were up for grabs, many of which were incredible. Apart from the substantial cash amounts, there were clocks, gold medals, handmade boots, hats, and even cases of tonic water, cigarettes, and tobacco.

I made sure that my father got a copy of the *Belfast Telegraph* to read the full details. It reported that people wanting to see the start of the race brought Belfast to a standstill, and when the high sheriff dropped the flag to set 401 runners on their way from the centre of the city, it went on to describe how a

Belfast butcher called Felix Furlonger set off at a sedate pace and was some distance behind the early leaders as they left the city along the Balmoral Road.

According to the *Telegraph,* if the crowd in Belfast at the start was excited, it was delirious in Lurgan as rain lashed down while they awaited the arrival of the first runner. Furlonger, headed by a posse of cyclists, arrived looking strong and stopped the watch at three hours, eight minutes and two and one-fifths seconds. The second-placed runner, Thomas McCullough, arrived five minutes later, with Corporal Sparkes holding on for third a further three minutes back.

My interest in running continued into the following year when London hosted the 1908 Olympics. The newspapers reported that the marathon provided the most famous incident of the Games. Italian Dorando Pietri, like Furlonger, started cautiously but came through the field in the second half of the race to put himself into second position by the 20-mile mark, four minutes behind South African Charles Hefferon.

Learning that Hefferon was suffering, Pietri further increased his pace, overtaking him at the 24-mile mark. He may well have been too rash because with little over a mile to run, Pietri started to pay for his efforts; appearing disorientated, he took the wrong route on entering the stadium.

He was redirected by stewards but fell to the ground for the first time, managing to get up with their help in front of 75,000 spectators. He fell four more times, and each time the stewards helped him up, before he managed to finish the race totally exhausted in first place.

It took him ten minutes to cover the last 385 yards out of his total time of 2:54:46. The American team immediately lodged a complaint against the Pietri on account of the assistance received from the officials. The complaint was accepted and Pietri was disqualified and removed from the final standings of the race. That meant that the second-placer, Johnny Hayes from Nenagh in County Tipperary, running in the colours of the United States, was made champion. Ireland was not permitted to compete in its own right at the time as it was not an independent country.

We were not taught much of the history of our own city, and I think this was the case in most, if not all, of the Catholic schools. I knew little, for example, of the Siege of Derry, despite the descendants of the Apprentice Boys, who shut the gates in 1688, still living in the city.

I was aware of two dates when there were great Protestant celebrations: 12 July to mark the victory of Prince William at the Battle of the Boyne and 18 December when the thirteen Apprentice Boys shut the gates in the face of the Catholic forces of King James II coming to take possession of Derry.

On the former date, crowds arrived in the city from all parts of Ireland and, dressed in military uniforms, marched to the accompaniment of their bands around the town in triumphalism. In 1905, a crowd broke away from the main parade and attacked the houses in my old street, only adding to the enmity between the two communities that resulted in a month or more of violence every year. It also added to the alienation of the Catholic community, who felt excluded from these celebrations.

The other date, 18 December, known as "Lundy's Day," centred on the burning of an eighteen-foot effigy of Colonel Robert Lundy, governor of Derry during the siege, who was regarded by the Protestant people as a traitor to their cause. They believed him to have "sold the keys of Derry for a bap" when he tried to negotiate surrender terms and had to flee the city through an orchard just outside the city walls.

The first red and leaping flames from the effigy was the signal to all Catholics in the vicinity to set fire to their chimneys, sending huge amounts of soot in the direction of the walls to settle on the clothes of those celebrating. Occasionally there would be a change of wind direction and the smoke would blow back and drift across the houses of the Catholics, much to the satisfaction of the Protestants.

However, there were occasions when both communities came together. I could not have been more than 10 or 11 years of age when the whole city turned out to welcome home the Royal Inniskilling Fusiliers from the Boer War in South Africa. The Royal Inniskilling Fusiliers, a regiment originally formed in 1689, had seen service at the contentious Battle of the Boyne, where Prince William of Orange had defeated the forces of James II.

They had also been present at Namur in France during the Nine Years War and at the Battle of Culloden, the Anglo-Spanish War in the Caribbean, the American War of

Independence, Waterloo, and the Peninsular War, amongst others.

Carlisle Bridge was filled to overflowing as the soldiers came marching across in advance of a service in St. Columb's Cathedral. They then returned to their barracks in Ebrington, just over the bridge in the Waterside, or east side, of the city. Although the Waterside was a part of our city, we rarely, if ever, went over there as it was considered to be Protestant territory and consequently not a safe place for a young Catholic. Some people even went further and suggested the Watersiders spoke with a different accent from us.

You could not help but be thrilled by the spectacle, and we played soldiers in the street for months afterwards. We marched along in time to an improvised drumbeat on the lid of a biscuit tin "borrowed" from someone's kitchen. It was the first time that being a soldier had appealed to me and became a memory that stayed in my subconscious.

The Catholic community was friendly to the British military at the time, and many from the community signed to escape unemployment. Others were simply attracted by the prospect of travelling to exotic places they had only read about or heard of from family and friends who had joined up before them. That attraction might diminish as events evolved in the next two decades.

The second example of the two communities coming together was when the Guildhall was burned to the ground on 19 April 1908. When we heard what was happening, we all rushed from wherever we were to catch sight of the building in flames. A fire brigade came, but they could not get it to work for some minutes, by which time the flames, aided by a strong wind, had gotten hold of the building.

Soldiers came, but even with their assistance, it was a lost cause. Londonderry Corporation had a lot to answer for, apart from an inefficient fire brigade. They failed to tackle a lot of the city's population, especially Catholics, living in squalid and overcrowded conditions, despite there being a glut of accommodation and many houses standing empty.

Sanitation and basic facilities such as running water were inadequate or non-existent. The austerity of the corporation rebounded spectacularly on this occasion when the lack of an adequate water supply or fire brigade led to the Guildhall's destruction. The home of the corporation had only been opened in 1890, and if there was ever an example of what my mother used to call "penny wise, pound foolish," this was it.

Our house in Nailors Row was typical of the housing in the city. It was cramped with such a large family. The situation improved a little when we had an extra bedroom in Donegal Place. All of the boys slept in one large bed with half of us with our heads at the top and the other half at the bottom. This was fine when we were all young, but as we grew older, our feet started to reach the face of the brother opposite you in the bed, which led to more than one scuffle at bedtime.

The girls had a separate bedroom, but with there not being as many of them, they had more space than us. The youngest children slept with our mother and father until they got too old and were ejected to either the boys' bedroom or the girls', depending on their gender.

The family home was damp, even in the driest times of the year, and ice formed inside the bedroom windows during the winter. Because of the cramped conditions of the housing and the poor heating, many children in the Bogside developed asthma or bronchitis, and there was hardly a day between November and April that someone in our house did not have a cough of some kind.

Perhaps the worst of us was my father, who used to have regular coughing attacks and frequently brought up a mixture of blood and mucous. We thought nothing of this at the time, but we did notice that his coughing became more frequent and lasted longer each winter as the years went by. These coughing attacks did not stop him smoking his favourite brand of cigarettes called Woodbines. He insisted the cigarettes helped his cough, and we knew no better but to take his word for it.

Almost as bad as the dampness were the rats. They did not quite fight the dogs and kill the cats, but they were everywhere. They terrified the children, and if they got into your attic or under the floorboards, it was impossible to get to sleep at night with their noise. Frequently, people moved to a new house when the infestation got out of hand, and there were apocryphal tales of rats biting babies in their cribs.

Certainly, food could not be left uncovered, and there was special vigilance during the autumn as it was believed the

LION FOR A DAY

rats came in from the fields looking for warm cover for the winter. Doors and windows were not left open so as to facilitate an easy entry, but they always seemed to get in anyway.

The corporation employed a rat-catcher who would come and put down rat poison, but they said he killed more dogs than rats. He would block any entry holes he could find on the outside of the house and tar over them. He said they did not like tar, but they still kept coming. The Brandywell area where we lived was reputedly one of the worst areas because of its closeness to the river and the country.

Our staple diet consisted of potatoes— spuds or "purties" as we called them. These were mostly served in their jackets, and we ate them with butter. On special days, we had mince, which was fried or cooked in a stew along with whatever vegetable was available at the time of year—onions, cabbages, and turnips being the most common. One of the most common meals was mince fried with onions and served with boiled spuds. Sometimes our mother fried the boiled spuds in the fat left from the mince, and we saw this as a special treat. Occasionally we had black puddings, with a shop on Creggan Road making a special variety that was much sought after throughout the city.

We did not wear shoes a lot of the year. This toughened up our feet on the hard cobblestones of the streets, and it was only when we were going to school in September that we would put on our boots for the winter. These were hand-me-downs, with only those at the top end of the chain getting a new pair. In truth, some of these "new" boots were second-hand, bought in one of the many small shops in Waterloo Street that sold used footwear and clothing to those who could afford them.

My father was, by his own description, a cattle dealer but always seemed to have a horse or two about him as well. He was a wheeler-dealer and seemed to have his finger in more than one pie. Whatever he did, he kept us fed and still had enough left over for a drink in the local bars, where he seemed to conduct a lot of his business.

But life was a struggle for many, as some had unusual ways of making an extra few bobs, such as our neighbour who kept pigs in his backyard, where he fed them on what we called "brock." This was the leftover food he collected two or three times a week from homes around the area. It was gathered into a huge tin bucket on the back of a cart drawn by a donkey that every so often dug its heels in and refused to move. A pantomime ensued, with our neighbour tugging and pulling the donkey to encourage him to start. The harder he pushed and pulled the donkey, the more steadfastly it stood its ground. Eventually, when forceful means were exhausted, the donkey would succumb to bribery in the form of a treat such, as a carrot or an apple.

Then one Tuesday night—7 May 1907—when we had just gone to bed, a knock came to the door to inform us that our father had collapsed and died from a heart attack in the bar at the end of Butcher Street. It was said to have been provoked by his bronchitis, which was no surprise to us given his coughing, but we were all shocked to lose him so suddenly at just 47.

He was in the company of our aunt, Mary Anne McCafferty, at the time, and she said he just passed out peacefully following one of his coughing attacks. He was brought to our house in the company of the priest. There was a woman in the district who laid out the deceased. She washed my father and dressed him in a shroud, before putting him on a bed of fresh linen. Blessed candles were lit all around the bed before the whole family and neighbours congregated for the rosary led by the priest.

We stayed up all night, as we did the following night, before burying him after requiem Mass on Thursday. Hundreds came to pay their regards and say a prayer for the repose of his soul, with everyone saying that they had never seen my father looking so well, while others remarked on how well mended he was!

The wake and funeral had a numbing effect on me. My father never had a serious illness his whole life. I'd never seen him sick in bed, yet suddenly, in the blink of an eye, he was gone and never to return.

After his death, with the elder brothers and sisters in employment, we continued to manage well for money. They had got jobs when they left school, but instead of going into the shirt factories, our girls had chosen to be hairdressers and two of my brothers became barbers. It was now my turn to find employment.

At least I was able to read and write quite well, which ran against the national trend at the time that only a small minority were regarded as literate. While the economy of

Derry was based significantly on the textile industry, this meant jobs for the women but not necessarily the men. As a consequence, for many years, women were commonly the sole wage earners, working in the shirt factories, while the men in comparison had high levels of unemployment. Although there was almost 100 per cent employment for females in Derry's shirt factories, the men of the family could be unemployed for long periods when no work was available.

The situation had been made worse for the male worker following the failed strike by the trade unions in a bitter dispute with the Londonderry and Lough Swilly Railway Company during the winter of 1903–04. The victory by the bosses led other employers to make pay cuts that resulted in increasing de-unionisation of the unskilled and a series of strikes in which workers only sought the conditions and wages elsewhere, but particularly in Belfast.

Because of the sectarian divide, there was no unified voice to demand workers' rights, despite trade unionists standing in local elections in 1896 and 1904. It was one of the few subjects on which Catholics and Protestants agreed and, on rare occasions, put forward a common voice.

The Catholic clergy had not resisted the rise of trade unionism but exercised a power over their community undreamed of on the Protestant side. It was not unusual for priests to co-operate with factory owners where they shared common interests and were able to set up clubs and societies within factories.

LION FOR A DAY

All these circumstances conspired against me getting work other than as a labourer with no job security. I was forced to take work that lasted only weeks or even days at times. If it were outside, where it was mostly, you could arrive in the morning only to be sent home on account of the weather or other reasons, and that meant no pay.

The consequence was that I was permanently short of funds, and when I did get money, I handed most of it into the house for my keep. The poor job market for men led to significant male emigration, and it was always at the back of my mind that this was a road I would have to take at some time in the future.

The triumphant return of the Inniskillings was still fresh in my mind. At the time, the Nationalist community had no antipathy to things British, even the military. Many young Catholics joined up each year. I knew a number of people, both family and older friends, who had joined up, and their tales of wars in South Africa, India, and other places were made to appear as huge adventures in the popular press and even in daily conversations. Against these dire economic circumstances, many from the Nationalist community enlisted in the British Army, where at least they were sure of being clothed and fed. For young single men, there was always the suggestion that enlistment was because they were either too lazy for work or because they had got a girl in the family way.

I had grown into a tall, skinny lad, and when I tried to join in 1910, the recruiting sergeant in Ebrington Barracks, where the Royal Inniskillings had been stationed, told me to clear off and pack twelve months of dinners into me. I took him at his word and returned a year later. This time I passed the medical in a canter, and on 27 November 1911, I was officially a soldier of the Royal Inniskilling Fusiliers. And more importantly, I was out of Derry.

I did the rounds of family and friends to wish them farewell but met with mixed reactions to my joining the British Army. Tensions were increasing at the time with a slow rise in Nationalist emotions and Irish politicians demanding home rule for the country.

For me, this was just a distraction because I was on my way to exotic places and adventure. After all, army life could not be any worse than hanging round Derry and going from job to job for poor pay. The following week, I and twenty-nine other recruits from Derry and district were taken to the St Lucia Barracks in Omagh, where we started life as Royal Inniskilling Fusiliers.

St Lucia Barracks looked cold and forbidding as we reported for training as soldiers of the First Battalion, Royal Inniskilling Fusiliers. The camp had been built in 1875, and when the Twenty-Seventh (Inniskilling) Regiment of Foot had been merged with the 108th (Madras Infantry) Regiment of Foot some six years later, it had become the depot for the Royal Inniskilling Fusiliers.

We were young men, mostly from Derry and the surrounding counties, and an officer escorted us to a large, whitewashed room where there were about twenty other recruits. A couple of what appeared old soldiers appeared from the other end of

LION FOR A DAY

the room. We learned later that they had served abroad and were known as "duty men." A corporal with sixteen years of service was in charge of us all. One of the duty men showed us how to fix our straps for drill purposes and told us what cleaning tackle we would need. He taught us how to fix our black kitbags and topcoats over the bed.

During the evening, we were taken around the grounds of the barracks, in which there were relics of former wars in which they had taken part. Our tour ended with a beer in the canteen. This led to several more, and several men got up to sing sentimental or comic songs. But when someone started on Orange songs, the corporal arrived to put an end to the session. It was just as well because we were up at 5.30 a.m. the next morning for drill. Thus commenced my life in the British Army.

For the next ten weeks, we learned to march, fire assorted weapons, throw improvised hand grenades, and generally become soldiers. Discipline and good order were drummed into us from morn till night. Although at the time we moaned and groaned, I must say that it stood us in good stead in the years that were to follow.

At the end of the ten weeks, we were pushed to the limit over a week in which we were required to march 25 miles in full battle order. Then we were tested on our ability in the use of a Lee Enfield rifle and bayonet, and this was followed by the dreaded assault course, in which "encouragement" was sometimes physical as well as verbal.

The week ended with a forced march of 10 miles in under three hours while carrying a full battle gear of pack, rifle, and sixty rounds of ammunition plus provisions for two days.

Amazingly when the passing out parade was held on the final day, the sense of pride we had in the regiment and ourselves was tremendous. Marching past the colonel as he stood on the saluting base, we felt 10 feet tall and fit as fiddles. I wondered what the Christian Brothers would have thought of me in my khaki uniform.

CHAPTER 3

THE EXPLOITATION OF INDIA

*The British conquest of India was the
invasion and destruction of a high
civilisation by a trading company
(the British East India company)
utterly without scruple or principle,
careless of art and greedy of gain, over-
running with fire and sword a country
temporarily disordered and helpless.*

—Will Durant

In 1600 the population of the Indian subcontinent was estimated at 140 million, of whom 100 million lived in the great sweep of territory between the Himalayas and the Deccan sultanates, which comprised Akbar's empire. The population of the British Isles was probably only 5 million at the time.

India was not in any way impoverished by such a large population. In fact, its strength was its abundant labour force, which generated much of the wealth of the ruling

Mughals. However, a complex system of assessment and taxation was in place, which saw the average peasant who tilled the land left with little to live on regardless of the size of the crop.

Nevertheless, industry and trade boomed thanks to the country's stability and a safe communication network of roads which are still evident today. Indian craftsmen and women turned out the finest gold and silver articles, jewellery, and textiles found anywhere in the world. Professional people abounded with an army of engineers, architects, and civil engineers engaged on massive building programmes.

Great Britain's exploitation of India began surreptitiously that year with the East India Company being incorporated by royal charter from her Majesty Queen Elizabeth I to trade in silk, spices, and other profitable Indian commodities.

In pursuit of these objectives, the company established outposts or "factories" along India's extensive coast but notably in Calcutta, Madras, and Bombay. To defend its personnel and premises by military means, it increasingly recruited soldiers. Its charter permitted it the right to "wage war" in furthering its business interests. In that way, trading posts soon became military fortifications as it expanded its commercial interests as much by conquest as trading activities.

The competing Dutch East India Company was founded two years later as other European nations set about getting in on the wealth. The French were to come a little later, but all opposition, including the Portuguese, who had been there before the British, were driven out by stealth and military might.

The EIC was assisted in its rise by the British government's supply of military and naval resources, loans from the Bank of England, changes in legislation when required, and supportive foreign policy.

Then began a sustained campaign of plundering India's riches and resources, which saw its economy fall from 27 per cent (in 1770) of the world's commerce to just 3 per cent by the time the British departed in 1947.

India enjoyed a 5 per cent share of the global trade in textiles in the early eighteenth century, but these industries were run down, with India continuing to grow cotton but mainly sending it to Britain.

This helped fuel the Industrial Revolution in Britain at the expense of decimating India's lucrative commercial activities. Indian handloom products had been in big demand throughout the world, but these were replaced by British ones, ironically produced from Indian raw materials, and exported back to India.

In the mid-eighteenth century, India's textile industry was world leader in innovation, creativity, and production, but when British traders took control, everything changed. They stopped paying for the goods in pounds sterling, opting to pay in local money extracted from Bengal, denying the native companies valuable foreign currency. This also pushed prices still lower, and they squeezed out buyers from other companies, so depressing the local market.

When the British manufacturers could not compete with Indian prices, soldiers of the East Indian Company stepped in and systematically smashed the looms of the Bengal weavers. Previously, the women had worked at home spinning and weaving while the men tilled the fields. But the removal of a substantial part of the family's traditional income threatened their existence, especially when their plight was exacerbated by droughts or other natural phenomena.

Because of over-cultivation, among other reasons, India suffered a series of serious crop failures in the late nineteenth century, leading to widespread famines which saw at least 10 million people died. Seeing famines as a threat to the stability of colonial rule, the East India Company began to concern itself with food shortages but failed to tackle the underlying causes: too many people relying on too little land, using outdated farming methods. The result was that rural poverty persisted and was a direct consequence of Britain's rapacious actions.

Textiles was just one of several Indian industries that was strangled by the British in favour of their own. India's once thriving shipbuilding industry was almost extinct by 1850 after the introduction of a series of laws by the British made it impractical to continue. The first ban came in 1813 after British shipbuilders petitioned the government and saw ships below 350 tonnes prohibited from sailing between British colonies and the UK. That immediately took 40 per cent of the Bengal boats out of the lucrative trade.

Other prohibitive laws were to follow. Earlier the company was given a monopoly on trade routes, including those formerly operated by Indian enterprises. Duties were charged on Indian merchant ships moving to and from Indian ports and not just foreign ones. The damage did not end there, with Britain seeing India as a cash cow from a taxation point of view. It was calculated that the British wrung out £18 million from India every year between 1765 and 1815. The directors of the East India Company were richer than most European kings and the company created, for the first time in Indian history, a landless peasant deprived of their only source of income aided and abetted by Britain's avaricious foreign policy.

Robert Clive, or Clive of India, was probably the most ruthless of the English adventurers. As a child and young man, he caused all sorts of trouble at a succession of schools, including setting up a protection racket among the local shopkeepers while attending Market Drayton Grammar School in Shropshire.

He captured and held a large swath of South India for the British East India Company, and the wealth that followed turned him into a multimillionaire. Hired by the company to return a second time to India, Clive secured the company's trade interests by dethroning the heir to the throne of Bengal, the richest state in India. With the monies he got in India, he was able to buy seats in the British Parliament for both himself and his family. He remains one of the most controversial figures in British military history. His achievements include establishing control over much of India, laying the foundation of the entire British Raj. It should be noted that he worked only as an agent of the East India Company and not the British government, although it was difficult ever to discern the difference between the two.

Clive was awarded an Irish peerage in 1762, being created Baron Clive of Plassey, County Clare. He bought lands in County Limerick and County Clare, giving the name Plassey to part of his lands near Limerick City. The current University of Limerick is built on the Plassey lands.

Contemporaries were especially concerned about the massive personal fortune Clive had accumulated in India. During a parliamentary enquiry in 1772, he was questioned about some of the large sums of money he had received while in the country but pointed out that he had not accepted anything that was contrary to accepted company practice.

He defended himself by stating, "I stand astonished at my own moderation," given opportunities for greater gain. The hearings did highlight the need for reform of the company, but a vote to censure Clive for his actions failed. Clive was appointed Knight Commander of the Order of the Bath and later appointed lord lieutenant of Shropshire.

Many modern historians have laid the blame on him for atrocities, high taxes, and for the forced cultivation of crops, which exacerbated the natural causes of famines. In particular, there was a great famine in Bengal between 1769 and 1773, which reduced the population of Bengal by a third.

American theologian Dr Charles Hall put it this way: "India starves that India's annual revenue may not be diminished by a dollar. Eighty per cent of the whole population has been thrown back upon the soil because England's discriminating duties have ruined practically every branch of native manufacture. We send ship loads of grain to India, but there is plenty of grain in India. The trouble is that the people have been ground down till they are too poor to buy it."

Many also believed that the activities of company officials were to blame for the famine, particularly the abuse of monopoly rights on trade and land tax. Most officials, as well as their official duties, also had side-lines which further impoverished the indigenous population.

These revelations and the subsequent debates in Parliament reduced Clive's political fortunes considerably. On 22 November 1774 Clive died, aged 49, at his Berkeley Square home in London. There was no inquest into his death, and it was variously alleged he had stabbed himself or cut his own throat with a penknife or had taken an overdose of opium. A few newspapers reported his death as due to an apoplectic fit or stroke. Others suggested it was linked to a history of depression and an opium addiction resulting from trying to minimise the pain of gallstones with the drug.

The voracious appetite of the British for colonising meant that by 1823 just about all of India was under their control, either directly or indirectly.

Some, unlike Clive, left a lasting positive legacy. One of these was Lord William Bentinck, who was appointed the first governor general of India in 1828 and continued as such until 1835. Bentinck was said to be a man of peace, discipline, and economy. He was a liberal reformist who took active part in the reform movement of England.

Lord Macauley described him flatteringly. "Bentinck infused into oriental Despotism the spirit of British freedom; who never forgot that the end of the government is the welfare of the governed." He was genuinely sympathetic towards the Indian people and to improving their lives. He started appointing Indians in company's service, a practice discontinued by Lord Cornwallis, who had a low opinion about their character, ability, and integrity.

In this way, he established a closer contact between the ruler and the ruled. Indians were appointed to the posts of deputy magistrate and deputy collector, meaning Bentinck took a giant step towards the Indianisation of the government service.

He increased the length of holdings in the North-West Frontier Province, encouraging tenants to make improvements to the land; he reorganised the judicial system in Bengal, including appointing a commissioner in each of the twenty divisions, and provided oversight of the judges; the beating of men with a whip as a punishment was ended in the Indian Army; and Persian was replaced by the local language in local courts and by English in the higher ones.

He also carried out a root-and-branch reform of the country's economics, increasing revenue and reducing expenditure, particularly on the military, where wages were reduced.

Perhaps his lasting legacy was institutionalising English as a medium of education in schools and universities, meaning for the first time there was a common language across the entire subcontinent.

Bentinck was also busy in legislating for social reform, principally the abolition of sati, whereby widows were compelled to throw themselves on the funeral pyres of their deceased husbands. Many widows died on the funeral pyre of their husbands while willingly believing this was the manner of joining him on the other side. But in many cases, the widow chose to die against her will in order to escape public criticism. In some places, the ignorant relatives forced the widows to die in order to uphold their own social prestige.

The next achievement of Bentinck was the abolition of the system of human sacrifice prevailing among hill tribes, and with the aid of his leading captain, William Sleeman, he eradicated organised thuggery carried out by a community of robber-murderers.

Raja Rammohan Ray, the great Indian reformer, and considered by many as the father of India, supported Bentinck's reforms and went to England to plead with the British government in favour of them. Bentinck held the highest rank among all the governors generals in India due to his various initiatives. His seven years rule came to be known as an "Age of Reforms." Dr Ishwari Prasad wrote, "Bentinck's glories were the glories of peace. His reign stands in sharp contrast to the years that preceded or those that followed it."

Subsequent Afghan, Sind, and Sikh wars occupied the attention of the British, but they got back on track after the appointment of Lord Dalhousie in 1848. He introduced new laws to give Hindu widows the right to remarry and to protect the inheritances of lapsed Hindus, usually converted Christians. Both impinged on traditional Indian practices but were seen as steps towards modernising and equalising the country's long-standing caste system in which an underbelly of society, the untouchables, were condemned from birth to a life of abuse and poverty.

He pressed on with major public works, roads, railways, telegraph networks, and irrigation systems. He did not allow the caste system to slow his progress, and there was a major outcry when railway carriages were brought into service that did not make provision for social exclusion of the "untouchables."

He insisted on "consolidating territories which already belong to us by taking possession of States that may lapse in the midst of them." By this he meant taking over the sovereignty of a state whose ruler was either manifestly not up to the job of ruling or died without a direct heir. This overlooked the established Indian right of a sovereign to choose his successor.

Dalhousie believed that it was the government's obligation "to take which is justly and rightly its due." It is unlikely that this would have passed the test of juris prudence, but he went on to seize seven states in as many years, greatly boosting the coffers of the East India Company. This greatly alarmed other rulers, such as the Mughal emperor who had already been demoted to king of Delhi with his successor being recognised as no more than a prince.

Never one to take a sideward glance, Dalhousie pulled off his greatest land grab on the eve of his departure from India when he annexed Awadh—or Oudh as the British called it. It was possibly the largest and probably the richest, but certainly the most loyal of all the states. Since the days of Clive, it had been the most compliant in accepting a list of territorial and financial demands from the company and supplied much of the manpower for its Bengal army. Awadh's confiscation seemed to call into question the justice and fair play on which the British prided themselves throughout the world.

It was that disregard of the local sensitivities in 1857 that led to one of the bloodiest and most controversial events in Indian history and marked a watershed in relations between the two countries. Even how it is remembered reflects this fracture in the relationship. For the British it was the "Sepoy," "Bengal," or "Indian Mutiny," but to Indians it was the "National Uprising" or the "First War of Independence." To the disinterested it was the "Great Rebellion."

Irish scholars have drawn comparison with the 1798 Rebellion, while Americans could be drawn to equate to something like the Boston Tea Party.

No single issue united the insurgents, many nursing age-old grievances that had provoked minor uprisings in the past. One thing is that the British had not learned from previous experiences and the sensitivities of the native Indians. While it is common ground that it started within the ranks of the Bengal army, it was not the first. Almost a century earlier, the company's Indian sepoys had refused orders and had been viciously executed by Hector Munro.

Now still smarting from Dalhousie's unjust annexation of Awadh, the Bengal sepoys were issued with new rifles which came with cartridges that had to be rammed down the barrel, but these had to be bitten first with the teeth. The cartridges were greased with a tallow which the sepoys came to hear included fat from both cows and pigs. The new ammunition could not have been more repugnant to the soldiers had they been smeared in excrement, with the Hindus revering cows while Muslims were paranoid of pigs. They were quickly replaced but not before the ordinary soldier interpreted the whole incident as another example of the insouciance of the British and another attempt by them to do anything to compromise the sepoys' religion and leave them open to conversion to Christianity.

It did not stop there either with rumour and counter-rumour spreading the length and breadth of volatile northern states of India. It was only a matter of time until the festering native distrust and British arrogance came together to spark a fire that would be difficult to extinguish and would affect Indo-British relations right down to the present day.

And the man who threw the match that was to light the volatile cocktail was the commanding officer at Meerut, an important garrison town about 60 kilometres from Delhi. He court-marshalled eighty-five Indian soldiers for refusing the offending cartridges and then humiliated them in front of the whole garrison. Predictably the following day, their comrades broke into the armoury and set to killing off the local European community as well as setting light to the tinder-dry huts of the camp and officers' accommodation.

The insurgents headed to Delhi, where they sought out the 82-year-old Mughal emperor Bahadur Shah II, a ruler with neither subjects nor troops. His backing for the mutiny gave it political legitimacy and triggered a number of other risings all over the country. It not only gained support from Indians in the military but also civilians who, without doubt, sought to rid their country from a foreign occupier and restore the old order in which the king of Delhi was a rightful representative. It also widened the enemy from just being the British troops but the whole establishment.

However, without any command structure, the mutiny started to disintegrate, and this allowed the British to retake Delhi, but such were the heavy losses they suffered that they thirsted for revenge. An indiscriminate pogrom of native Indians and a free hand in looting only added to the city's misery. Two of Bahadur Shah's sons and a grandson died in prison, allegedly shot while trying to escape, and the last Mughal was exiled to Rangoon, where he died a lonely death without the reverence or honour that should have been accorded his standing.

The insurgents, with inferior weapons and no structure, were incapable of holding the strongpoints north of the Narmada River. South of this, they enjoyed little support, with the Madras and Bombay armies remaining loyal to the British. The Sind in the north-west were indifferent.

Kashmir's new maharaja supported the British, and in the east, Bengal and Bihar had been taken out of the conflict by the early arrival of troops previously deployed in the Persian Gulf and China.

This meant the rebellion sunk back to where it had begun with Lucknow now replacing Delhi as the centre of the rebellion and Nana Sahib, the chosen heir of the last peshwa, replacing the Mughal as the symbolic head.

The loss of the peshwa's pension gave Nana Sahib a grudge against the British, and although he may have exerted little authority over the insurgents, nevertheless he accepted the role of peshwa, albeit maybe reluctantly.

Either way, it was in that position that he accepted the surrender of four hundred British in Kanpur after three weeks of siege. He offered them safe passage back to Allahabad, and they were taken to boats for their voyage downriver but were massacred when they boarded.

It may have been set off by a few Indian soldiers letting off a few shots by way of celebration that triggered a chain reaction by their comrades fearing they were coming under fire. Only two officers and two Irish soldiers managed to survive by jumping in the river and making their way to Allahabad, where they related news of the massacre.

Against a background of reports of horrific retaliation by the British and rumours of an avenue of gibbets all along the road to Allahabad, Nana Sahib took under his personal protection the two hundred women and children from the

British garrison at Napur. With the British forces advancing and the leaders of the mutiny considering escape, an order was issued for the execution of the women and children. The task proved to be an antipathy to regular soldiers; the job was undertaken by five bazaar soldiers, including two who were butchers by trade. The barbaric nature of the slaughter was only matched by British reprisals. From there the Crown forces were able to march on to Lucknow, which the insurgents had seized in June 1857 when the 750 British soldiers and 1,400 loyal Indian soldiers and servants as well as five hundred wives and families had holed up in a fortified area centred on the British residency on the edge of town. They were surrounded by approximately 10,000 mutineers and supporters.

Diaries of the captives inside the compound reflect how the spirit of free enterprise, a hallmark of the British Raj, flourished despite the abject conditions, with many starving while others dined lavishly accompanied by sherry, champagne, and claret. A relief forced its way through in September but got trapped inside the siege, only exacerbating the situation in that there were many more mouths to be fed and no more food to do so.

Eventually, a second relief force succeeded where the first failed and broke into the rebel stronghold with the ensuing slaughter knowing no bounds. Women, children, and rebellious sepoys met with the same indiscriminate savagery, with even those wishing to surrender being met with a bayonet.

The Cawnpor (Kanpur) Dinner, six inches of cold steel, was meted out to all to such an extent that the elephants dragged out 2,000 corpses to be buried in a mass grave. Very soon, the other pockets of resistance met with the same fate. Whilst the events in Kanpur were quickly relegated to the recesses of people's memories, the besieged in Lucknow were immortalised in word and verse and came to epitomise the ethos of British imperialism. Their plucky, backs-to-the-wall spirit would be marked by a flying of the Union flag at the residency for the remaining ninety years that Britain occupied the country.

George Nathaniel Curzon was perhaps the best equipped ever to fill the role of viceroy when he was appointed in 1899. He had obsessed with India since his school days attending Eton. He openly admitted that it was the job he most wanted in his career. Perhaps it helped that the residence of the viceroy in Calcutta had been built a century earlier by Wellesley and based on Curzon's family home Kedleston Hall. For Curzon, India's appeal rested in its status as "the Jewel in the British Crown." India's history fascinated him, and he was probably the most familiar with its languages since Warren Hastings in the late eighteenth century.

He worked long and hard, but he terrorised rather than inspired, and his caustic wit damaged rather than amused those around him. To his credit, he did build more railways and carry out more ambitious irrigation projects, especially in the Punjab. He presided over the partition of Bengal in the face of much opposition. It would later be revoked, but the final straw for him came when he had a dispute with Lord Kitchener over the status of the military member of the council in India. Both wanted control, and when the government would not back him, he resigned and returned to England in 1905. He is also remembered for presiding over a famine in 1899–1900 in which several million died of starvation.

By this time, the British had a standing army of 430,000 men in India, with Irish regiments, the Connaught Rangers, and Inniskilling Fusiliers being almost ever-present. A fresh batch of young Irishmen would soon arrive to boost their numbers and experience a way of life never imagined by them in their home country.

CHAPTER 4

FROM DERRY TO DELHI

It is far better to live like a lion for a day than to live like a jackal for a hundred years.

—*Anonymous*

It had been a year since I enlisted, and finally I was aboard ship and bound for India out of Avonmouth. Our departure for India had been delayed on account of the First Battalion being deployed in China after arriving in Tientsin in November 1909.

One company had been dispatched to guard the British Legation in Peking in the wake of the Boxer Rebellion, and apart from the British, there were also troops from the USA, Holland, Germany, France, the Austro-Hungarian Empire, Russia, and Japan—all guarding their respective legations.

In mid-1911, the battalion had embarked for a posting to India, but when the political situation rapidly deteriorated, they were suddenly recalled to Tientsin. Such was the

LION FOR A DAY

urgency of the mission that all the winter clothing was left in the hold of the troopship. Little happened until Chinese troops started to burn and plunder Peking, at which point the Inniskillings were sent to their aid. A parley was successfully negotiated between the British military and the rebels, meaning the Inniskillings could withdraw without suffering any casualties and embark for their original posting in India.

Our daily routine changed little on board ship. We continued to have reveille at 6 a.m. and did some drills and exercises to maintain our fitness. Breakfast was generally an hour and a half later. The journey took some weeks, and apart from brief stopovers in Gibraltar, Malta, and Alexandria, we spent all that time on board. We were not allowed ashore in Gibraltar but had two days in Malta while we received fresh supplies.

Between 9 a.m. and 11 a.m. there were more drills, followed by a bathing session in canvas tanks filled with seawater. We would then lie on deck relaxing, and many, like me, read. Some of the men wrote letters home to pass the time, with these always being posted at our next stop.

I scribbled a few lines to my mother to let her know I was well and to enquire about my brothers and sisters but must admit it was hard work for me at the start as I was not accustomed to putting my thoughts into words, let alone writing.

After dinner, there would be lifeboat drills and rifle inspections. We also ran so-called marathons in our bare feet around the perimeter of the deck, while other men took part in boxing contests in the middle. It came as a surprise to me how it took little out of me to run for an hour or more without stopping, and I was usually well in front of the rest by this time. There was also a choir, but for the sake of the ears of the other soldiers, I kept far away from it.

The downside of life on a ship, apart from the initial seasickness, was the queues. There was a queue outside the toilets in the morning, there was a queue to fill up the water bottles from the freshwater tap, and there was a permanent queue outside the canteens to buy buns or cigarettes.

We changed into lighter uniforms after entering the Mediterranean. That helped, as the sun had been strong since we left Gibraltar despite it being winter. We now all had a "V" on our chests where we had left our shirts open. Now when we relaxed in the afternoons, we tried to sit in the shade as we played cards, wrote letters, or did whatever to pass the time.

We had our first fatality between Gibraltar and Malta when a young recruit died. He had caught a chest infection shortly before we sailed and it had developed into a more serious condition: pneumonia. I recalled this was common in Derry and could be brought on by the damp conditions in which a sizeable proportion of the population lived, particularly in the Bogside and Brandywell areas.

Even the best doctors on board could not save him. What I had not realised was that someone seemingly so young and strong could catch pneumonia, much less that it would prove fatal. I did not know then that this was something that was to strike closer to home in the near future. Our young comrade in arms was buried at sea just after six o'clock in the evening, prior to us reaching Malta. Some said that if he could have held on, he might have recovered now that we were in warmer climes. I'm sure his parents back in Portadown would not have been expecting the telegram they were to receive in the next week or so.

The ship continued its passage eastward, skirting along the North African coast. We were able to see villages and destroyed castles in Morocco and Tunisia as we made our way towards our next stop in Malta, where we were amused to be met on our arrival by a flotilla of small vessels selling a wide selection of wares of every description. One of these had a sign on its awning saying, "My father was an Irishman." One of the lads shouted down, "It wasn't me! This is my first time here!" which met with laughter on all sides.

We were astonished by the number of small Maltese boys who were swimming in the harbour and diving under the hulls of the huge ships before reappearing on the other side. Some of the other soldiers threw pennies in the water and the young swimmers were able to dive and recover these without any apparent effort, let alone discomfort. I thought they would not be quite as impressive in the cold, murky waters of the Foyle, but such was their skill, I may have been wrong.

We were allowed to disembark in Valletta, and I was able to spend a day in a fascinating city. We were rowed ashore on little boats with awnings of various colours to keep away the

MALCOLM MCCAUSLAND

flies. I was soon struck by the vista of the long, steep streets of the Maltese capital that led down to the harbour where we were anchored. I was also stuck by the herds of wild goats driven through the streets by wild-looking herders who would stop their charges to give a pennyworth of milk to someone who wanted it.

Despite a subsequent stopover in Alexandria, it seemed an interminable journey until we arrived in Bombay. There, we were taken ashore by tenders and spent our first full day on land for some time in the troop sheds, while we waited for a train to Deolali, which at that time served as the depot for all troops arriving in the country.

Deolali would come to enter the English vernacular because it had previously been the holding camp for the men who had completed their service and were awaiting transport home. The wait could be as much as six months, depending when their finishing date happened to fall in the calendar. During this time, they had no duties, and if the hanging around caused them to do odd things, it was said to be the "Doo-lally tap." Eventually saying that someone had "gone doo-lally" came to mean they had gone a little mad.

The practice of holding the expired soldiers in one location had just come to an end before our arrival with them being sent directly to ports of exit to await transport home. Although it was autumn, it was still warm and we needed just a single blanket over us, but the hard metal beds made it difficult to get the rest we needed before the upcoming journey to our camp in Secunderabad.

LION FOR A DAY

That night we were on the train for the 100-mile journey to Deolali and arrived there just as it was getting light. We were issued ground sheets, blue rugs, and Indian kitbags. There were quite a number of men waiting there from other regiments who had completed at least twelve years of service, and we were quick to ask them about India.

We were talking to one of these while an Indian servant swept around his tent. The old hand asked the native to do another task, and he replied he would when he had finished his sweeping. The soldier drove his fist into the native's abdomen and roared at him that when he was asked to do something, he should do it immediately. As you guess, the language was fairly colourful, and the Indian ended up on the ground, writhing in agony.

The soldier's tirade did not end there either. He launched into a torrent of abuse in a foreign language that I took to be Hindustani. Eventually the native got up slowly, still shivering in fear, and it was obvious the soldier's tongue had inflicted greater damage than his fist. He made several salaams to the old soldier and started what he had been asked to do. We were shocked by the treatment meted out, but the old soldier merely explained.

"This country is going to the dogs. The natives are getting more cheeky by the day. Not that long ago, I would have half killed that native, and if he had complained, no one would have listened to him. Now the commanding officer would punish you for ill-treating them. For that reason, I always punch them in the stomach so that they don't have any marks to take to the CO.

Besides, most of the natives on the plains have enlarged spleens, because of their poor diet, and a good punch to the mid-drift hurts them more than it would us. You men probably have six or seven years to serve here, and if you want to see it out, you will feel the same as I do. You will soon find out that if you are down on them, they will respect you more. Treat them kindly, and they will interpret it as weakness on your part. What is won by the sword is held by the sword, and don't you ever forget that."

We left Deolali the following night, and it took us five days to reach Secunderabad, travelling at a terribly slow pace by night and resting by day in improvised shelters along the way. Facilities at our camp were basic, and although the days were warm, the nights were bitterly cold. We laid our waterproof sheets on the bunks with our two blue blankets over them, and then we got in between the blankets. The cold caused many a man to wet his bed, but thankfully I was not one of them. I suppose I had been hardened by the cold winters in poor housing back in Derry.

We had changed our money into Indian currency with the Parsee money changers while we had been waiting in Durban. It was not hard to get the hang of it with one rupee worth about a shilling and fourpence, an anna one penny, and a pice one farthing. We had been told that India was "the land of milk and honey," and we were determined to make the most of it.

The regiment had its own bakery, dairy, and bazaar, which contained the dwellings of natives who attached themselves to the regiment in much the same way as the camp followers

LION FOR A DAY

of ancient armies. Obviously, the bakery and dairy supplied us with our daily bread and butter, but the bazaar offered for sale everything from contraceptives to bicycles.

Every day before breakfast and tea, the natives came around with trays carrying pats of butter and small cans of milk. "Mucking wallah! Dood wallah!" they shouted, meaning butter and milk in Hindustani. A pat of butter cost one anna, while a pice purchased enough milk for a mug of tea. Nearby the natives set up stalls every day and sold fresh meat, bacon, eggs, pork sausages, and vegetables. Everything cost little or nothing; in fact, a man could eat of the best for a few annas each day, while our pay was one rupee. That meant most soldiers had more than enough left for their daily beer, a bit of gambling, and even a visit to the local brothel at the weekend.

The Indians who waited on us hand and foot were only paid a pittance; native sweepers cleaned our bungalows, including the latrines, for four rupees a month, which was less than tuppence per day. The cooks were paid five rupees, although they were always supervised by the battalion's own chefs. The native barber, or Ana, would shave you twice a day for two annas a week. Every section of men had their own boys for cleaning their boots, for which they were paid four annas each week by every soldier for whom they worked. All of the washing was done by the dhobis, and each soldier had twelve annas a month deducted from his pay. A man could send fifty pieces for wash each week in the nearby river, and the white would come back sparkling bright without using soap.

One of the dhobis, called Surinder, spoke exceptionally good English as he had worked out his time as an indentured servant in South Africa. Some government official had recruited him during his time in India and had taken Surinder with him when he was transferred to Pretoria. Surinder stayed after his period of indenture had finished and earned some money, which he assiduously saved and brought back home with him to Secunderabad.

Now aged about 60, he had a small holding of land and a young wife. He worked for us to earn some extra income as he could not have survived what he produced on his parcel of land. He told us that he had three young children, all under five years of age, and despite his advancing years, his wife wanted more sons but not daughters. He was remarkably well informed about events and politics happening all around the globe. I could never discover where he got his information.

He used to say to us, "You Irish are under the British yoke just like us Indians, but a young lawyer in South Africa, Mahatma Gandhi, will come back to lead us to freedom. Mark my words." He always ended his serious pronouncements with "mark my words" to lend a note of gravity to them.

Our captain, Gerry O'Sullivan, very obviously had a soft spot for Surinder, and despite the gulf in social standing between the pair, they could frequently be seen engaged in conversation together. I think the captain relied on Surinder for local information and in that way avert any disturbances.

LION FOR A DAY

While he might have been in good books of the captain, he was very obviously loathed by Sergeant Howcroft of our company, who gave him a hard time. Then again, Howcroft gave all the natives a hard time. "The only good Indian is a dead Indian," he would say when he was not satisfied with something they had done or not done. Howcroft was from a place called Leigh, near Manchester. It was not clear how he ended up in the Inniskillings, but he had been with them in China. Somebody said that he had been in the East Lancashire Regiment and was going to be kicked out of the army for something he did. Instead they transferred him to the 'Skins, who were short of men at the time.

Surinder did Howcroft's washing for him, but he was never content with it and continually complained to anyone who would listen. Worse still, whenever he was drunk, which was fairly often, he would vomit over himself or even mess his trousers. Surinder told me that this had been going on for some time.

"Anton, Howcroft sahib, very cruel man," he said. "Some mornings, he call me and throw vomity shirts, shitty underpants, and trousers in my face. He say, "Come here, you black f**ker. Clean them, or I'll beat you senseless.""

This was going on for some time before Surinder had his revenge. He took Howcroft's soiled and shitty clothes to the river, where he beat them against the rocks until they were almost threadbare with small holes all through them. He brought them back to Howcroft who was furious, but Surinder explained the clothes were old and that was the reason for the holes.

Howcroft could do nothing with us all watching him, but it was obvious he was fuming and would not leave matter there. He did change his dhobi from Surinder to another younger man but did not treat him any better than he had poor Surinder, who seemed to have had the last laugh after the months of humiliation.

The natives seemed to manage very well on these poor wages, needing only a turban on their head and a cloth to cover their loins. Many were rearing a family on these wages, but they could exist on two meals a day: flour mixed with water made into thin cakes called chapatis for breakfast and curry along with rice for their dinner at night.

I came to learn that some fed their daughters well because at 12 or 13 they would command a good price, if in good condition, from either one of the local brothel owners or some older man looking for a young female concubine. When the young women had served their usefulness or became infected, they would be pitched out on the street to live out the rest of their pitiful existence begging or selling sex to the lowest and most desperate in society. Most were dead through various diseases associated with their work before they reached 30.

Every morning around breakfast, natives came around the huts selling live hares, wild cats, or on the odd occasion, a jackal. Many of the men kept dogs, and those with greyhounds would buy the live game for anything between four and six annas, the latter being the price of a jackal. After breakfast they would line up their dogs of all shapes and sizes before releasing the hares, cats, or whatever for a live course out along the plains adjoining the camp. The hares were given a decent chance to make their escape, but on the barren plain, there was no refuge, and I cannot remember even one being able to get away alive from the dogs. The wild cats, about twice the size of their domestic cousins, usually suffered the same fate, although on occasions, being much craftier than the hares, could escape down a gulley formed by a sudden flood after a rainstorm.

The jackals were shown no mercy and were taken to an enclosure, where they were pitted against two or three of the fiercest dogs. Normally the jackal was a bit of a coward, but when he realised there was no escape, he would retreat to a corner and literally fight for his life. Nevertheless, in ten or twenty minutes, he or she would usually be dead. Though on one occasion when we were waiting for the *gamewallahs* to come and take away the carcass of the dead jackal, someone threw a bucket of cold water over him, and to our shock and surprise, the jackal jumped up and took off into the nearest thicket and was never seen again.

"He who fights and runs away lives to fight another day," piped up one of the old hands, at which point we all burst into laughter. But it was something I was never to forget. "He who fights and runs away lives to fight another day!" was etched on my subconscious for the rest of my life.

The annual monsoon season arrived around the middle of July, and for five or six weeks, there was nothing but rain. We managed to drill during lulls in the storms, but generally we hung around and marked time by playing cards, writing home, and other pastimes. When the mist lifted and it stopped raining, normally distant objects seemed much closer and the plains looked like a vast ocean with islands dotted here and there. Because of the humidity, it was difficult to get our clothes to dry, and an extra ration of charcoal was given to each room for the log fires.

Our regular route marches were suspended during the rainy season, and we relied more on our daily drills to get fighting fit. When the rainy season was over, it was back to our weekly route marches that could last between one day and three days, the duration being limited by the amount of rations we could carry. It had been decided by the medical authorities that in the Indian climate, the maximum pack we could carry was 52 pounds, including the rations for three days. This did not mean that some soldiers did not manage this weight, and often we lightened the load for a colleague by carrying some of his rations. The officers frowned on this but at the same time turned a blind eye in the interest of avoiding the poor unfortunate being put on charges, only adding to his misfortune.

Sport played an important part in battalion life, with football and boxing the most popular. Strengthened by the return of First Battalion from Peking, I was in the battalion team that won the football cup in 1913. It was open to all the regiments serving in India at the time, and we repeated the feat the following year. We also won the marathon (cross-country) both years, lifting the Challenge Cup open to British units in the Ninth Division.

Our cross-country team had to consist of one officer who was Captain O'Sullivan, two non-commissioned officers,

LION FOR A DAY

and seventeen men from ranks, with the distance being between 6 and 7 miles. Earlier we had beaten the King's Shropshire Light Infantry in the preliminary round at our home course around the plain, where our dogs used to chase the hares and other prey. The Dublin Fusiliers, the Camerons, and the Buffs finished behind us in that order in the final.

The first year was my debut in a competitive race of the kind, and I started too cautiously, leaving myself too much ground to make up in the second half of the race. Nevertheless, I was delighted to be the third man home, helping us win the inter-regimental competition. I did not know the first two finishers, but I heard they were both accomplished runners back in England. And one of them was said to be a member of the famous Birchfield prior to signing up for the Buffs.

The second year I made no mistake and was delighted to finish half a minute ahead of the nearest finisher. The officers footed the bill back at the camp bar, and we celebrated until the early hours of the morning, well past our normal bedtime. We were still up early for reveille in the morning, albeit still half asleep and most of us nursing a very sore head.

I was especially popular back in the barracks from those soldiers who had bet as much as a week's wages on the result. I made a small fortune myself with a couple of mates finding eager takers among the men from the other regiments who were convinced of the merits of their own respective champions. Of course, I was well rewarded, for the win and sporting achievement was always well appreciated by the top brass who revelled in the reflected glory of the men under their command. The First Battalion of the Inniskillings was no different; henceforth, I always found myself excluded from the more unsavoury duties assigned to the average private.

Unfortunately, I did not have much time to enjoy the privilege because we were all summoned to the drilling ground late one afternoon in August 1914. This was usually a time that we were allowed to do our own thing, so we knew something was up, especially when we saw that the commanding officer, Major F.G. Jones, had come to address us.

He took up his position on the bandstand, and we could see by his manner that the matter was grave. His officers stood expressionless behind him when he opened by saying that we had probably heard that Austrian Archduke Franz Ferdinand had been assassinated at the end of June in the Bosnian capital, Sarajevo, by a Bosnian Serb. He said that this did not directly affect Great Britain, but because of a number of complicated alliances among various countries, it meant we were now at war with Germany.

The day before we left I was able to win the cross country championship for a second time. Not so pleasant was hearing that Surinder had been found dead at the side of a nearby lane. He had been making his way home in the evening after working in the camp and it seemed he had been set upon by someone and beaten to death with a cudgel that had been left bloodstained at the scene of the crime. Someone said they remembered Howcroft keeping a cudgel under his bed for his protection, but he brushed off all insinuations that he had anything to do with Surinder's death. In fact, he seemed nonplussed about the Indian's death. "I don't know what all the fuss is about. One less dhobi isn't going to make any difference to the British Empire, is it? Anyway, as I've always said, the only good Indian is a dead Indian."

We had a quick collection for Surinder's widow. Then a few of us, led by Captain O'Sullivan, called with her to express our condolences and give her the proceeds of our collection. It was the first time we had met her; she was a beautiful young woman, probably in her late twenties. It was sad to see the young children in their little cabin knowing they would never see their father again.

We started with our long train journey back to Durban the following day, still with heavy hearts, thinking of poor Surinder, his widow, and their young children. What would the future hold for them without a breadwinner? Our sadness was only abated knowing he would have had some savings which would help them through what would be some tough times.

I watched as we passed village after village with hungry, desperate people at every turn. Men and women stood at the doors of rudimentary shacks surrounded by children, sometimes naked, at times with distended stomachs due to hunger—and always without hope of escaping this poverty. We thought that there was poverty in Derry, and there was, but nothing like this.

CHAPTER 5

GETTING READY FOR WAR

What have you done for Ireland? How have you answered the Call? Are you pleased with the part you're playing in the job that demands us all? Have you changed the tweed for the khaki to serve with rank and file, as your comrades are gladly serving, or isn't it worth your while?

—1915 First World War recruitment poster

Although the commanding officer informed us in August 1914 that war had started in Europe, we had to await replacements and it was not until 15 December that year that we finally embarked for home.

The journey from Durban was naturally slow, owing to the war footing, the convoy having to move at the speed of the slowest vessel for protection. We spent Christmas at sea and passed it like any other day, although we were given extra rations to mark the occasion.

LION FOR A DAY

The only remarkable event occurred on our third night out of Bombay when the cry went up, "Man overboard!" A group had been playing cards at the back of the ship when they heard sounds of a struggle on the deck above them followed by a loud splash of someone entering the sea. Alarmed, they looked back into the water to see someone wearing a uniform bobbing up and down and shouting frantically for help.

They could not recognise who it was on account of the darkness, with there being no moon that night and all lights on the convoy extinguished for security. Within a couple of minutes, the shouting had stopped and there was no sign of anybody in the water.

Captain O'Sullivan had been the first person on the scene but was unable to find anyone who had witnessed what had happened. He had a roll call put in place immediately, but it was maybe half an hour before everyone on board was rounded up for inspection and all the names called.

Initially, three people were missing, but this came down to just one when two men were found asleep under the stairs on one of the decks, rather the worse for wear having taken a little too much to drink. Where they had got the alcohol from was one question, but no one was really interested in finding out, with the more pressing task of discovering exactly who had gone over the side.

Eventually, it was narrowed down to Sergeant Howcroft. They checked his berth in case he was asleep, or drunk, and the other places he could have been but didn't find him.

Somebody said that they had seen him up on deck, but nobody had witnessed him going overboard. Occasionally, in rough waters, a rogue wave would take someone with it, especially on the lower decks, but we were sailing through the tranquil waters of the Gulf of Oman. Finally, the ship's captain declared Howcroft "lost at sea." The padre said a few words at an informal ceremony that a few of us attended out of a sense of duty, but nobody shed any tears. The circumstances of his drowning remained a mystery.

On arrival back in England at Avonmouth in January, we were immediately transferred to camp in Rugby, where we joined the Eighty-Seventh Brigade of the Twenty-Ninth Division. Originally, the Royal Fusiliers and the Lancashire Fusiliers were to be billeted there, but at the last minute, orders were changed and the King's Own Scottish Borderers, the Border Regiment, and we, the Royal Inniskilling Fusiliers, were sent.

When news of our impending arrival got out, there was a small crowd waiting to welcome us at the L & N-W Railway Station. They must have been surprised at our appearance because, whilst we were still wearing our Indian sun hats, we had also donned great khaki coats to shield us against the cold, biting wind.

We marched immediately to what I learned later to be the Abbey Street and Oxford Street quarter of the town, where we were to be billeted with the local people. It was the first time the army authorities had used this type of accommodation, but as the local paper, *The Rugby Advertiser*,

LION FOR A DAY

reported, "Tommy Atkins is an adaptable fellow, and will no doubt settle down to the new arrangement."

It was tough experiencing a British winter again after a two-year absence and having enjoyed the warmth of India in the interim. I know I was not alone in these sentiments. We all missed the Indian servants who had attended to all our "needs."

Everyone found the billets comfortable, and the families with whom we were billeted could not do enough for us. It was soon obvious to us that the people of the area were friendly towards the military and very patriotic. The local hospitality even extended to the provision in the town of five "Welcome Clubs" where soldiers could go to play games, have a cigarette, read newspapers and magazines, or simply enjoy a much-appreciated cup of coffee in the morning.

An Anglican Church service was arranged to welcome us to the town, which only the Church of Ireland soldiers were required to attend. I do not think the people of Rugby realised that these only numbered three hundred out of the seven hundred in our battalion, with the remainder comprising an equal split between Presbyterians and Roman Catholics.

I was assigned to lodge with Albert and Vera Middleton, who looked to be in their sixties, near the railway station. Their two sons had joined up with the Northamptonshire Regiment when the war broke out and had been sent to the Western Front. Unfortunately, the elder brother, Albert Junior, or Bertie as they called him, had been killed within weeks of his arrival on the front line. The other brother, Charlie, was still there and the father and mother were genuinely concerned for his safety.

Albert scanned the newspapers every day for news of the war to see how it might affect his surviving son. My arrival coincided with a period of anxiety for them as they had not had a letter from Charlie for several weeks, which they said was not like him. I tried to reassure them that this might be normal in times of war and that we had only sporadic communication with our Second Battalion, who were also in France. I am sure having lost one son; it could not have been easy for them.

The townspeople were aware that "the Skins," as we were known, had a top-class regimental band; already the people of Rugby were relishing some musical treats during our sojourn. They were not disappointed either, with the boys giving a concert each Sunday afternoon in Caldecott Park, close to the centre of the town. Despite the cold weather, hundreds flocked to hear the music, which included a good selection of Irish tunes.

I think for many of the locals it was the first time they had heard a drums and pipes military band and they were obviously enthralled as the attendance grew by the week. Every week, they finished with a medley that included "The Rose of Tralee," "When Irish Eyes Are Smiling," and "The Mountains of Mourne." These had always been part of the band's repertoire and reflected that we had soldiers in our ranks from all parts of Ireland. The sound of Irish

LION FOR A DAY

ballads brought a tear to the eyes of many who, like me, were thinking of home.

I soon found out that there was quite a large Irish community around Rugby due to people coming to work on the railways since their advent in the 1870s. Once boasting one of the longest platforms in the country, Rugby station was a major hub in the English railway system.

St Marie's Catholic Church was full for Mass every Sunday, and I soon realised that there were people from all over Ireland. This, and lack of tension, may have been two of the reasons that I took a liking to Rugby from the very start. It was the first time that I was anywhere where I did not feel stress. I had grown up in a city where two communities were continually at each other's throats, and in India, I had been part of a garrison holding down British rule. But here there was neither enemy nor enmity.

We very quickly fell into our routine of daily drilling at the ground, which was kindly lent to the army by Rugby FC, and the Saturday after our arrival, we went out on a route march that took us over three hours. We left from beside the famous Rugby School, where William Webb Ellis picked up a football and ran with it, inventing a game that the school give its name to and spread all over the world. Rugby School was also where cross-country running in the form of paper chases developed. Thomas Hughes describes in his book *Tom Brown's Schooldays*, based on his days at Rugby, the Crick Run which started in 1837. That commenced outside the school gates and headed towards Clifton and Lilbourne, then on to Crick, Kilsby, and Barby before ending back at Rugby School.

As we set off, we could see the young toffs with their top hats through the school gates, as we headed off on a route that followed a similar course to the Crick Run. Passing through the countryside, with farms scattered here and there, reminded me of long, Sunday afternoon walks with my brothers out to Carrigans in County Donegal, about 5 miles from our home in the Bogside. We had a brief stop to make a brew and eat something in the village of Crick, where the citizens turned out in numbers to greet us. From Crick, we returned via Hillmorton, once again meeting with a warm reception, and back to Rugby for our evening meal. Although many had complained about these marches, especially in the heat and humidity of India, it gave us an excellent opportunity to get to know the area. The more time I spent there and the more I saw, the more I liked Rugby.

The local newspaper did a feature on the regiment in which they interviewed a number of the rank and file, one of whom complained of the change in climate. "It's a bit cold after the hotter parts of India where we have come from; but I suppose we will soon get used to it." The regiment's sporting prowess was also highlighted, particularly the soccer team, which was one of the strongest in India and had secured the inter-divisional cup for two seasons in succession. Our communicative NCO, as he was described, told the newspaper that we would be quite keen on a match, if possible, with the Borderers, who also had a particularly

LION FOR A DAY

good team. He suggested that the gate receipts could be donated to one of the relief funds.

Our man was also full of praise for the Inniskilling Fusiliers' cross-country team and pointed out that we had won this competition for two successive years. His words may have influenced the local sports clubs, including Rugby FC, allowing us free use of their grounds for training.

It was not all positive though. Lieutenant Colonel F.E. Jones, from the regiment, also posted a notice in the same issue pointing out that the pay of a soldier could not be stopped for a private debt and advised the town's inhabitants that if they allowed soldiers to "contract debts," they would do so at their own risk.

We were used to having our pay docked for any number of items—beer, tobacco, and cigarettes being just three. The officers were keen that the practice should not be extended to local shops to avoid any ill will against the military if soldiers left town without settling their accounts.

We were also surprised to read in the newspaper that at least one of our comrades had already "met his fate" in Rugby and intended to lead a local lady to the altar at an early date. I found this hard to believe given the short time we were there, but a chance meeting that evening was to make me change my mind.

I was back in the house on my own. The Middletons had gone out to a prayer meeting when I heard a knock on the door. I opened it to find a very pretty young woman on the doorstep. She appeared just as surprised to find me answering the door.

"Who are you?" She got the words out before me.

"Private Anthony Hegarty," I stammered in reply, admiring her dark eyes and perfect white teeth.

"Are you always so formal, Private—?

"Hegarty, sir. I mean miss." I could see I was stammering as I tried to get my breath.

"I'm a friend of Albert and Vera. My name's Gertie. I went to school with Bertie, and I just came around to see if they had heard from Charlie. I know they were worrying, him not having written home or anything."

"They've gone out to a prayer meeting. You'd better come in. I don't think they'll be long." I was back in control of my speech.

"And what would the Middletons think if they came home and found me here on my own with a Scottish soldier?"

"I'm not Scottish. I'm Irish—"

"But you've a Scottish accent—"

"No, I haven't. I'm from Derry, or Londonderry, in the north of Ireland. We all speak this way—"

LION FOR A DAY

"What do you mean Derry or Londonderry? Can you not make up your mind where you're from?"

I thought, *This is a saucy one*, and was about to launch into an explanation of why the city had two names when the Middletons came around the corner.

"Good evening, Gertie. I see you've met our young Irish soldier," said Mrs Middleton. "Handsome isn't he?"

Now Gertie stumbled. "Ah ah ah, I suppose so, but he isn't sure where he comes from. It's Delhi or Londonderry or something."

The Middletons and I all burst into laughter, while Gertie blushed in embarrassment. I was able to take a glance at her figure and noticed her comely hips and adequate—shall we say—chest compartment.

"You better come in, girl," said Albert as he moved past me with Vera in his wake.

We all sat down, and although it was almost 9.30 p.m., we had a cup of tea and a slice of Mrs Middleton's best sponge cake.

When it was time for Gertie to go, I saw her to the door and plucked up the courage to suggest that we might go for a coffee some day when she was free. She readily agreed, and a date was set for that Friday morning, when she said she came to Rugby to do the shopping.

As we made our preparations for war, we were aware that there was pressure at home for more volunteers. The Home Rule Act permitting an Irish Parliament had finally become law, but its enactment was suspended until the hostilities against Germany and its allies were resolved. It was initially believed that this would only take a few months and the men would be home by Christmas.

Catholics were being urged by John Redmond, leader of the moderate Irish Parliamentary Party, to join up on the understanding that Ireland would secure its own parliament on their return. He saw the Allied war as an effort to restore "the freedom of small nations," such as Belgium on continental Europe. Redmond's own brother was one of many to answer the call, and whole new divisions were formed, such as the Tenth Irish, based in Dublin.

We knew that Home Rule was anathema to the Protestants, who perceived it as Dublin rule. Thankfully, with a common enemy, it did not drive a wedge between the religions in the Inniskillings, but at home, the Ulster Volunteer Force had been formed to fight against any form of home rule, with Dublin lawyer Edward Carson the political head of the resistance.

Mass rallies were taking place in Derry and other cities and towns throughout the nine counties of Ulster. On occasions, these gave rise to violence, which certainly heightened the tension between the two communities.

The position of the UVF was strengthened when officers in the Curragh Camp mutinied, making it clear they would not move against the force even if ordered to do so. At the same time, the UVF was being turned into a real fighting force by the huge imports of arms smuggled into the country and distributed to the branches of the organisation in all nine counties.

However, not all Catholics subscribed to Redmond's analysis, and there was a strengthening movement advocating that Irishmen should not join up to fight in what they described as Britain's war. While it was said that the recruitment figures in Derry were in line with other places, Sinn Fein and more radical groups continued to campaign against recruitment.

The polemic split families, including my own, with many of my neighbours in the Bogside joining Sinn Fein and actively campaigning against recruitment to the British Army. Rumour and counter-rumour proliferated, with anti-recruitment voices stating that Catholic soldiers would be used for the more arduous and dangerous assaults, while Protestants and mainland troops would be kept in safer positions.

Prior to our departure for the Dardanelles, we were part of a huge parade of troops in Stretton-on-Dunsmore, close to our temporary camp in Rugby, which we knew from our marches. King George V took the salute from the 2-mile line of 16,000 troops, men of the newly formed Twenty-Ninth Division, made up of twelve infantry battalions, including ourselves and other Irish regiments, such as the Royal Munster Fusiliers and the Royal Dublin Fusiliers.

Although some were drawn from the Territorial Force, most of us were part of the regular army and recently returned from overseas service in the British Empire. We were there to show our readiness for war, although, in truth, none of us knew what we were going to face.

Figure 2: King George V (centre) inspects the British 29th Division at Dunchurch prior to its departure for Gallipoli (https://commons.wikimedia.org/wiki)

Around mid-morning on 12 March 1915, the royal party arrived by train at the nearby Dunchurch station. The king mounted his horse, Delhi, before riding past the troops, who stood four men deep, to the inspection point near the intersection of the London Road and the Fosse Way. The king reached the crossroads at 12.15 p.m., where he remained on his horse as the Twenty-Ninth Division marched east along the London Road.

LION FOR A DAY

Unfortunately, our all too short stay came to an end on 16 March. There were tears of joy and sorrow in the Middleton household. They had received not one but three letters from Charlie earlier that day. The sorrow was to see me leave, because even in that short space of time, I had become one of the family. And I think they sort of saw me as a replacement for Bertie.

Mrs Middleton organised a little get-together by way of a send-off for me. As Gertie had been "stepping out," as Mrs Middleton called it, she was invited. Her employer, Mr Payn, gave her the night off as his housekeeper, and she was invited to stay over as the Middletons did not want her travelling back to Crick, where she worked, late at night.

I could see that Gertie was close to tears most of the evening, as I was too, but we each tried to put a brave face on it. It was a surprise for me when I felt a warm body enter my bed long after we had all retired, but it was Gertie's way of saying goodbye in turbulent times.

In the morning, she was gone, and there was a little note attached to the pillow. "Don't forget to write!" We did not even have a few more moments together before I left for the assembly point at the railway station.

Sometime later, we boarded the *RMS Andania* in Avonmouth for the Greek island of Lemnos. She had been a Cunard passenger liner, launched in 1913, but had been requisitioned as a troop ship by the war office earlier that year. I learned some time later that she continued in that role before reverting to a passenger liner on the Liverpool-New

York route in 1917. She was torpedoed and sunk by German submarine *U46* two miles north-east of Rathlin island the following year with the loss of seven lives.

Unknown to us at that point was that our mission was to invade the Gallipoli Peninsula as part of the plan championed by Winston Churchill, then First Lord of the Admiralty. The strength of the battalion on boarding the vessel was twenty-seven officers and 999 other ranks, having absorbed the three hundred or so new recruits since returning from India. We embarked along with the other regiments who, like us, were made up of veterans and complete novices.

The sea trip was a complete contrast to my earlier journey to India. Whereas two years earlier there had been no urgency and we were all filled with the excitement of discovering far-off lands, this time we sensed the urgency. We barely stopped in Gibraltar, other than to take on supplies, and only the officers were allowed to disembark at Valletta.

Then, after a two-day stopover, we were on the high seas again, arriving at the end of March in Alexandria, where the whole battalion disembarked and marched to the rest camp at Mex.

It was difficult to acclimatise to heat, and we were soon undertaking our drills again. We left again in early April and reached our destination, Mudros, on the island of Lemnos, in another day or so.

By this time, we knew that we were going to invade the Gallipoli Peninsula, but we had been encouraged by our officers in Alexandria telling us that the Turks were extremely poor fighters and would put up little resistance. I took this with a pinch of salt, recalling that they had earlier said that the war in Europe would be over by Christmas. They were not right then, and as we were to find out to our cost, they were not correct on this occasion either.

CHAPTER 6

THE POLITICS OF WAR

A nation which makes the final sacrifice
for life and freedom does not get beaten.
—Mustafa Kemal Ataturk

Once the dominant force in Asia Minor, Greece, and the Mediterranean, by the start of the twentieth century the Ottoman Empire was in decline. Internally, the autocratic Sultan Abdul Hamid II had been deposed by the Young Turks in 1909 and replaced by his younger brother Mohammed V. Although the new Sultan remained the titular head of the country, it was the Young Turks, a peculiar collection of revolutionaries and opportunists, who called the shots in no less dictatorial manner than the deposed sultan.

A triumvirate headed the Committee of Union and Progress (CUP) that ruled the empire, comprising Mehmet Talaat Pasha, Ismail Enver Pasha, and Ahmed Djemal Pasha. They were known as the Three Pashas. Mehmet Talaat was regarded as the leader and the shrewd political operator. He had risen by stealth to assume head of the cabal, despite spending time

LION FOR A DAY

in prison for subversive activities. After the revolution of 1908, he was elected as a deputy to Parliament and subsequently held important ministerial posts. He gave up his hopes to form an alliance with traditional enemy Russia and, after delaying as long as possible, turned to the Germans, and worked with Enver to enter the war on their side.

Jemal Pasha was a professional army officer who displayed skills as both an administrator and a propagandist. After the coup of 1913, he became the important governor of Constantinople and was influential in formulating foreign policy for the government. His preference was to join in an alliance with France, but his efforts failed, and he eventually joined his fellow Pashas in favouring fighting in alliance with Germany.

Enver Pasha was also a professional army officer and had dreams of expanding the Ottoman Empire. He was one of the organisers of the 1908 Revolt that deposed the sultan and advanced rapidly afterwards, serving with distinction as attaché to Berlin and in the Tripoli War. He led the coup that gave the Young Turks full power in 1913 and entered the cabinet as Minister of War. The most pro-German of the Young Turks, he played the key role in joining the war on Germany's side.

The change of regime failed to halt the decline in either the country's fortune or its reputation as it suffered a crushing defeat in the Balkans to an alliance of Bulgaria, Greece, Serbia, and Montenegro in the wars of 1912–13. The political and economic disintegration left Turkey open to exploitation by the larger European powers. To halt the decline, they began to draw up plans to strengthen the navy after attempts to construct Ottoman-made battleships such as *Abdul Kadir* had ended in failure. So, the Ottoman Navy Foundation was established with the aim of commissioning new ships in British shipyards through public donations rather than having them built locally. Two ships were ordered in 1912 from shipyards in Britain as part of the Strengthening the Navy project, which was funded by public subscription. Even housewives in Istanbul were said to have donated their jewellery to pay for them.

However, when the vessels were completed on the eve of World War I, with the Turkish crews already in the northeast of England to take possession of them, the British first lord of the admiralty, Winston Churchill, ordered their requisition. He gave the order that if any Turkish crew on Tyneside tried to board the vessels, they would be dealt with by force. In that one act, he probably pushed the Ottoman Empire into the Central Alliance, especially given the already strong German influence in Istanbul. Churchill cabled Enver, "I deeply regret necessity for detaining Turkish ships because I know the patriotism with which money has been raised all over Turkey."

He went on to promise the return of the ships and full compensation for the delay in delivering them "when the last German officer and man shall have left Turkish Territory definitely and finally" and asked that Turkey remain neutral in the then current war. This referred to Enver having brought in German advisors some time before to modernise and restructure the Ottoman military.

LION FOR A DAY

Enver refused to even accept delivery of Churchill's message, and the die was cast at that point. No money was refunded to the Turks, the British setting it off against some alleged historic debt owed by the Ottoman Empire. After that, the Germans played on the anti-British feelings in Constantinople and shrewdly gifted the Turks two modern battleships, the *Goeben* and *Breslau,* to compensate them for their loss.

The British and French politicians had shown little desire from the outset to engage with the Young Turks, or even accept them as the rulers of the Ottoman Empire, preferring to give their tacit support to the older and more conservative politicians in Constantinople. The stakes were high. If they could oust the Young Turks, they were guaranteed a friendly neutral government and with it the end of the German threat in the region. On the other hand, if the triumvirate stayed in power, the British and the French would be in the tricky position of switching their affiliations in midstream.

In contrast, the Germans had been quick to take advantage of the situation by rowing in behind the Young Turks and, through the German Military Mission, had actively infiltrated the Turkish Army. They had sent a general, Liman von Sanders, to head the mission, and he had proven to be an inspired choice. Calm and steady by nature, he had overseen the arrival of German officers, technical experts, and instructors, first in groups of tens and twenties and then in their hundreds.

The mission took over the munitions factories and manned the guns in the Dardanelles, and von Sanders turned out a regiment of Turkish soldiers in new uniforms and armed with the latest rifles that could match anything in Europe. By August 1914, the Young Turks believed that their lot would be best served in any conflict aligning with the Germans.

Meanwhile, as the war dragged on into late 1914 and reached stalemate on the Western Front, with both sides entrenched in a conflict that seemed would never end, an alternative plan was needed by the British and French to unblock the logjam. It was suggested that the Russians should invade Germany from its north coast, but there was opposition to this. The deployment of forces in the east would leave the Allies weak in the west, endangering France and putting England at risk of an invasion.

Lord Kitchener was one of those initially opposed to the plan to attack the Ottoman Empire on its home territory, pressurising it to withdraw its forces attacking Russia on the eastern flank. The added bonus of taking Constantinople was that it would secure a sea route to and from Russia that would be open year-round as opposed to that through the Baltic, which was ice-bound for a greater part of the winter.

It is hard to convey to a modern reader the esteem in which Kitchener was held by the British people. It was with awe more than respect, which is why his face was used on recruiting posters. Born near Listowel, County Kerry, the son of a military man who had recently moved there, Horatio Herbert Kitchener had made his reputation through military campaigns. He first gained fame for winning the

Battle of Omdurman and securing control of the Sudan and was rewarded by being made Baron Kitchener of Khartoum.

He was chief of staff during the Second Boer War in South Africa, and his scorched-earth tactics brought him success but also notoriety. His setting up of concentration camps resulted in deaths of between 18,000 and 28,000 men, women, and children, mostly through epidemics. This only added to his reputation, and in Britain he was regarded as a war hero. His term as commander-in-chief of the army in India saw him quarrel with Viceroy Lord Curzon, who was eventually forced to resign.

At the start of World War I, he became secretary of state for war, a post that meant he was in the cabinet. He was one of the few to foresee a long war, of at least three years, and on that basis organised the largest volunteer army that Britain had ever seen. He was never regarded as a great strategist but relied on his gut feeling to dictate his actions.

Kitchener changed his mind about attacking the Ottoman Empire in late December 1914 when a message was received from Britain's ambassador in Petrograd, Sir George Buchanan, informing that the Russians were in difficulty. Reportedly they had suffered over 1 million casualties and were running short of rifles and even ammunition.

Grand Duke Nicholas, commander of the Russian armies, had asked "if it would be possible for Lord Kitchener to arrange for a demonstration of some kind against the Turks elsewhere, either naval or military, and to so spread reports as to cause Turks, who he says are very liable to go off at a tangent, to withdraw some of the forces now acting against the Russians in the Caucasus, and thus ease the situation of the Russians."

In Kitchener's judgement, the only place that an intervention might aid the Russians and precipitate the withdrawal by the Turks of forces from the east would be in the Dardanelles, particularly if Constantinople could be put under threat. The following telegram was dispatched to Petrograd: "Please assure the Grand Duke that steps will be taken to make a demonstration against the Turks. It is, however, feared that any action we can devise and carry out will be unlikely to seriously affect numbers of enemy in the Caucasus, or cause their withdrawal."

Brief as the message was, it committed the British to action, and both Churchill and First Sea Lord Fisher got down to deciding what action should be taken. Fisher felt an attack on Turkey should be undertaken but would only be effective if carried out immediately. He proposed that all the Indian troops and 75,000 of the British soldiers in France be embarked in Marseilles and landed, along with the Egyptian garrison, on the Asiatic side of the Dardanelles. The Greeks were to attack the Gallipoli peninsula and the Bulgarians were to march on Constantinople, while a squadron of Britain's old battleships would be sent as support to the land forces in the straits of Marmara.

Jackie Fisher, as he was commonly known, had the ear of Churchill, who had brought him out of retirement to become first sea lord. It was Fisher who was first credited with using the now familiar expression OMG, although he

LION FOR A DAY

said, "Oh! My God!" He and Churchill were great friends as well as professional colleagues, but that friendship was to be pressed to breaking point in the following weeks.

Fisher was reluctantly persuaded of the merits of the plan, which included using some of Britain's ships that were due for scrapping to mount a naval attack on Constantinople, but believed they had to be accompanied by a larger military force. But Kitchener was adamant that no troops could be spared from the Western Front, meaning the assault would have to go ahead with just 75,000 troops. The composition of the flotilla was agreed at a meeting in the war office, but Churchill, who stayed late, added two submarines overnight. This seemed to be the straw that broke the camel's back for Fisher, who resigned the following morning.

The basic flaws in the Entente's plans did not become immediately obvious. Naval guns could not usefully engage unseen targets, being constructed to train only on visible objects and on a level plain with them. In contrast, military guns could be used on both seen and unseen targets. This had recently been illustrated in October and November 1914 when the Germans had tried to bombard Antwerp from the sea. Nevertheless, the Gallipoli Campaign went ahead on 17 February 1915, with forces from the Entente powers seeking to take control of the straits by attacking the Ottoman forts at the entrance of the Dardanelles.

Two days later, they began their first attack in the Straits of the Bosporus, with *HMS Queen Elizabeth* leading an assorted fleet of British and French vessels in a long-range bombardment of Ottoman coastal artillery batteries.

Inclement weather hindered the full effectiveness of the shelling, grounding the eight aircraft from *Ark Royal* they had planned to use for spotting the key positions of the enemy's defences. This period of bad weather slowed the initial phase, but by 25 February, the outer forts had been reduced and the entrance cleared of mines. The Royal Marines were then landed to decommission the guns at Kum Kale and Seddulbahir, while the naval bombardment shifted to batteries between Kum Kale and Kephez.

On 18 March, the Entente, comprising eighteen battleships with an array of cruisers and destroyers, began the main attack against the narrowest point of the Dardanelles, where the straits are 1 mile wide. Although suffering some damage, the plan seemed to be going well, and minesweepers were ordered along the straits to be followed by the main fleet. It was then the French battleship *Bouvet* struck a mine, causing it to capsize in two minutes, with just seventy-five survivors out of a total crew of 718.

The minesweepers, manned by civilians, retreated under Ottoman artillery fire, leaving the minefields largely intact. *HMS Irresistible* and *HMS Inflexible* struck mines, and *Irresistible* was sunk, but most of its surviving crew was rescued. The *Inflexible* was badly hit and withdrawn. There was confusion as to what caused the damage with some blaming torpedoes from German submarines. *HMS Ocean,* sent to rescue *Irresistible,* struck a mine and was abandoned before making its way to the seabed.

The French battleships *Suffren* and *Gaulois* fared no better, suffering damage when sailing through a new line of mines

LION FOR A DAY

placed secretly by the Ottoman minelayer *Nusret* ten days before, highlighting the poor reconnaissance by the Entente intelligence. The losses forced the admiral in charge, Kildare native John de Robeck, to sound the "general recall" to protect what remained of his force.

During the planning of the campaign, naval losses had been anticipated, which was why they sent obsolete battleships, but leaders but did not expect this humiliating defeat by a supposedly depleted land force. Allied attempts to gain control of the straits and open the way for an attack on Constantinople using naval power were terminated, due to the losses and bad weather. This failure not only resulted in the heavy losses of ships and men but, perhaps more fatally, tipped off the Turks that another attempt would be made to occupy the peninsula, giving them more time to prepare their defences for a second assault.

The Entente changed strategy and planned to capture Gallipoli by land. The clarion call was sent out to, among others, the crack Twenty-Ninth Division, currently stationed in Rugby, which was previously being held in reserve for action on the Western Front. The British and French believed that the superior numbers of their forces would prove decisive, particularly in view of the perceived poor quality, inferior weapons, and low morale of the Ottoman military.

But when the Turkish needed a hero, they found one in Mustafa Kemal Pasha. The native of Salonika in northern Greece was just 22 at the time and had chosen the army as a career despite his father, a minor bureaucrat, wanting him to take up a trade. His second name Kemal, meaning "Perfection," was given to him by his mathematics teacher "in admiration of his capability and maturity," but according to others, it was because his teacher wanted to distinguish between two students who had the same name. His biographer, Andrew Mango, suggested that he may have chosen the name himself as a tribute to the nationalist poet Namik Kemal. He was obviously not offended by the soubriquet as he assumed it as part of his name.

Kemal graduated from the War Academy in 1905 as a captain, and although he was involved in revolutionary politics from his graduation and had formed his own political group, he was overlooked by the Young Turks movement when they came to power. Kemal led the Turkish forces in the war against Italy in east Libya in 1911–12 and subsequently served in the Balkans, rising to the rank of lieutenant colonel. He was then a military attaché in Sofia until the German head of the Ottoman army, von Sanders, had the vision and foresight to put him in charge of the Nineteenth Division, the main reserve unit on the Gallipoli peninsula.

When Kemal received official word of the Entente landing on 25 April, he was exercising his troops on top of a hill. He received orders to send one battalion down to confront the invaders but realising the significance of the landings and the importance of holding the high ground, he gambled by sending the entire Turkish Fifty-Seventh, one of his best regiments.

Kemal's military genius was to serve the Turks well, spreading his reputation throughout the Ottoman Empire. Turkish troops were considered weak and inept but were galvanised by an inspirational leader. They made the British and their allies in the Triple Entente wish they had never seen the Gallipoli peninsula. He and his German advisors were quick to realise that guns placed strategically along the ridge that formed the backbone of the Gallipoli peninsula could dominate and overcome a much larger force arriving on the beaches some distance below.

That, along with Kemal's inspirational leadership, was the keys to the Turkish success and the Entente's humiliating defeat. However, the incompetence of the leaders of the Entente forces would only be brought to the British prime minister's attention by a courageous young Australian journalist whose son would go on to be a worldwide media mogul.

CHAPTER 7

WAR IN GALLIPOLI

He who fights and runs away
May live to fight another day;
But he who is battle slain
Can never rise to fight again.

—*Oliver Goldsmith*

"Hegarty!"

"Here, Sarge," I replied as I jumped up from the quiet corner that I had found up on deck to escape the cramped cabin I shared with three others deep in the bowels of ship.

I had just finished writing a letter to Gertie. We had received our mail earlier in the day and I was daydreaming as I admired her smile in the photo that she sent me.

"Hegarty, you're to report to Captain O'Sullivan. He's up in the command room on C deck. And by the way, it's 'Yes, Sergeant' and not 'Sarge,'" admonished Willie Smyth, a career soldier from Belfast.

LION FOR A DAY

"Yes, Sarge. I mean yes, Sergeant," I stuttered. "On my way. He didn't say what it was about?"

"No, he didn't, but I only got the message second-hand to send you to him."

Captain Gerald Robert O'Sullivan was from County Cork. A tall, handsome man who was well over six foot with a mischievous twinkle in his brown eyes, he had been the officer on our successful cross-country team in India. He also played a bit of football and accompanied us when we went away to matches against other regiments. He had even played on a couple of occasions when we were stuck for numbers and had proved to be a solid centre half in the take-no-prisoners mould.

He had told us once on an away trip that his father had been a soldier and he had been sent to school in England before going on to Sandhurst Military College. At home during the summer in Douglas, he had played hurling and Gaelic football for the local club side.

When he was in familiar surroundings on away trips, he would lapse back into what I took to be a Cork accent, not unlike that of Brother O'Connell, who had taught me at the Christian Brothers. Captain Gerry, as we fondly called him when he was not listening, always seemed to wear his hat cocked slightly to the one side, and his tie was rarely fully tightened, giving him an air of unconformity.

On away trips and off duty, he was regarded as one of the boys, which was unusual because there was generally a class

MALCOLM MCCAUSLAND

gulf between the officers and the listed men. But we always felt reassured when he was in our company because he had got us out of one or two scrapes.

On one occasion, we had beaten the Royals East Kent (the Buffs) regiment, who we regarded as our main rivals in India, at their base, and we had celebrated well past curfew in a local establishment. Gerry, as he allowed us to call him on these occasions, had surprised us by singing "A Nation Once Again" and "The Boys of Wexford" during our singsong, and I could see our Protestant mates giving each other a knowing glance. We were trying to sneak in through the perimeter fence at the back of the camp of the Queen's Own Cameron Highlanders when we were halted by an officious sergeant major who seemed intent on locking us up in the guardroom. Captain Gerry appeared. He was always the last out of whatever establishment we were in and was about five minutes behind us.

"I'm sure, Sergeant Major, you have better things to do than lock up these brave Irishmen," he said in his best Sandhurst accent, albeit with a slight slur on account of the drink taken.

Although not in full uniform, the sergeant was quick to recognise from the pips on O'Sullivan's shirt that he was talking to an officer and quickly backed off.

"Yes, sir. I'm sorry. I didn't see you there. I wish you all a good night, and by the way, I've not seen any of you and you haven't seen me."

LION FOR A DAY

It was reports of incidents like this that spread like Chinese whispers among the rank and file that made Captain Gerry loved by all. We would have followed him to hell and back, as much out of affection as duty. It is just we did not realise at the time that that loyalty would soon be tested.

By now I had reached the command room, where I knocked on the door. I recognised the voice of Captain O'Sullivan telling me to come in. He was sitting at a table at the far side of the room with Colonel Koe and Colonel Matthews but moved across to a chair near the door as I entered.

"Private Hegarty reporting for duty, sir!"

"At ease, Private," he said making himself comfortable in what looked like an exceptionally large armchair. There was a pleasant smell of coffee in the room as the other officers continued their conversation at the table.

"I'm looking for a volunteer, Hegarty, and I know you're the man for the job. But there's no compulsion on you to take it. It's purely voluntary, and if you say no, there'll be no harm done."

"What is it?" I asked as curiosity got the better of me. At the same time, I remembered the old adage from growing up in Derry and going to the Christian Brothers. "Never volunteer. Never own up."

"All hell is going to kick off here soon and I need a messenger who is fast and can run all day. The signallers aren't going to be effective in this light and terrain, and we'll have no telegraph wires when we land to send signals by Morse. I need someone that I can trust to carry messages by hand, and you were my obvious choice as our Derry greyhound and cross-country champion. But I can't order you. It's purely voluntary."

"I'd be delighted to," I blurted out before I even thought to ask for more details.

"That's good. Come along here this time tomorrow. I'll brief you fully and give you a revolver and messenger's bag. In the meantime, I'd appreciate it if you said nothing to anyone."

I saluted and went back to my spot on the deck. My mind was racing away with the implications of what I had just signed up for: a messenger. I'm reminded now, on reflection, of the Greek shepherd who had brought the message of victory to ancient Athens.

"What was that all about?" asked one of my cabin mates, Mickey O'Neill from Belfast.

"Nothing much. He was just thinking about organising a football match or something," I said. "Want a game of cards? You must have some money left that I haven't taken off you yet."

I reported back the following day. This time, Captain O'Sullivan was on his own and sitting at the table on the far side of the room, looking at what appeared to be maps. He reached into a drawer and pulled out a service revolver of the kind given only to officers, along with spare bullets and a smallish black satchel with a shoulder strap and the regiment's insignia burned into the leather.

"You won't be able to bring your pack, so you'll have to live off the rations of other soldiers for maybe a few days," he explained. "And your rifle will be too heavy and cumbersome for you, which is why I've given you a revolver for your protection. I want you to be at my shoulder at all times when you're not running a message. I'll give you your final instructions tomorrow morning. Do you understand?"

"Yes sir," I said as I saluted.

"Oh, before you go, I suppose you heard that Rupert Brooke died on Skyros?"

My face must have looked fairly blank and uncomprehending as he continued.

"He was from Rugby, where we billeted before we came out here."

The penny dropped.

"Yes, sir. He lived just around the corner from where my young woman lives. She pointed out his house to me when we were out walking one evening. But I must confess I'm not really a fan of poetry."

"You have a young woman in Rugby? That was fast work, Hegarty! I hope you're as quick with my messages. Now off with you," he said with a smirk.

"Yes, sir. Thank you, sir. I promise I'll not let you down." I saluted and left as he turned away. It was obvious despite his good humour that there were serious matters on his mind as he returned to the maps on the table.

Two hours later, the order came to prepare to go ashore the following morning at five o'clock. I dug out the revolver, made sure it was oiled for action, and put the spare bullets in my tunic pocket. I would not be able to carry rations, so I got a bag of raisins from the store and put these in the messenger's bag along with a metal canteen of water. I was ready for action, but of what kind I was unsure. The other men were given two days' rations and two hundred rounds of ammunition. We were told that Colonels Koe and Matthews were the officers in command; Captain O'Sullivan was to answer to the former.

We were up at five o'clock the next morning and went ashore at Hellas Bay in an assortment of small crafts and barges. On Captain O'Sullivan's orders, I accompanied him on one of the boats at the front, and we were among the first to hit the shore at about 9 a.m. We were met with a hail of bullets from Turkish troops hidden well above us on the slopes overlooking the beach. We quickly moved 600 yards inland along with the First Battalion of the Border Regiment and started to dig in, taking up a position overlooking and protecting the beach.

Meantime, we could hear all hell breaking loose farther up the coast as the battleships fired on the Turkish land positions, with the enemy giving as good as they got from guns mounted inland on the ridge overlooking the coast. It would be some time later before we heard about the carnage inflicted on the East Lancs and the Anzacs farther up the headland.

The Turks attacked our positions that night, but we repulsed them quite easily and received orders to advance the following morning, which we were able to do, meeting surprisingly little resistance. We continued a few miles inland when the captain gave the order to dig in and have some food. He signalled me to come with him and a few other officers, and we carried on inland on foot, scrambling up the steep slopes towards the top of the ridge as far as the outskirts of the town called Krithia. At one point when we had reached the summit of a ridge, he stopped, turned to us, and pointed far across the water which was now in vision.

"I don't expect this means much to you, but if you look very carefully across the strait, you can pick out the ruins of Troy. It was one of the finest cities in creation but fell on account of one man's lust for another man's wife. I hope there is not a parallel in this mission."

"Paris and Helen?" I said before realising it.

"Hegarty, you never cease to surprise me. How did you know about Paris and Helen?"

"Sir, the Christian Brothers taught us some Greek mythology."

"Those Christian Brothers have a lot to answer for," he said as he continued on towards the village.

MALCOLM MCCAUSLAND

We were close enough now to see the locals going about their daily business, totally ignoring the war that was going on around them. Only half a dozen Turkish soldiers could be seen holding the town.

Captain O'Sullivan beckoned me towards him.

"As I feared," he said. "The signallers can't get a line, and I need you to run a message back to control for me. Tell them that we can take Krithia if they send me another five hundred men immediately. Wait an hour for an answer, but if none is forthcoming, come back as far as the line where the men are dug in."

He scribbled down a note in a little book he took from the inside pocket of his tunic, tore it out, folded it, and gave it to me.

"Show them this," he said. "And away you go now, like the wind."

It was liberating being able to take off without the weight of a pack. I careered headlong down some gullies, clambered slowly down the faces of some slopes, and sprinted along the flat when the opportunity arose. A couple of times, I thought I was going to fall over, but I reached the shore in little over an hour. I quickly spotted the command tent that had been erected in the shelter of the cliffs and dashed inside.

I sought out the commanding officer, Lieutenant Colonel Jones, and gasped out my message as I dug out the captain's note from my satchel at the same time. He took the slip of paper and I was dismissed with the instruction to return in thirty minutes. I spent the time well, obtaining a fresh supply of water and some food to carry with me on my return journey. Even after only two days of our landing, I was told to go easy with the water as it was in short supply.

Figure 3: The command ships anchored just off the beach at Gallipoli. Anton ran messages from the front lines to the beach when required. It was on the beach that he met the journalists to whom he related events that led eventually to the withdrawal of troops from the peninsula.

Sitting close to the command tent, I could hear the news coming through about the disastrous landings on the other beaches. An NCO was reporting in horrific detail how the Lancashires were decimated on W beach, suffering six hundred casualties from 1,000 men, many of them mowed down as they were disembarking the boats. Those who escaped the enemy machine guns got caught up in barbed wire laid below the surface of the water since the first assault on the peninsula a couple of months earlier.

This slaughter was replicated farther up the peninsula, where the Anzacs—soldiers from Australia and New Zealand—but also including the Twenty-Ninth Indian Infantry Brigade got caught on the beach under enemy fire and without any cover other than a small ledge of two to three feet where the sand met the land. The general opinion was that the top brass could not have picked worse points for landings if they had walked the whole coast. The maps they were given were inaccurate and out of date. Worst of all, the Turks were far from the pushovers we had been led to believe from our officers when we were briefed prior to the invasion.

I re-entered the command tent, as instructed, after half an hour, only to be informed that there was no response yet received to Captain O'Sullivan's message. The communication had been delivered to the overall commander, Sir Ian Hamilton, a Scot, who was well liked by the men but already had the reputation as a bit of a ditherer. It seemed he preferred books and poetry to guns.

As instructed by Captain Gerry, I took to my feet again to tell him that I had not got a response within the sixty minutes. This time it was much harder going as I had to climb all the hills that I had freewheeled down earlier. I eventually found our lines as darkness descended and quickly realised that the Turkish snipers were now in place as sporadic shots rained down on our positions. I located the captain, pistol in hand, on the top of a small rise in full view of the enemy. The captain was one of those men I met in the war, maybe only one in 10,000, who seemed to have this air of invulnerability, who never thought that they would be shot, unlike the rest of us, who lived in a constant state of fear.

"No reply?" he asked.

"No reply, sir."

"Well, feck that," I heard him whisper under his breath. "Damned we could have taken that town, and we might not get as good an opportunity again," he continued to mumble as he came down from his vantage point.

He had now been left second in command, and leading our left flank, after the death of Colonel Koe, while the other joint commander, Colonel Matthews, headed up our left flank. I passed on the information I had gained about the other landings, which obviously did nothing to improve his mood in any way.

"Well done, Hegarty. You're dismissed," he said after a pause to take everything on board. "Come back in the morning. Get yourself some food and water," he added. He pointed me in the direction of the other men, as an apparent afterthought, his mind clearly preoccupied with other matters.

For the next three days, there was a relative calm with only occasional sniping, but on the night of 1 May, the Turks mounted a fierce attack. Thankfully forewarned, we were prepared to meet fire with fire. Bombers comprised the Turkish first line, and they were promptly bayoneted on the parapet before the main attack began. On the captain's order, the main body of our men waited until the Turks were within thirty yards before opening rapid fire and quashing the attack. When dawn arrived, we saw the extent of the damage we had done by the numbers of dead Turks piled in front of our lines. Farther distant in a dip in the ground, a party of Turks was seen sheltering. Fire was opened on them, and they showed a white flag. A total of 142 officers and men were captured and seemed pleased to be out of the conflict.

I thought by now that I would have been redundant as a messenger because the signallers had come and put down wires for communication. Whilst these sunk down into the mud on the Western Front and remained out of sight, because of the hard terrain on Gallipoli, they stayed on the surface and were easily cut by marauding Turks. For this reason, I was kept on standby and was soon ordered to take word of our success and a request for reinforcements back to the command centre on the beach.

Lieutenant Colonel Jones welcomed the news, and as he was still waiting on orders from Sir Ian Hamilton, he decided to accompany me to the front lines to assess the situation himself at first hand. On his orders, we advanced the following morning at 7:30, but progress was slow on both flanks. Then the battalion on our right retired in some confusion and the order came for the whole line to fall back to the trench from which we had advanced. Lieutenant Colonel Jones was struck by a shell while reorganising the men on the right of the Inniskillings, but the wound did not seem fatal at that stage. He received some initial treatment before being taken to the beach and evacuated with the

LION FOR A DAY

other wounded on the *HMHS Caledonia* to Alexandria, Egypt. We learned a few days later that unfortunately he had succumbed to his wounds whilst on the voyage and, like so many other men, was buried at sea. Loss of our leader did our already sinking morale no good at all.

By this time, I was back on the beach and had recovered my main pack, which had been kept for me in the supplies tent but found it had been left at the bottom of a barge. It had got soaked through, ruining most of my rations and soaking all my clothes. I hung my great coat out on a bush to dry, and when I returned, I found that a sniper's bullet had pierced the back of it right between the shoulders. I counted this a lucky escape, but the coat was to prove even more fortuitous several days later when I was running a message late in the afternoon when darkness fell as suddenly as it usually did on Gallipoli. One minute it was bright, the next you were in total darkness.

I got hopelessly lost and ended up in a trench with bodies from armies strewn along the sides. I could hear Turkish voices approach from the opposite direction and was about to turn on my heel and run like hell when I realised there was a small contingent of Turks approaching from the other side as well. I did not know what to do when I remembered that crafty old jackal in India. I quickly donned the coat and threw myself prostrate on the ground.

The smell from the corpses was sickening, and I ended up staring eye to eye with a dead fusilier. I recognised him as one of the new recruits who had joined us at Avonmouth. The two groups of Turks made slow progress towards me, and as they got closer, I could see they were going through the pockets of the dead, presumably for cigarettes and valuables.

I came out in a cold sweat as I watched them slowly approaching me, methodically stripping the dead of their possessions with grunts of pleasure when they found something of use or value. Finally, they reached my length and I could feel someone rifling through the pockets of my great coat. I held my breath and prayed they did not feel my body heat which would mean the end of me. Discovering nothing as I had moved my things to under my belly, they moved on to my dead recruit friend. They seemed pleased with their finds.

By now, the two groups had met and exchanged pleasantries. I could smell the strong aroma of Turkish cigarettes being lit as they engaged in what appeared to be a light-hearted conversation. I was saying Hail Marys and Our Fathers, prayers I leant as a child, under my breath because this lot was not going to take a prisoner. It would be a bullet in the back of the head if I was rumbled.

After what seemed like hours, but was probably only a few minutes, both groups returned towards the respective directions from which they came. To say I drew a long sigh of relief would be an understatement, and when I felt it safe to do so, I took off again at top speed, aided by the moon that was now out. I could clearly see the sparkling sea in the distance and headed in that direction. Being badly astray, I hit the beach somewhere south of the East Lancs' position but was able to work my way back to our encampment. After delivering my message, I got some water, which was

LION FOR A DAY

in increasingly short supply, and food from the stores, before settling down for the night under what I now felt was my lucky great coat.

The following day I returned to the lines to find us now under heavy shelling from guns on the high ground. The order came sometime later to withdraw to the beach, bringing the first phase of our invasion to an end. The Turkish snipers did not relent, and you did not dare to put your head above the low ledge along the fringe of the beach. The snipers seemed to be everywhere. I had run across one on my travel some days back. He was dug in the whole way up to his neck directly behind a bush for cover. He did not see me as I approached him from behind, and I was able to slip away unnoticed. I reported his position and I think a small party was sent to sort him out. They must have been successful because his foxhole was empty the next time I went by the spot.

As well as the shortage of water, the flies were now becoming a problem. You could not eat your food without it being attacked by them before it got to your mouth. This gave rise to all sorts of stomach complaints and diarrhoea. The only respite from them was after dark, but then the rats started coming in from no man's land between the trenches, where they had been feasting on the dead corpses. This brought back bad memories of rat-infested houses in Derry.

My good luck did not last forever and ran out in the most freakish of circumstances. I went out to the karsey. No one lingered there on account of the smell, but during my brief stay, I heard a bullet ricochet off the rock above me followed by an excruciating pain in my left hand. I looked and the blood was pouring out of it. I immediately made it to one of the hospital tents on the beach, where they had to apply a tourniquet to halt the bleeding. Instead of being greeted with sympathy or even compassion, the medical officer in charge of the field officer interrogated me as to how I had got the wound. I explained about going out to the karsey and hearing a ricochet and feeling the sharp pain in my hand, but my story seemed to be met with some scepticism.

"Do you know you're the fifth soldier to come in here today with a wound to the hand?" He stared me intently in the eyes as he asked the question slowly and deliberately, emphasising the word "hand."

"No, sir, I didn't know that, but my wound is genuine. I think they are targeting our latrines."

"Do you know the punishment for self-wounding?" he continued.

"No, sir, but I didn't self-wound," I responded as blood continued to pump out of my hand.

"A firing squad at dawn, Private!" He continued to stare me in the eyes.

With that, several more stretchers came through the door of the large canvas tent.

"Orderly, take this man and have him treated," said the medical officer as he turned to presage the new arrivals.

LION FOR A DAY

I was treated by a second doctor, who told me that it looked like the bullet had done more damage on account of it being a ricochet rather than a direct hit, shattering several bones and tearing tendons. This doctor also said they might have to amputate the hand from the wrist, but I resisted the suggestion and asked if they could just bandage it up for me.

But it was not that simple, they said, with the possibility that I might get an infection or even gangrene. Fortunately, there was a boat just about to leave for the hospital ship and they put me on a barge and took me out to it. The medical staff on the ship made a similar diagnosis but unusually deferred to my wishes and staunched the bleeding, giving me an injection of morphine to kill the pain.

Luckily for me, they decided to ship me on to Alexandria for further treatment and recovery. I learned that they often amputated hands and feet when it was not absolutely necessary but simply because it was easier and faster than allowing the wounds to heal with the possible danger of infection. It was also thought to be a deterrent to stop men shooting themselves in the hand or foot as a means of getting out of the war. It may not have been a highly effective deterrent, given the number of one-handed soldiers I was about to play cards with while convalescing in Egypt.

On board the hospital ship, it soon became apparent that it had been previously used to transport the mules and horses to the peninsula and that now their stalls, still uncleaned, had become "wards." Our transport carried 1,600 wounded, including three hundred stretcher cases, with just four doctors working heroically to treat them. We overtook another small ship on which the wounded lay uncovered on the deck all the way to Alexandria, a journey of three nights, while in other vessels the wounded were accommodated in holds without ventilation.

"Do you think it's God's punishment?" asked the man in the bunk next me as I settled in for my first night on the ship.

"Do you think it's God's punishment?" he repeated as I realised the question was addressed to me.

I looked across and recognised Billy Smyth underneath the bandage that circled the upper proportion of his head. He and his brother Sam were from Glendermott, over the bridge in Derry from where I grew up. They were among the new recruits who had joined us in Avonmouth before our departure for Gallipoli.

"What do you mean, Billy? I asked tentatively.

"Do you think this is God's punishment? I mean for centuries we have gone to all parts of the world and enforced our will. We've shot and killed, taken anything of value. Mr Churchill took the two ships from the Turks that they had bought and paid for, and then he sends hundreds of thousands of men and ships to attack them in their homeland. Imagine if some nation did that to us."

I was going to say that it did happen to us in Ireland around seven hundred years ago, but I decided that perhaps it was not the best time to open that can of worms.

"Never thought of it that way, Billy, but you're right," I said, taking the easy option.

He grunted and turned over to go to sleep, and that was the end of his philosophising.

When I went to wake him in the morning, he did not stir. Prodding him with my good hand, I realised he was cold and stiff. He had died during the night from his wounds. And he was not the only one. When we reached Alexandria, there were perhaps three hundred dead on arrival. The hospital staff were appalled at what they discovered when they boarded the ships. Many men were filthy and bloody just as they had left the battlefield days before. Their bandages were unchanged, and their wounds were gangrenous and septic. Nevertheless, I was glad to be off that peninsula and attended by the wonderful nurses who worked tirelessly sixteen hours a day.

CHAPTER 8

BACK IN THE FIRING LINE

I hate war as only a soldier who has
lived it can, only as one who has seen
its brutality, its futility, its stupidity.

—*Dwight D. Eisenhower*

I may have escaped the horrors of war for a few months, but I could not get away from the bad news. I had barely been admitted into the hospital in Alexandria when I received a telegram from my mother to tell me that my brother had died on 12 May.

The telegram would have reached me earlier, but it had lain in the comms tent for a couple of weeks before they realised that I had been wounded and transferred on the hospital ship to Alexandria. In the end, the slip of paper was brought to me by a nurse who obviously knew, from the expression on her face, she was the bearer of bad news. I read it time and time again until it sunk in.

LION FOR A DAY

> Sad news. Your brother Joe died 12 May 1915.
> Acute pneumonia. Died peaceably after short
> illness. God rest his soul. Love and God bless.
> Mammy

I thought about our poor mother, who would have just buried her son, aged only 23, when she got a telegram informing her that another son was wounded in a far-off war. I am sure this recent loss must have brought back the memories of the other children she had lost over the years.

I had written to her shortly after my arrival in hospital, to reassure her that it was only a hand wound and I was very much alive. She must have wondered why I never mentioned Joe's death. I sat down and wrote a follow-up letter explaining the delay in the telegram reaching me and reassuring her again that I would be fine. Obviously, I was shocked, but I also felt helpless being so far from home at a time like this and unable to console my poor mammy at a time when she needed support. But then I realised, like most Derry mothers, she was strong in every sense and had always been the rock of our family.

That was not the end of the bad news either, with Corporal James Somers coming through among the wounded with more sad tidings. He was originally a Munster Fusilier but transferred across to the Skins First Battalion when we were billeted in Rugby and joined my company. He informed me that Captain Gerry had died in action. That came as quite a shock as I never imagined that he would not survive the war to return safely to his family. James said that the captain had been wounded earlier fighting a trench full of Turks on his own but refused to leave the action to go to the hospital ship for treatment. He had the doctor bandage up a flesh wound in his forearm and was back on duty the following day. I could picture him gung-ho despite his wounds, rallying the men to go forward, himself at the front leading by example.

He did not learn anything from the incident because he took fifty men with him several weeks later to capture a hill held by the Turks. According to James, who was with him, Captain Gerry stormed up the steep slope while throwing hand bombs in front of him, and although they captured the hill, the captain was hit by a sniper and killed instantly. He had been recommended for the highest military honour, a Victoria Cross, but it seemed poor recompense for the life of such a brave officer and exceptional human being. I felt like I had lost two brothers in a matter of weeks.

Somers, being a modest Cavan man, whose family had now settled in County Tipperary, failed to tell me that he had also been recommended for a Victoria Cross. I had to hear this from another of the wounded, Barney Donaghey from my hometown, who in fact had grown up in the street next to me. I challenged James about his modesty the next time our paths crossed in the rehabilitation.

"What's this about you getting a VC?" I taunted him, knowing now that he had held a trench in the face of severe enemy attacks.

"It was nothing."

LION FOR A DAY

We did learn details of his encounter some evenings later when a group of us were gathered and another of the wounded was able to tell us more details.

"He beat Turks out of our trench, and he had four awful hours at night," his colleague explained. "The Turks swarmed in from all roads, but he gave them a rough time of it, still holding the trench until reinforcements arrived with a good supply of hand bombs. James then grabbed a handful of these and almost single-handedly drove the enemy out of their positions overlooking our line. When it got light the next day, it was shocking to see the dead. There lay about 3,000 Turks in front of our trench, and the smell was absolutely chronic. You know when the sun has been shining on those bodies for three or four days it makes a horrible smell. A person would not mind if it was possible to bury them. But no, you dare not put your nose outside the trench, for if you did, you would be a dead man."

When James was recovered from his shoulder wound, they sent him home to convalesce for some weeks and they used him at several recruiting rallies in Ireland to encourage enlistments. Although we knew that huge numbers were signing up in the cities like Dublin and Belfast, only a dwindle came forward from rural locations.

Meanwhile, my hand was slow to mend. It took two months of recovery and gentle exercise before I was able to clench my fist again, and only then with pain. I had hoped they would send me home to recover, but I think with suspicions that I had self-wounded, they passed me fit to go back to Gallipoli. They told me that because my hand was still not

MALCOLM MCCAUSLAND

fully functional, I would be given general duties behind the lines.

As it turned out, I joined a squad of men who were given the chore of digging latrines, which had to be well out of sight of the enemy snipers. The Turkish sharpshooters had made a fine art out of killing men while they were doing their ablutions. When we had first landed, everyone had done whatever they had to do wherever they could find a quiet spot. This meant that it soon became impossible to go in any direction without stepping in someone's faeces. This, the flies, and the scores of dead bodies and dead animals had led to epidemics of various stomach complaints and dysentery. At one time, as many as 40 per cent of the land forces could be *Hors de combat* through illness.

Water was also in short supply, and with no source on the peninsula, it had to be brought in from Lemnos in huge tanks. But there was still never enough, and consequently what there was had to be rationed. The water itself was bitter and gave us all sick stomachs, which led to vomiting and added to the dehydration. They then decided to put potassium permanganate to the water to sterilise it, but they must have gotten the amounts wrong because nearly everybody, myself included, got the most awful fit of stomach cramps and diarrhoea.

The food was no better. Without refrigeration facilities, there was no fresh meat for the men and no army bakery to supply fresh bread. Instead, the men had to exist on a diet of bully beef and hardtack biscuits. The beef was like sliced corn beef and came in distinctive tins, while the hardtack

LION FOR A DAY

was a mixture of wheat flour, water, and salt. By baking the biscuit multiple times, all moisture was drawn out of it. Not surprisingly, hardtack was not a favourite for anyone who had to eat it and was often referred to as "tooth breaker."

Being in the service unit on the beach meant I met all sorts of characters. Possibly the most unique was an Englishman who came to be known as "the man with the donkey," later made famous in a painting by Horace Moore-Jones. John Simpson was a muscular, young private from the north-east of England who had been a fireman in civilian life.

He became a stretcher-bearer in the Third Field Ambulance, and having carried heavy men down the steep slopes, one day he chanced upon a donkey nibbling on some grass in a gully and decided to use the animal to carry wounded soldiers back to the temporary field hospitals. Showing no concern for his own safety, day in day out, he ventured into no man's land to retrieve wounded soldiers. Despite being under enemy fire at times, he conveyed hundreds of men back for treatment with the aid of his donkey. For weeks, the soldier and his donkey, with a Red Cross bandana tied around its head, became a familiar sight by day and night as they ran their errands of mercy up and down the ravines and gullies between the front line and the beach.

Sadly, one day, Simpson was shot straight through the heart. He was buried in the evening at the bottom of Shrapnel Gully. His donkey was adopted as a pet by the Indians of the Sixth Mountain Battery, who had nicknamed Simpson Bahadur, meaning "the bravest of the brave." I went to his burial service as we had exchanged salutations on a number of occasions without ever getting to know each other any better. I think he must have had Irish connections because I learned at the service that he was known as Murphy to his mates.

The priest, Fr O'Reilly, read a letter that had arrived for him from his mother shortly after his death. She wrote, "My dearest son, hoping and trusting that the Lord in His great mercy will guard and protect you in these terrible times and hear my prayers for you." He went on to relate how Simpson always carried a picture of his mother with him. Indeed, most of us carried the picture of a loved one, for solace when we were enduring the most difficult of days or nights. I always had the photo that Gertie sent me on my person, along with a set of rosary beads my mother had gifted me before I left for the army. Both were great sources of comfort in trying times.

Meanwhile, with my digging duties completed, my next assignment saw me on guard duty outside the comms tent, where one day there were two war correspondents hanging around hoping to get an update on the latest attacks by our troops. One of these was an Englishman called Ellis Ashmead-Bartlett, which I read from the identity card he wore around his neck, while the other was a young Australian named Keith Murdoch.

I heard them discussing the terrible aftermath of the August offensives on Krithia and the Suvla Bay landings. They made no attempt to lower their voices, and it was quite obvious that they were sceptical about the whole military operation on Gallipoli.

LION FOR A DAY

"Sirs, excuse me for interrupting, but we could have taken Krithia within two days of our landing," I said meekly.

They seemed taken aback by the interruption, and I could see them looking at my sleeve and recognising that I was a lowly private.

"And what makes you say that, soldier?" asked the Englishman somewhat condescendingly as he peered over the top of his slightly twisted glasses.

"Let him talk, Ellis," said Murdoch in his very obvious Aussie accent. "What makes you say that, Private?"

I went on to relate about us landing and meeting extraordinarily little resistance, being able to move inland to within sight of Krithia, and Captain O'Sullivan asking for permission to take the town, which very obviously had only a few defenders. I pointed out the lack of a timely response and us being forced to withdraw to our first line of offence. I went on to tell them about Colonels Koe and Matthews, who could not agree on which was in command.

I said that not even the ordinary Tommy could understand why we had landed at the point of the peninsula and not the other end, where we would have had command of the strait as well as breaking the Turks' supply lines. The more I talked, the more the pair nodded in a mixture of agreement and incredulity. Our conversation had to ended abruptly when an officer who obviously had overheard the conversation popped his head out of tent. I ducked around the corner before he nabbed me while the journalists went off—I expect to write up their reports.

I did not see either of them again for about a month when I was on sentry duty and the Englishman Ellis came along with a different war correspondent to the comms tent. He remembered me and, when no one was looking, nodded me to the one side.

"I put what you told us in an uncensored report, but they intercepted the document in Marseilles," he confided. "Murdoch has now left for England, and he told me he is going to write his own account. I'm not sure what will happen with that but thank you for sharing your experiences with us."

We were given a week's break in Imbros at the end of September, where we were inspected by the overall commander, Lieutenant General Sir Ian Hamilton, before returning to the Hellas Bay front that very same day. By now, the autumn had arrived in Gallipoli and we seemed to be enjoying an informal truce with the Turks. Neither side was initiating any assaults, and while the occasional sniper could be heard, it seemed more intended to tell us they were still there rather than to inflict any damage.

Such was the lull in hostilities, football was started in the reserve area at Cape Hellas, and we beat the King's Own Scottish Borderers 1–0 after extra time in the first round of the Dardanelles Cup. This was quite an achievement as many of our opponents still had players from the KOSB FC who had played in the Irish League in 1903–04 season, having earlier been in the Leinster League while stationed in Dublin.

There was extra needle to the match, with us being aware that the KOSB had been involved in the Bachelors Walk Massacre the previous year in Dublin. The carnage took place when a column from the regiment was accosted by a crowd of protesters on Bachelors Walk in the south of the city. The troops retaliated against the demonstrators, who were described in newspaper accounts as being "hostile but unarmed," with rifle fire and bayonets, killing four and injuring another thirty civilians.

The massacre followed the purchase of 1,500 rifles and ammunition for the Irish Volunteers in Germany to counter the Protestants smuggling much larger consignments of guns into the north of Ireland. Whilst the Protestants had been allowed to import and distribute their arms with little interference, the reaction from the British ruling authorities this time was to attempt to seize the entire shipment bound for the south, setting off the protests from Republican sympathisers.

Our match looked to have passed off peaceably despite the rancour, until we were coming off the pitch at the end when one of the Scots shouted, "At least we sorted you Paddies out in Dublin!" That was the spark that lit the flame, and within seconds, it was an eleven-a-side, no-holds-barred brawl that lasted at least ten minutes before troops on the side-line, under orders from the officers, stepped in with weapons raised to put an end to the fight.

None of us, even the Catholics, had much time for the Republican agitators at home, but as they say, blood is thicker than water and we reacted instinctively. And fair play to our Protestant mates, they piled in on our side without hesitation and great gusto, despite many of them sharing the same surnames and ethnicity as our Scottish adversaries.

I think we all realised that things were changing at home and, especially for us from the Nationalist community, old emotions were being awakened. And it was only going to get more obvious in the years ahead.

It was noticeable by this time that our numbers in the peninsula were diminishing, with wounded men being shipped off never to return. Some had died, but we preferred to believe that those taken away in hospital ships were enjoying their recovery in the land of the pharaohs. Certainly, nobody was returning, and we assumed they had been transferred to other units.

Another indicator that our days in Gallipoli were ending came when Hamilton was relieved of his command towards the end of the October. We heard the usual platitudes from the officers after Hamilton sent a message as to how much he was honoured to command such a fine force, etc. The fighting men were used to receiving praise from the top brass before being sent out to die in what it had become clear was a totally botched and foolhardy campaign.

Initially the impression was that Hamilton had been an outstanding commander of the Mediterranean Forces, but that opinion was now changing as we read our mail and newspapers clippings sent to us that painted a picture of an affable man who could not make a decision. Going through the clippings that were passed around among us men, I was surprised to read an article in *The Times* by Keith Murdoch. He outlined the danger and squalor in our lives, the sickness, the monotonous food, and lack of water. Worst of all, he wrote, was the general air of depression that permeated through every man jack of us. But his clearest message was that the British forces were using nineteenth-century tactics on a twentieth-century battlefield. In other words, we were lions led by donkeys.

Winter announced its arrival at the end of November in dramatic but grim fashion. A rainstorm preceded a heavy snowfall as an icy gale from the Russian steppes saw temperatures plummet. Trenches were obliterated, guard posts flooded, and men drowned, while others, weakened by illness and inadequate clothing, simply died from the cold. I was glad again of my great coat. While we suffered huge casualties militarily at Hellas Bay, losses due to the weather at Anzac and Suvla Bay exceeded those suffered during the fighting.

Unfortunately, one of those to succumb to the cold was Sam Smyth. He was brought in on a stretcher, cold and shivering, but did not last any time. It had been his brother Billy who had died from his wounds on the hospital ship just four months earlier, and I am sure a second bereavement in such a short space of time would leave his family in Derry's Waterside totally distraught.

The only good thing to come out of this was that it brought home to those sitting in warm offices in Whitehall that this war was not going to be won any time soon, if at all. Therefore, it came as no surprise when we heard just before Christmas that both Hellas and ANZAC beaches had been successfully evacuated without loss. We feared that when this became obvious to the Turks, they would launch an assault on us that would drive us back into the sea. Thankfully, this never happened, and it seemed that they had endured enough of this futile conflict as we had. We had a hearty Christmas Day thanks to parcels posted from home by the organisers of the Inniskilling Fund. Better followed just before the New Year, when we were informed that we would be leaving in early January.

As a first step towards the evacuation, we were to move all our baggage and equipment to the beach. We went about it with the vigour of schoolboys in the last week at school before the summer holidays. We fashioned all sorts of devices to make the enemy believe we were still there long after we had departed. We laid booby traps and landmines and dressed up dummy soldiers that made excellent use of old and worn uniforms.

The most ambitious devices were the "clockwork rifles" that we loaded and fixed facing the Turkish positions. Needing 7 pounds of force to pull the trigger, a tin containing 6 pounds of sand was hung from the trigger. A second tin, with a small perforation and containing water, was suspended immediately above the sand. The water dripped slowly, but when the weight of the can of sand, plus water, reached 7

LION FOR A DAY

pounds, the trigger was activated. Less sophisticated was the removal to the beach of all arms, ammunition, and equipment so as not to be of use to the enemy.

Finally, we heard that it was Z day, the date of our departure. All our devices were now in place, the rifles were set to fire some hours after our evacuation, and the dummy soldiers were in the trenches to discourage an early Turkish attack that would disrupt our withdrawal. Being in the front line, we carried little equipment or clothing, which made it easier, and the exit was planned in three trips to our ship waiting off the coast. Our feet were muffled with blankets and sandbags to eliminate the noise of our boots, and the men for the first trip were assembled at dusk in the reserve trenches.

They moved off right on the scheduled time and were conveyed on a lighter, a flat-bottomed barge to the *Staunch*. Back on the shore, we waited patiently for the return of the transport, and the second batch left at 11.45 p.m. with 1,100 men safely on board the *Staunch* when the destroyer sailed for Mudros at 4 a.m.

I was one of the men from our company. There were six detailed from each, who remained behind to fire rifles in various locations to confuse the Turks. We completed our task by midnight, leaving the automatic rifles to their work, and as we returned down towards the beach, we dragged barbed wire "gooseberries" into the communication tunnels to block any advance by that route.

The whole of the rear party met at battalion headquarters before going down to the beach to await our transport, which was delayed because the navy had not been able to cope with all the people waiting to embark on the lighters.

While we were waiting, we watched with sadness while the veterinary officers shot hundreds of mules that we were not able to take with us. It was one of the most sickening things I ever saw, and I thought of what my father could not have done with those fine animals. He could have sold them to the well-to-do farmers out in the prosperous Laggan area in east Donegal and lived off the proceeds for the rest of his life. Meantime, I was sitting on a rock on this God-forsaken beach while waiting for transport to get out of this hell.

Eventually, our turn came and we boarded, but by now the sea had become much rougher and we were tossed about like a cork on the waves. When we about a mile from shore, we were ordered to stand under the metal awning covering the deck of the ship for shelter. No sooner than we did so, there was a huge explosion of armaments on the beach and we could hear pieces of metal raining down on the tin roof above us. The danger did not end as the rough seas not only made us all seasick but broke our line to the mother vessel, setting us adrift on the increasingly angry waters.

Strangely, no one seemed overconcerned. We were just that glad to get off Gallipoli. We remained adrift all night until the *Scorpion* got a line to us and took us in tow to Lemnos, where we transferred to a tug that conveyed us on to Mudros and safety.

CHAPTER 9

TRENCH WARFARE

*And towards our distant
rest began to trudge.
Men marched asleep. Many
had lost their boots,
But limped on, blood-shod.
All went lame; all blind.*

— *"Dulce et Decorum Est"* by Wilfred Owen

After a brief stopover in Mudros, it was aboard ship again before arriving six days later at Suez camp, near Alexandria. The warm winter sun lifted our moods, and we were relieved to be soon back to our normal routine of reveille, pack inspections, and drilling.

We were told that during our time in Gallipoli, the First Battalion had 267 killed, 1001 wounded, and seventy-nine still missing, probably never to be found. Of the original battalion that had come from India, we were now only two officers and 114 men remaining. We knew too that our war was far from over, being already informed that our next deployment would be on the Western Front in Europe, where the Kaiser's crack troops awaited us. Despite being far away from the constant threat and danger experienced in Gallipoli, we were still constantly on our guard, ready to dive for cover at the least unexpected noise.

From conversations, I also knew it was more than me who was having trouble sleeping. Most of us were waking up in the middle of the night and unable to get back to sleep again. I suppose it was this sensitivity to danger that helped us survive in Gallipoli, not underestimating the craft learned from that old jackal in India who faked death to avoid death.

Nevertheless, we were determined to enjoy every minute of our stay in Egypt. Taking stock of our belongings, we realised that we lacked many items that in peaceful times we were used to laying out for kit inspection. Ordinarily, we would have had to pay the considerable cost of their replacement, but in these exceptional circumstances, we were promised free replacements.

Our clothes were also in poor condition after our exploits in Gallipoli, and we were assured we would get new uniforms when supplies arrived from England. Worse still, we had not received any pay for months, though fortunately I had kept some local currency from when I was in hospital and was able to supplement our drab army diet with fruit, which was abundant in the local markets.

I was able to renew my acquaintance with Barney Donaghey, who like me was from Derry and had been a childhood hero of mine. A semi-professional footballer when the war broke

LION FOR A DAY

out, he immediately volunteered for military service and joined the First Battalion of the Royal Inniskilling Fusiliers.

We had been in Gallipoli together but in different companies. We met when we both played the football match at Hellas against the King's Own Scottish Borderers. Shortly afterwards, he had received a head wound from shrapnel and been transported from Gallipoli a few weeks before our withdrawal. He had been in a field hospital at Tanta and was now recovered and back to normal duties.

During a long career, Barney Donaghey had played for Manchester United, Burnley, and a host of Irish clubs, as well as making one appearance for the Irish international team. I remember, as a boy, watching him play for Derry Celtic when he terrorised opponents on the wing with his speed and dribbling ability. Standing only 5 feet, 4 inches, and weighing 10 stone, he was a real will-o'-the-wisp and had run riot in our match against KOSB. But for our failure to convert the many opportunities he created; we could have won quite handsomely.

I made the most of the free time to resume my long walks twice per week. I had not done these since we were in India, and they took me to within sight of the pyramids and the other ancient Egyptian monuments. Every second day or so I went down to the exercise ground, and following the guidance from an old and now tattered book on training called *Pedestrianism, Health and General Training* I had picked up in the camp, I finished with a few sprints to improve my speed, which had never matched up to my stamina.

Despite having little or no money between us, Barney and I decided we would visit Alexandria, getting there by walking and the occasional lift in an army vehicle. I still had a few local coins left totalling five piastres, worth about a shilling at the time, which bought us some fruit and two sweet cakes in a market, as well as strong coffees in a café.

We ate the fruit and cakes fairly rapidly but took our time in the cafe, where we sat among Arabs who appeared to be fairly well off, judging by their robes and fezzes. Several of them hired hookahs, with their glass water containers standing on the floor, and smoked through the long, flexible tubes leading up to the mouthpiece which they gripped between their teeth. A look of contentment settled on them as soon as the smoke started to flow through their lungs.

Other customers were less tranquil as they talked loudly among themselves, while a few intrigued me by counting circular strings of beads as they said their mumbled prayers. Later, I learned that they were of the Coptic Church, an eastern branch of Catholicism.

By now, we were penniless and wandered aimlessly around the town, taking in the sights and smells of the busy city. By chance we passed through Rue Des Soeurs, commonly known to British soldiers as "Sisters Street," which was notorious for its brothels. We were approached by a number of girls, some maybe as young as 11 or 12, who quickly lost interest in us when we made it clear we had no money. Undaunted, we finished up the tour of what was a fascinating city before making our way back to our camp by sundown and just in time to have our bully beef and hardtack for supper.

LION FOR A DAY

We received orders the following morning to prepare for a train journey of about six hours to Cairo, and after breakfast, we marched to the railhead, where we loaded on to the wagons a great number of canvas bags containing tents, quantities of shovels and picks, and provisions. We filled our water bottles for what promised to be a long, hot rail journey.

The luck of the draw saw some men travel in roofed carriages but most of us boarding open wagons, while the officers and senior NCOs occupied a coach with proper seating. At times we suffered from the full overhead sun, but the scenery more than compensated with frequent views of the Nile.

Frequently, the workers in the plantations stopped their work to look at us and, in what we were told was a mark of respect, raised their robes to display their genitals. "Balls to you too, mate," said one of my mates.

After some hours, we got off the train at a railway halt with several small buildings and a short, wooden platform and immediately set to unloading the baggage and other equipment on board. Then hard biscuits and individual tins of corned beef were handed out with large containers full of strong tea appearing shortly afterwards. We were able to draw breath and survey the locality, and I was able to pick out a small, level plain where I could train.

Nearby, an ox turned a large, wooden wheel, walking in innumerable circles to drag a chain of leather buckets into and out of a well. These buckets disgorged their contents into a large, metal container whose overflow poured into a wooden duct and supplied the irrigation system of channels throughout the plantation.

Not that far away, we could see a village that we later learned was called Beni Salama, the same name as the railway halt. It seemed to comprise mainly small, mud huts that housed the poor folk who worked on the cotton plantations and reminded me of the villages near our camp at Secunderabad—or Krithia for that matter.

We hauled the tent bags some distance away from the railway and commenced erecting these in parallel lines, with an equal distance between them as marked out by the officers with ropes. The larger marquees proved more difficult, but we still completed our task comfortably before the sun set.

We had each been given two blankets, and being extra tired, we were soon were off to sleep—no nightmares that night. Some poor chaps were assigned to mount guard and scare off intruders, such as the jackals and other wild animals, that lurked around our tents.

The next few days, we continued to work hard, putting the camp in order on our diet of hard biscuits, corned beef, and dried, shredded veg, with a little jam and a small amount of cheese once or twice a week when further supplies arrived. Each day, a train brought in a new load of tents to be unpacked and fresh battalions arriving to fill those tents. Then the Royal Engineers arrived, trained tradesmen for the most part, and things really looked up. They brought tools and a huge quantity of sectional piping and standard-sized

LION FOR A DAY

rectangles of the framed matting we had often seen used to build reed or cane huts in India.

In what seemed no time at all, they put up showers, ablutions, and cooking shelters in endless lines between camp and the river. They also constructed a purifying plant way over by the river to remove the human waste. Now we were able to have a cool shower whenever we wanted and really needed in the hot and humid conditions.

Barney and I made the most of our leisure time. He was not particularly keen on accompanying me on my long walks but was an enthusiastic training partner when it came to the calisthenics and sprinting. He could put two yards on me in the first ten of any sprints, and it was obvious that he had always looked after himself, being a teetotaller and non-smoker. Practically everyone in the company, apart from the two of us, smoked, and they maintained a cigarette was great source of relaxation and good for your health. Neither Barney nor I had ever taken to them. Maybe it was that both of us had grown up surrounded by so many people who had suffered bronchitis and other chest problems.

Although now 33 and considered well past retirement age, Barney said that he hoped to return to Derry Celtic for one last season, which he said would be his swansong as a player, before moving on to management. Already a couple of Belfast clubs had asked him to join their training staffs before he had decided to join the army.

It was remarkable how quick our fitness improved while exercising in the warm climate, but sadly we were soon on the train back to Alexandria and boarding the transport ships for France.

The mood on board this time was similar to when we were going to Mudros in advance of the invasion of Gallipoli, except now we would be facing the Germans, who were probably the best trained, best armed, and best disciplined soldiers in the whole world, except for the glorious Twenty-Ninth Division of course.

We had lost so many close friends and colleagues to the resolute Turks, and inevitably we were going to lose even more to an even more formidable enemy. Even our officers, usually full of gung-ho, seemed quiet and contemplative. No one spoke of the imminent war, and we tried to escape our own thoughts by writing letters home. Barney, who had a wife and four children, still found time, after sending each one a separate little note, to practise with a football up on deck to *keep his hand in,* as he put it.

We arrived at Marseille on 18 March, having been given a ration of rum the previous day to celebrate St Patrick's Day. We made the long train journey in France north to the battle lines and were brought up to the front in converted London buses.

It was my first time to ride on motorised transport, and they said it would put paid to the horse as a means of carriage. We were told that the strength of the battalion was twenty-nine officers and 745 men before taking over our first trenches from the South Wales Borderers. The Welsh regiment's first battalion had been involved in France since 1914, while their

LION FOR A DAY

second battalion had been in Gallipoli and returned from Egypt at the same time as us.

Whilst there is generally a certain friction between regiments, we had got on well with the Taffs, who enjoyed their beer and a good singsong. Many of them had Irish surnames, like Sullivan and Ryan, being descendants of Irish who had come over to Wales at the time of the famine.

Even coming from Gallipoli, we were not prepared for the sights we encountered. Decaying corpses and body parts of man and beast lay strewn on the cratered no man's land between the two lines, and they continued to be mutilated by the ongoing shells landing there. The stench from these was abhorrent and no doubt led to diseases being transmitted to both sides of the conflict.

Most of the trenches had mud up to the ankles, with a little raised shelf about 2 feet wide along the side from which to fire at the enemy. It was also on this shelf where we had to sleep. There were hundreds of sappers busy burrowing under the no man's land and underneath the enemy's trenches.

These men had experience of tunnelling and were mainly ex-coal miners and labourers who had dug out the ground for the London Underground system.

Occasionally, our tunnellers would meet Germans burrowing the opposite direction and a desperate hand-to-hand fight to the death would ensue in the pitch blackness underneath our feet. Other times, tunnels would collapse, and the men would be interred in a tomb of their own making.

Thankfully, after a week, we were moved out of the front and into billets at Acheux, where the regiment was also brought up to full strength with a draft of new recruits from home. We spent the next couple of months familiarising ourselves with the methods of war, which in many ways had changed markedly since our days in Gallipoli.

Innovations like the deadly flamethrower were shown to us. It spewed out flames that extended 20, maybe 30 yards, and incinerated everything in its path. God help the man who got in its way. It was also said that a motorised vehicle, called a tank, was being developed that was almost impregnable to shells and would drive straight over the enemy's machine gun positions. It would also be armed with two deadly machine guns, and its deployment would be a turning point in the war—and, for that matter, in the manner future wars would be fought.

At the same time, news was coming from home about a major incident in Dublin. On Easter Monday, a group of Irish Republicans staged a rebellion across the city. They had proclaimed the establishment of the Irish Republic and, along with some 1,600 followers, seized prominent buildings in Dublin and clashed with British troops. Thankfully, the insurrection had been suppressed, but not before more than 2,000 people were dead or injured.

It was reported that the general public had no sympathy with the Rising, but that was changing, with the leaders of the rebellion being executed on a daily basis. The shooting by firing squad of James Connolly, who had to be tied to a chair on account of his wounds, provoked a huge change of sentiment, with the executed leaders now being hailed as martyrs in some quarters.

The Germans were obviously aware of what had taken place, and they used placards to taunt the Munsters, who were in trenches opposite them.

> *Irishmen! Heavy uproar in Ireland; english [sic] guns are firing at your wives and children! 1st May 1916*
>
> *Interesting war-news of April 29th, 1916. Kut-el-Aara has been taken by the Turks, and whole english [sic] army therein—13,000 men—taken prisoners.*

The Irish troops responded by singing Irish songs and "Rule Britannia" before sending out a raiding party, a number of whom were badly wounded, to crawl across no man's land and seize the placards which they brought back to their own trenches. Although the Munsters were quick to show their loyalty to king and country, a sense of growing distance was becoming obvious between the Catholic soldiers and those from a Protestant background, even in a traditionally mixed regiment such as the Inniskilling Fusiliers.

Whilst in the past a group of men playing cards would have been split between members of both religions, it was becoming increasingly common to see all Catholic schools and all Protestant schools. It was clear from letters and newspapers that attitudes at home were changing, and it was having a marked impact on recruitment.

There was growing discontent too that the Irish regiments were being consistently given the most dangerous assignments, and the impression formed that an Irish life was valued at less than an English one. This was not just the enlisted men who were saying this as I overheard a conversation between two officers in which they were voicing similar concerns.

"The Irish are always at the front," said a captain in the Royal Irish Regiment to his counterpart in the Munsters. "Whatever is on, they say, 'Send the Irish; they are the boys to get the Huns on the run.' It's not good enough, and the men are beginning to realise it as well."

Much later, it came to our attention that the Germans had listening posts beneath their front lines from which, by the use of special equipment, they were able to intercept British and French telephone conversations. These remarkable verbatim records, written in perfect English, include the ruminations of one disgruntled Irish officer who, just two weeks before the start of the Battle of the Somme, is heard saying, "You think we Irish people are only here for doing your bloody work. The way we are being threated [sic] is absolutely a shame to civilisation."

Meanwhile, we had moved back into the trenches in mid-May in order to continue our training for a great assault on the Germans that we were informed would come sooner rather than later.

We were given the impression that the artillery guns would flatten the resistance first and that we would be able to

LION FOR A DAY

walk unharmed through no man's land before driving the Germans back into a retreat. Most of us recalled similar talk about the Turks before we landed in Gallipoli and took this with a rather large pinch of salt.

I was back in the third line, known as the reserve line, and I volunteered, despite my CBS schooling, when they called for runners to serve as messengers. I had enjoyed doing the role in Gallipoli, and because of my previous experience, I was chosen. Although we had field communication points in the front line, with a telephone to report back to command, quite often the flimsy cables got broken, either through enemy shells or someone accidentally tripping over them.

Whilst they were buried deep in the mud, offering them protection, it was a devil of a job finding the break when things went wrong, and it was easier to simply to lay a new cable. But this took time, and the messengers were brought into play, running written notes from the front through communication trenches all the way back across the three lines to the officers in charge.

The trenches had been dug in a zigzag design so that if hit by a shell, the impact did not travel more than a few yards, but it also meant that I never managed to get into even a trot as I moved along the trenches.

Unlike Gallipoli, where the terrain was firm for the most part prior to the storm that came in from the east, here I was squelching through the mud, at times above my ankles. I could see why many of the men who had been serving in the trenches for a prolonged period suffered a condition called trench foot on account of their feet being constantly wet.

Affected feet became numb, turning red blue as a result of poor blood supply, and started to give off a decaying odour if the early stages of necrosis set in. As the condition worsened, the feet swelled up even more and could lead to gangrene, and that meant amputation.

Another hazard was the rats. There were hundreds, even thousands, of them. When there was a gas attack, they went berserk, and you could meet a small army of them coming down the tunnel towards you at top speed and shrieking at the top of their voices as the mustard gas attacked them. If you did not get up on the shelf, you would have your legs taken from under you with deadly consequences as they piled over you, completely out of their minds with the poisonous vapours.

Even when there was no gas, they were never far away. One officer went to sleep one night only to wake up in the morning to find he had no buttons left on his jacket. Made of bone, the rats had nibbled them away during the night while he was sleeping. You could not leave food out for even a minute or they would descend on it and eat it within minutes.

More frightening was the number of men I encountered standing alone in some quiet spot of the trenches with their eyes seemingly standing in their heads. At times they would be shaking uncontrollably, but all seemed to be totally

LION FOR A DAY

oblivious to what was going on around them until a shell exploded near them when they would go into convulsions.

Some would scream for loved ones, others would cry out for mercy, some would grab a gun and try to go over the top to attack the enemy single-handedly, but the greater majority covered their heads and went into a foetal position in the mud.

I tried to engage in conversation quite a number of times with someone in this state, but it was difficult to get a coherent response.

Despite being obviously fatigued, they seemed to find it difficult to sleep and dwelt in some twilight zone between life and death. They relied on their comrades to feed and look after them and to put on their gas masks when there was an attack.

It was obvious this was not some sort of contrived ploy to escape the action. These men were casualties of war just as much as those with gunshot or shrapnel wounds. I happened upon a doctor one day on my errands and asked him about these men.

He said this war had produced an army of emotionally damaged soldiers who could no longer bear the incredible destructive force of modern mechanical warfare and that the diagnosis and treatment of mental diseases confronted military doctors with new challenges.

My ears also pricked up when he said that the condition had been become so prevalent that a special hospital had been set up in Rugby to treat the sufferers of the disorder.

Our artillery pounded the enemy trenches for a solid week at the end of June, and we were told to prepare our equipment for an attack on 1 July. My own orders were to be on duty at one of the communications points on our front line, nicknamed the White City on account of the chalk soil, which faced the great German fortress position Beaumont Hamel.

On the morning of the appointed day, there was a huge explosion to our right, and it was later reported that it could be heard as far away as London. It was a huge bomb smuggled along tunnels burrowed under the German lines and was supposed to render their defences ineffective.

The first wave of troops was ordered over the top shortly afterwards, and I watched their progress on a trench periscope. They took off at walking pace but had not travelled more than 50 yards until they came under intense crossfire. The Germans, contrary to what our generals had planned, emerged unscathed from their trenches within a couple of minutes of the huge explosion.

Our intelligence officers had not known that the German trenches were as deep as 30 feet in places and lined with concrete and sandbags. The week-long bombardment had done minimal damage to them but had instead served as a warning to the enemy that a major attack was imminent. During this time, the Germans had set up their guns aimed

LION FOR A DAY

diagonally across the no man's land for maximum effect, causing untold damage to our troops, who were caught in a crossfire immediately on emerging from the trenches.

That resulted in the first wave of troops soon disappearing dead or wounded within a few minutes. The whistles sounded for the second tide to get ready, and by now the cries and screams of the injured and dying were coming from the 300 yards of territory between the two lines. I saw Barney moving towards me along the trench to go in the second wave as the German shells started to come thicker and faster.

"God bless, Barney," I said. "You'll be fine." And as he took up his position, I added, "You'll be back in Celtic Park playing again before you know it."

He tried to say something, but the words wouldn't come out for him, just an unintelligible mumble as he blessed himself and started to scramble up over the side of the trench, which on account of his height was a little more difficult than for others.

I followed his progress anxiously through the periscope, but he did not get halfway across no man's land until he seemed to suffer a direct hit from a German shell and disappeared in an explosion of flesh, blood, and bone. His body was never found.

CHAPTER 10

WE SERVE NEITHER KING NOR KAISER

*The present duty of every Irish man
is to stay at home and fight, if at all,
for the welfare of his own country.*

—*Constance Markiewicz*

It started as a very normal Easter, even though Britain had been at war for almost two years. Huge congregations packed the churches in Dublin on Good Friday, 1916, for religious services, despite unseasonably low temperatures and the risk of rain.

Many people looked forward to doing their Easter duty and the end of a long and cold Lent. The newspapers were full of war reports. The French were on the offensive in Verdun, one of the most bloody and protracted battles of the entire war, having held off the German advances earlier in the month. Russian forces were also gaining the upper hand in the east, but it all seemed a million miles far away from a hustling and bustling Irish capital, probably the second most important city of the British Empire.

The imperial mentality was obvious in the *Daily Express,* in which there was an article by Mr Edmund Candler from the banks of Tigris River extolling the fighting qualities of the Jat people from Hisar and Rohtak in the Punjab region of India. The Jat regiment was then, in the aftermath of the failures in Gallipoli, fighting the Turks in Mesopotamia, modern-day Iraq, but had also been involved on the Western Front from as early as the start of the war.

The colonel of the regiment was reported as saying, "The Jat is primarily a farmer and it was during the reconstruction of the Indian Army in 1893 that the Jats were built up again into a fighting race. A good regimental officer can make anything he will out of the Jat. It takes earthquakes and volcanoes to turn a regiment of all those hard-bitten men out of a position they have been given to hold."

Like Ireland, the subcontinent had been a rich recruiting ground for the British Army, the military arm and enforcer of a British government whose writ ran large throughout the known world.

Three soldiers were featured in the press following acts of gallantry. Lieutenant William Griggs, a well-known English jockey, was the first to arrive in a motor attack to rescue the Tara prisoners in the hands of the Turks. Griggs had his best year in the saddle in 1907, when he rode sixty-seven winners, with major victories during his career including the Chester Cup, Stewards Cup, the Lincoln, and the Goodwood Cup. He would survive the war to win his one and only Classic, the 1,000 guineas, in 1920.

The Reverend E.N. Mellish had been awarded the Victoria Cross "for most conspicuous bravery. During heavy fighting on three consecutive days he repeatedly went backwards and forwards, under continuous and heavy shell and machine gun fire, between our original trenches and those captured from the enemy in order to tend and rescue wounded men."

In contrast, Captain R.G. Kerr of the Seventh (Service) Battalion of the Royal Inniskillings Fusiliers was presented with a parchment praising his bravery and recognising his good work in France.

Like today, sport took up much of the newspapers, with the Irish Grand National at Fairyhouse on Easter Monday being eagerly anticipated, as was the Dublin Show in Donnybrook later in the week. In the meantime, the Easter weekend had seen a multitude of fixtures in a number of sports take place. Soccer matches were popular with the sporting public, and there were close-fought contests both in Dublin and Belfast. Shelbourne, who suffered only two defeats during the regular season, those being at the hands of Bohemians in the Leinster and Irish Cups, clinched the Leinster League title with a facile 3–0 win over Chapelizod.

Up north, in the Gold Cup, decided on a league basis, Irish Cup winners Linfield easily disposed of Glenavon 4–1, while both the Distillery v Glentoran and Belfast Utd v Cliftonville matches ended as scoreless draws.

Reigning All-Ireland hurling champions Laois went down to a shock defeat to Clare by 4–2 to 5–4 at a Christian Brothers' Centenary Tournament in Thurles.

And in an "Old Crocks" Rugby match at Lansdowne Road to benefit the war charities, Ulster overcame Leinster by two goals and a try to two tries. A huge crowd turned up for a match that featured a healthy presence of former internationals despite the "threatening weather."

Against this backcloth of normality, it came as quite a shock, not only to the British authorities but to the general populace, when they heard on Monday that a group of Irish Republicans, numbering as many as 2,000 men and women, had occupied a number of key buildings around Dublin, including the General Post Office on Sackville Street (now O'Connell Street) in the centre of the city.

The Irish Volunteers and Citizen Army, styling itself as the Provisional Government of the Irish Republic, had jointly proclaimed an Irish Republic, with Patrick Pearse reading the proclamation outside the GPO to mark the beginning of the Rising. Despite being poorly armed and against superior numbers, they held out before the insurrection was crushed by the British.

Although British spies had infiltrated many of the organisations taking part and the authorities knew something was being planned, they were still taken unaware. They may have been lulled into a sense of security by a notice posted in the *Irish Independent* a few days earlier by Eoin Mac Neill, chief of staff of the Irish Volunteers, which had stated that all military manoeuvres over Easter had been cancelled.

The notice was genuine enough, but while the lack of arms and volunteers would have caused most strategists to pause, the Military Council was largely made up of idealists and not tacticians. They were zealots who decided that they had to rise up in order to create a spark, which they hoped in turn would light a fire that led to what they saw as the shackles of British rule being cast aside for good. The only concession they made was to postpone the start by twenty-four hours from the Easter Sunday to the following day, 24 April.

The British were blissfully unaware of this and had scaled down security at Dublin Castle, the headquarters of British rule in Ireland, so that staff could enjoy the Easter weekend break. It meant Dublin Castle was virtually undefended and could have been seized by the rebels with minimum force, had they known.

The Rising began at noon when rebel forces assembled outside Liberty Hall on the banks of the River Liffey. From there, they split up and marched to the various preselected locations that they immediately seized against little resistance. The rebels hoped that once they had begun the rebellion, thousands would join them all across Ireland, but poor communications meant that the word did not get through to many parts of the country, where activists were prepared and waiting to take action.

The rebellion fell through in the north of the country before it had even started. Denis McCullough, the commandant of the Irish Volunteers in Belfast, awaited news of German help and a call to arms that never came.

Patrick McCartan, dispensary doctor in Gortin, County Tyrone, only got the signal on Easter Monday, the day the rebellion began. He was to lead the men of Tyrone to Belcoo in County Fermanagh to meet up with the men of Mayo and Donegal, to hold the line until the Germans invaded, but this never happened.

Worse was to follow when police raided the home of McCartan's father in Termonmaguirk, near Carrickmore, and seized 6,000 rounds of ammunition, which they reportedly carried off in triumph, crippling the movement in east Tyrone.

Matters were equally chaotic elsewhere. In Donegal, seven men mobilised at Cashelnagor and cycled to Creeslough, where they met Seamus McNulty. Here they joined up with twenty-six more men who possessed twenty-six rifles and six revolvers, but there was no specific plan to follow as they were still awaiting orders from Dr McCartan, which never came.

In Derry, Roisin O'Doherty had brought a dispatch from Dublin the previous Thursday instructing the OC, Seamus Cavanagh, to muster his men on Easter Sunday. He ordered his volunteers to meet at John Doherty's shed near the distillery at the top of William Street; they amounted to seventeen in number, and they waited until 5.30 a.m. until hearing of the countermanding order and went home.

The south Derry men travelled by bicycle to join up with the Bellaghy volunteers but had no guns to bring with them. They were joined by a Newbridge contingent, and from there they travelled to Coalisland on Sunday afternoon, only to find that the Belfast volunteers had gone to Cookstown and the manoeuvres had been cancelled.

Meantime, the British authorities were quick to make up for lost ground and called up all soldiers presently on the island of Ireland, whether on active service or leave. "Report immediately to barracks" notices were flashed up on cinema screens throughout the country. The Third (Service Battalion), based at Ebrington Barracks in Derry, were in the middle of a sports meeting being held in the nearby St Columba's Field when the word came. The occasion, organised for the men and their families, included the usual running and jumping events as well as a mock-up of the famous battle at Rorke's Drift during the Boer War.

A body of the men had dressed up as natives and painted their faces black. Such was the urgency of the summons that they did not have time to change before boarding a special train at the railway station bound for Dublin. Some of them arrived in Dublin with their faces still blackened, giving rise to a rumour that black soldiers had been brought in to quell the uprising. The battalion would suffer two casualties in Dublin during its brief stay: Second Lieutenant Charles Crockett was accidentally shot by a British sentry and Private Francis Knox was killed in an accident.

By Tuesday afternoon, the commander of the British forces in Dublin, Brigadier General W.H.M. Lowe, had gathered up 5,000 troops, vastly outnumbering the insurgents, who had barely 1,600 troops at their different locations throughout the city.

In addition, the British were much better armed and trained, many of the troops having come through gruelling campaigns abroad. The British numbers were boosted even further the following day when the Sherwood Foresters arrived at the port of Kingstown (Dun Laoghaire). They marched on Dublin and ran into rebel forces on Mount Street Bridge, suffering more than one hundred casualties before finally breaking through the rebel lines.

With vastly superior numbers now at his command, Lowe was able to cordon off the areas around the rebel positions, cutting off supplies and communications in a move intended to force them to surrender.

Heavy artillery was moved into place and began shelling the insurgents' strongholds. The patrol ship, the *Helga,* sailed up the River Liffey and started shelling Liberty Hall, the HQ for the Rising, but anticipating this, the rebels had managed to leave the building.

When the British realised this, they turned their attention to Boland's Mills, where one of the rebel commanders was Éamonn de Valera, who would later become president of Ireland. The heavy artillery on the *Helga* made their work easy for the British against an enemy who could do nothing to defend themselves against the bombardment. After pounding the occupiers of Liberty Hall and Boland's Mills into submission, the *Helga* then directed its fire to the GPO, where the rebels, led by the inspirational James Connolly, continued to hold out despite the overwhelming odds against them.

By this time, General Sir John Grenfell Maxwell had taken over ultimate command of the operation from Lowe, who sent out a stern warning on Friday announcing, "Most rigorous measures will be taken by me to stop the loss of life and damage to property which certain misguided persons are causing by their armed resistance to the law. If necessary, I shall not hesitate to destroy all buildings within any area occupied by rebels."

It was not an idle threat as Maxwell ordered another bombardment, and although the GPO itself was not severely damaged, several other buildings in the vicinity of Sackville Street were reduced to rubble. Despite this, the Connolly-led Irish forces in the GPO continued to resist, but Connolly was then wounded in the leg by a ricocheting bullet and lost a lot of blood. Still under heavy fire, the roof of the GPO caught fire and the rebels were forced to flee the building. Gallantly, both Pearse and Connolly stayed on until everyone had escaped to safely.

On Saturday, Pearse and the rest of the insurgents found themselves in a temporary headquarters at a shop on Moore Street but were surrounded by British troops and had no way out. They also realised that they could not fight on for any amount of time, given a shortage of ammunition and the risk of precipitating an unacceptable level of civilian casualties.

Faced with these stark facts, the Military Council had no alternative but to surrender. A nurse named Elizabeth O'Farrell was asked to convey the message, and wearing the insignia of the Red Cross, she walked up Moore Street carrying a white flag. General Lowe agreed to see her and told her to tell Pearse and the rebels that they must agree to an unconditional surrender.

O'Farrell brought back the message and returned less than an hour later with Pearse, who agreed to the general's terms. Pearse took his sword from his side and handed it to Lowe as a formal gesture that the rebels were laying down their arms.

Pearse was then taken to see Maxwell, now titled the commander-in-chief of British forces in Ireland, so the terms of the formal surrender could be drafted into document form. However, Maxwell, a military man known for his arrogance, was not in the least gracious in victory, a trait that would later prove to be his undoing and result in him becoming known as the man who lost Ireland.

He had all the rebels rounded up and incarcerated in Kilmainham Gaol. He decided the insurgents must be tried by military court with death sentences meted out to everyone involved in the Rising. Very soon, the executions started, and whilst public opinion had initially been almost unanimously against the Rising, this changed with the day and daily executions, including that of a terminally ill Connolly, who was shot while strapped to a chair.

The rebels, who had been vilified by nearly everyone, became heroes and martyrs for the cause of independence, but more importantly, they awoke a flame of nationalism that would lead to a form of independence for Ireland within a few years.

The Rising would also herald the end of the moderate Irish Parliamentary Party (IPP), led by John Redmond, that had campaigned for self-government (or "home rule") for Ireland within the United Kingdom of Great Britain and Ireland.

The IPP had been the dominant political movement of Irish nationalism from 1870 up until this point. Donegal-born Isaac Butt founded the Home Government Association in 1870, which was succeeded in 1873 by the Home Rule League, and then nine years later by the IPP. All of these groups campaigned for home rule in the British House of Commons and, under the leadership of Charles Stewart Parnell, had almost succeeded when William Gladstone's Liberal government introduced the First Home Rule Bill in 1886, only for the bill to be defeated in the House of Commons after a split in the Liberal Party.

After Parnell's death, Gladstone introduced the Second Home Rule Bill in 1893 that was passed by the Commons but defeated in the House of Lords. When the Lords' veto was removed in 1911, the Third Home Rule Bill was introduced in 1912, leading to the Home Rule Crisis. The legislation was enacted, but its implementation was suspended until the conclusion of the war, with Catholics urged to sign up for the British Army in the meantime.

Northern Protestants were opposed to home rule from the outset, fearing they would be subsumed into what they perceived would be a Catholic parliament in Dublin. For this reason, the first bill resulted in serious riots in Belfast as early as the summer and autumn of 1886 in which many were killed.

Ulster Unionists were also vehement in their opposition to the Third Home Rule Bill, introduced in 1912, as was the case in 1886 and 1893. "Home rule" was synonymous with "Rome rule" in their minds and would lead to economic decline and threaten their cultural and industrial identity.

Edward Carson and James Craig, leaders of the Unionists, organised an "Ulster Covenant" against the "coercion of Ulster," and in January 1913, the Ulster Unionist Council instituted the Ulster Volunteer Force (UVF), consisting of men who had signed the Ulster Covenant. They wanted to co-ordinate the paramilitary activities of Ulster's Unionists, as well as to give military backing to the threats of the Ulster Covenant to resist implementation of the Third Home Rule Bill.

Subsequently, Carson made a tour of Ulster, reviewing Orange and Unionist Volunteers who had been drilling in considerable numbers in various parts of the province. Huge crowds turned up at these meetings, not just in Belfast but in provincial centres like Dungannon and Cookstown and even small towns like Raphoe in County Donegal, where in October 1913, Carson addressed a crowd of 1,500 Ulster volunteers replete in Baden-Powell hats and improvised uniforms.

Carson promised the Raphoe volunteers that he would provide each and every one of them with a rifle, and he was able to deliver on that promise the following April when the *Clyde Valley,* disguised as the *Mountjoy II*, whose namesake had broken the boom to end the siege of Derry over two hundred years earlier, discharged a huge cargo of arms and ammunition that was quickly distributed by various means of transport to volunteers all over the province.

The Larne gunrunning put the gun back into Irish politics and pressure on the Irish Volunteers, who had been working on their own plan. It also heightened the suspicions of Nationalists, who felt that the authorities had double standards in that they turned a blind eye to Unionist militants while applying the rigour of the law to those from the other side.

Certainly, after the events in Larne, many new members flocked to join the Irish Volunteers, formed in late 1913. At the outbreak of World War I, the government requested all arms and ammunition of the UVF for the war effort, with units of the organisation joining en bloc the Thirty-Sixth (Ulster) Division to fight on the Western Front.

The picture was not so clear in the Nationalist community, with the Irish Volunteers split into the larger National Volunteers, who followed Redmond's call to support the Allied war effort. In this way, he believed they would ensure the future implementation of home rule. And many heeded his call by voluntarily enlisting in Irish regiments of the Tenth (Irish) Division or the Sixteenth (Irish) Division of Kitchener's New Army.

Joe Devlin, Irish Parliamentary Party MP for West Belfast, campaigned tirelessly in his native city for recruits to the Sixteenth (Irish) Division, and huge crowds turned out on the streets of Belfast to wave farewell as the first batch of recruits from the Irish National Volunteers, accompanied by Nationalist bands, paraded to the Great Northern railway station to leave for France.

Many other Irish Volunteers opposed Redmond's strategy and actively campaigned against enlistment. Their slogan was "We serve neither King nor Kaiser, only Ireland."

Prominent among the latter faction was a well-to-do farmer called Robert (Bob) Hales, from near Bandon, County Cork, who had been active in the Irish Land Wars and was a member of the Irish Republican Brotherhood. He had five sons, who all resisted enlistment and even drilled local men around the roads in Bandon, much to the displeasure of recruiting officers in the area.

The family was prepared to play their part in the Easter Rising but, like so many, received the order to stand down in the days prior to the planned rebellion.

The outbreak of World War I had transformed the Irish political thinking and provided the fertile ground on which the seeds of rebellion were able to take root. Within weeks of Redmond's call for Irishmen to join the ranks of the British Army, all seven future signatories of the 1916 Proclamation attended a meeting at the Gaelic League offices in Dublin, at which it was agreed to hold an insurrection at some point before the conclusion of the war. In doing so, the architects of the Rising were merely reviving an established Nationalist slogan that England's difficulty was Ireland's opportunity.

In addition, Nationalists had long believed that the law was not being administered even-handedly between the Ulster Protestants and the Catholics in the rest of the island. This opinion was reinforced by what became known as the

Curragh Mutiny, which occurred in March 1914 at what was the principal base for the British military in Ireland.

It was one of the few occasions since the English Civil War that a part of the British Army openly intervened in politics.

There had been a growing rumour that there would have to be some military action against the Ulster Volunteers to prevent a widespread outbreak of violence in the north when home rule came into effect. Many officers, especially those with Irish Protestant connections, threatened to resign or accept dismissal rather than obey any order to act against their northern kindred.

The secretary of state for war, J.E.B. Seely, and chief of the general staff, Field Marshall Sir John French, issued a statement saying the whole matter had been a misunderstanding, but they were forced to resign after amending it to promise that the British Army would not be used against the Ulster loyalists.

It is widely thought of as a mutiny, though no orders actually given were disobeyed. The affair boosted the Unionist confidence but only hardened belief of Irish Nationalists that they could not expect support from the British Army. This, in turn, increased support for the Nationalist cause and led to more recruits to join one or other of the paramilitary forces. The Home Rule Bill was passed but put on hold at the outbreak of war and led the British government to consider partition in Ireland instead.

The Nationalist sense of grievance was heightened later that year. While they felt that a blind eye had been turned to the

LION FOR A DAY

import of arms at Larne, the authorities had acted with an iron fist when the Asgard unloaded arms for the Nationalists in Howth. The harbour master informed the authorities, and the Dublin Metropolitan Police were called out, later to be supported by a detachment of the King's Own Scottish Borderers (KOSB), who had been dispatched from their barracks at Kilmainham.

The opposing factions met at Clontarf, where a riot ensued. Mirroring, only in reverse, the Curragh incident, many policemen refused to obey orders to disarm the Volunteers. This was followed by another confrontation with the military detachment in which hand-to-hand fighting involved bayonets and rifle butts. It is not clear if the Volunteers fired shots, but they did manage to smuggle away safely the greater amount of the arms to a nearby Christian Brothers' grounds with the loss of only nineteen rifles seized by the police. These would later be returned when a court ruled that they had been confiscated illegally.

Unfortunately, that was not the end of confrontation. By this stage, a crowd had gathered, and when they saw the Nationalist sympathisers beating off the soldiers, they began to heckle and jeer.

Later, when some soldiers from the King's Own Scottish Borderers were returning to their barracks and had reached Bachelors Walk, they encountered a hostile but unarmed crowd that started to taunt them. An officer who had joined them en route was unaware that the soldiers had their guns ready to fire and gave them the order to face the crowd.

Whilst the officer was addressing the civilians, one of the soldiers fired a shot that precipitated his colleagues letting off a volley of shots. Three people were killed instantly and another thirty-eight were injured, with one man dying later of a bayonet wound. Among the wounded was Luke Kelly, a 9-year-old boy who would survive and later father a son by the same name, who would go on to be a famous musician and singer with the renowned group the Dubliners.

Another gunrunning attempt was thwarted by the British authorities in the week leading up to Easter 1916. Germany offered the Irish 20,000 rifles, ten machine guns, and accompanying ammunition but would not afford them any German officers.

Although the quantity of arms fell short of what they had desired, and despite the lack of military expertise, they still went ahead with the plan. The German weapons never landed on Erin's shores after the Royal Navy intercepted the ship transporting them, a German cargo vessel named the *Libau* that was disguised as a neutral Norwegian vessel.

All the crew were German sailors but were cleverly disguised, with their clothes and effects all Norwegian. The arms ship was escorted into Queenstown (present-day Cobh), County Cork, where Captain Spindler scuttled the ship by pre-set explosive charges on the morning of Easter Saturday, 22 April.

It was the loss of these arms, on which they had been heavy reliant, that forced Eoin MacNeill to cancel the proposed uprising the following day. However, it did not deter the idealists from taking up the gun on Monday. The rest is history.

CHAPTER 11

THE WAR LINGERS ON

"Escaping goblins to be caught by wolves!" he said, and it became a proverb, though we now say "out of the frying-pan into the fire" in the same sort of uncomfortable situations.

—J.R.R. Tolkien

"Tony! Tony! Wake up!"

I could hear a voice in the dim distance.

"Wake up, please!" The voice seemed to be getting louder. It seemed familiar. It could not be Gertie. I was dreaming again. Slowly, deliberately, I opened my eyes, in dread at where I might find myself. I was met by a bright light. I put up my hand to shield my eyes and furtively started to look around me.

"Is that you, Gertie? Have I died? Are we in heaven?"

MALCOLM MCCAUSLAND

"No, you're in St John's military hospital in Rugby. You've been here two weeks and I didn't know. I thought you were dead since I haven't heard from you in months."

I was starting to become fully conscious of my surroundings and detected a whole gamut of emotions, from relief to anger, in Gertie's voice.

"The doctors say you were in state of daze. They have a fancy name for it, but it means you are shell-shocked from the war."

"How did I get here?" I asked. "And why did you think I was dead?" My two questions came out without my drawing breath.

"Well," Gertie said before pausing. "Where shall I start?"

"Why not at the beginning?" I responded without thinking.

"Well, your mum got a telegram at the start of—it must've been August—to say you'd been wounded in France and were being sent home to a place called Oh-Ma or something."

"Omagh?"

"Yes. You were being sent back to the infirmary in Oh-Ma along with the rest of the wounded from your regiment, but when your mum checked with the hospital, you weren't there. After two weeks, you still hadn't arrived, and when there was still no word of you after a month, she got in touch with your regiment in Londonderry.

LION FOR A DAY

"They checked, and they couldn't find you in Omagh, and they couldn't find you among the list of people who came back on the boat or the train. So they then thought that there might've been a mix-up and in fact you were not one of the wounded but one of the missing, presumed dead. Your mother sent me a telegram telling me the bad news, and I cried my eyes out for days."

She continued, gasping for breath: "Then a nurse knocked at our door to say there was a wounded soldier in the hospital who was saying our address when he was delirious. She asked if I knew a private Hegarty because there was someone mumbling something about me in the hospital.

"I came down here immediately, but they wouldn't let me see you until I had spoken to the doctor. But he wasn't on duty until today, so I had to wait two full days not knowing if it was you or not. The doctor explained that you were admitted in early August suffering from that disease."

"Neurasthenia?"

"Yes, that's it. He said you were shell-shocked and they did not really have a cure or treatment for it. He explained that it was common among the troops at the front and while they used to treat it with electric shock treatment, they now just recommended plenty of rest. He said you were in sort of delirium and were not communicating, and you frequently went into a fit of shaking.

"He said you were having fits of shaking and were waking up in the night and shouting, 'Rats! Rats!' You'd jump out

MALCOLM MCCAUSLAND

of bed and try to shake them off you until the nurse assured you there were no rats in the ward, and then you'd go back into a sort of half sleep, half daze again.

"The doctor did not know why you were sent here and said you must've boarded the wrong transport when they brought you back to Harwich. That's how you ended up in Rugby."

She paused again to breathe: "The doctor said too that he'd never before met anyone with your condition who had such an enormous appetite. He said all you did was eat, and then you'd sleep usually for ten to twelve hours at a time. He said because you were not able to talk, they only learned your name from your identification papers.

"They say you kept mumbling in your sleep, 'Gertie, Pennington Street,' and this had been going on for weeks. Very few of the nurses are from around here, and they thought from your accent that you were talking about your girlfriend somewhere in Scotland.

"It was only when one of the auxiliaries from here heard you that she identified that Pennington Street was in Rugby and she knew a Gertie Turland who lived there.

"That was a week ago, but she only called two nights ago when her shift was over. My mum answered the door, and she came in saying, 'Gertie, there's a girl at the door and she says that there's a wounded soldier asking for you in the military hospital.'

LION FOR A DAY

"I replied, 'Mum, you know I'm still trying to get over Tony's death. How could you say such silly things?'

"'I think you better talk to her anyway. She's called here on her way home from the hospital, no doubt after a long day at work.'

"I went to the front door, and I recognised that it was Sally O'Driscoll, whom I'd known at school."

"'I'm sorry for bothering you like this, Gertie, but there is a sick soldier in the hospital, and I think he's been mumbling your name and address in his deliriums for weeks, maybe months. I only heard him for the first time today. He sounds Scottish or Irish. The nurses thought he was referring to a girlfriend back home, but I knew you lived in Pennington Street and I should tell you.'

"By this time, I had reached for my coat and had it half on. I didn't even take time to thank Sally before I was on the road down here, half walking, half running, but as I said, they wouldn't let me in. From the description they gave me, I knew it was you."

And with that, Gertie leaned over and was kissing me on the face. "I'm so glad you're alive," she said as she sighed.

By this time, the rest of the patients in the ward, at least those sufficiently well enough, were watching what was happening. The matron had come through the door and was about to evict Gertie, but when she caught the tail end of the story, even that tough old bird melted.

169

"Well, normally I would ask all visitors to leave by this time, particularly, but in the circumstances, I'll give you both another fifteen minutes, especially when you're obviously having such a remedial effect on this young soldier."

"Do you not remember any of this?" asked Gertie with a degree of incredulity.

"No. Nothing," I replied. "I just remember being down a very dark hole. It was like a mineshaft, and there were rats, great big ones, and every once in a while, they would try to crawl over me. I would have to shake them off. Then I thought I heard your voice—far, far away. Then I could see a light above me, and I started to rise, slowly at first, but very gradually I made it to the top, and you were here sitting by my bed. I thought I had died and gone to heaven, but I know now I'm in an even better place.

"Gertie, you don't know. I've been to hell and back this last couple of years. I thought I'd never live through it all, much less see you again. But thank God, you're here and I'm still alive. Are you sure we're not in heaven?"

The matron allowed Gertie to stay another hour, and I was able to tell her more about what I had experienced. I told her about Captain Gerry, my mate Barney, the two Smyths from my hometown, and others who would not be coming home. Gertie listened wide-mouthed as if I had been reading to her out of a horror book. From time to time, I could feel her grip tighten on my hand as I related some of the more harrowing bits.

LION FOR A DAY

To make room for the increasing number of casualties coming in, and because of my sudden recovery, a couple of days later they moved me to a rehabilitation ward. Gertie was allowed to come and go more or less whenever she wanted on her days off. Her employers, Mr, and Mrs Payne, were very understanding and gave her the evenings off from her job as housekeeper of Silsworth Hall so that she could visit somebody they regarded as a war hero.

Her dad and mum even came to see me, and the Middletons, who brought the good news that their son Charlie was still alive and well. Mrs Middleton remarked on how thin I had got. Mr Middleton said I was a hero, unlike that lot in Dublin who he regarded as a disgrace to Ireland and the British Empire.

Newspapers were delivered to us every day to catch up on the situation, not only in Ireland but also the Western Front, where no one seemed to be making any progress. The war that was supposed to end by Christmas looked like it would now go on forever.

By the start of September, I was allowed out each day to exercise, and by the middle of the month, official word came through that I should report back to the regiment's headquarters in Omagh. I broke the news to Gertie, who was disappointed that we would not be able to spend a first Christmas together, but she understood that my mother would want to see me too, particularly so given the amount of time I had been away.

In the meantime, we spent as much time together as we could, and from the money I received in backpay, we were able to go out and buy a ring to formalise our engagement. I left it almost as late as possible to head home to Ireland, and I almost ran into trouble when the sailings from Heysham to Larne were cancelled for two days due to storms.

I reported at the St Lucia Barracks and was given a month's leave to complete my recovery before returning to assist in training the new recruits before they left to join the battalions fighting in France.

From Omagh, I made the short journey on to Derry, before walking up Carlisle Road towards the Bogside in my full uniform and carrying my possessions in my backpack. I noticed nothing unusual until I came across a group of young men standing on the corner of Bishop Street and Carlisle Road close to the Bogside. I heard a spit and felt the moisture of a spittle coming my way as I passed them. I thought I must be mistaken, but shouts of "Traitor!" and "Turncoat!" followed me all the way down Hog's Folly onto the Lecky Road.

All was tranquil after that, and I quietly knocked on the door of my mother's house around 10 p.m. as a cold and biting wind blew in from the nearby River Foyle. My mother came to the door herself, and it took her some seconds to recognise me as I had not told her I was coming home for Christmas. She stood shocked for a second before throwing her arms around me, which was very unlike her to show much outward emotion.

LION FOR A DAY

She went back to the kitchen and knelt down in front of her picture of the Sacred Heart. "Thanks be to Mary, Mother of God, that she has brought you home safe and sound," she prayed. "We thought we had lost you, but now you're found. Thank you, Blessed Mary, Mother of God."

She sprinkled some holy water and, in the best Derry tradition, put the kettle on. "You must be hungry. I've some soup on the range made for tomorrow, but you can have some. There's plenty to go around everybody. Really there's not so many of us anymore," she said.

By that, she was alluding to my late daddy and Joe, who had passed away the previous year, but also some of the others who had moved out to start their own families: John, who had gone to Dublin, and David, to Tralee. Both had opened barber shops in their respective chosen destinations.

Nevertheless, we had a quiet family dinner together and toasted absent friends. In the afternoon, we followed the Derry tradition of visiting the graves of loved ones. Wishing to avoid the situation, I had experienced the previous night, I put on some of Joe's clothes, which had been kept by my mother in a trunk and sallied out with the rest of the family to pay my respects. I was able to reacquaint myself with the city once more. Dressed in normal street clothes, I moved through the quiet streets without anyone remarking on my presence, which put me at ease after my previous experience.

I spent the early part of January in Derry, getting back into a routine of long walks in the afternoon, which took me out the Letterkenny Road to Carrigans and back, or up the stiff climb of the Braehead and over Sherriff's Mountain and back by the lonely roads of Creggan Hill—with its marvellous, panoramic views over Derry—and right down Lough Foyle, which I had not seen the equal of on all my travels since leaving home over five years earlier.

During this time, I took the opportunity to go over to Emerson Street in the Waterside area of the city to meet the parents of the two Smyth brothers—Willie-John and Sammy—who had died in Gallipoli. I thought it best not to relate the details of their deaths to James and his wife, Annie. I merely extolled their great qualities, although I did not really know either of them very well, and how they had given their lives for our country without hesitation. I am not sure if I convinced myself that the cause was worth dying for in the circumstances, but they said they were greatly comforted by my visit, but they were now concerned about another son who was serving with one of the English regiments in France.

Visiting Barney Donaghy's widow did not go as well. She was bitter about losing her husband with four young children running around the house.

"I told him not to go. I told there were enough single men to do the fighting," she said. "But nothing would do him but he'd go. Barney seemed to think it was just another game and said he'd be back by Christmas. But I had the feeling he'd never be back. He had everything going for him here. He could have got a job in football anywhere, and now I have these four wains to rear on my own."

LION FOR A DAY

I recounted some of the experiences that Barney and I had shared, like our sightseeing tour of Alexandria, the football matches, and Barney's dedication to keeping himself fit, regardless of where we were at the time. I'm not sure it helped her any, but I felt better for trying. She was, probably rightly, bitter about losing her husband, and there were plenty of people who would have agreed with her.

In the final few days of my leave, my sister Cathy asked me to attend a funeral Mass with her. "You know I don't like going to these things on my own," she pleaded. I agreed and put on Joe's best suit, and then we headed out to the Long Tower Chapel one Friday morning.

"Whose funeral is it anyway?" I asked perhaps somewhat belatedly on the way up through the Bog.

"Mary Kelly's sister, Kate. She was a bit older than me at school, but Mary and I are best friends and we work together in the shirt factory. Mammy said you used to do a line with Kate, did you not?"

"I can't remember her, and I don't remember walking out with her."

"That's funny because Mammy says she has a photo of the two of you taken somewhere you went together on a trip."

"Are you sure it's not one of our brothers? Joe was a great man for the girls. What happened her anyway?"

MALCOLM MCCAUSLAND

"She got pregnant and, not being married, there was the usual hullaballoo from the hypocrites. It brought a lot of shame on Mr and Mrs Kelly, who my mammy says never left the chapel rails. Anyway, she had to go into Nazareth House to have the baby, and the nuns told her the baby was stillborn. But Kate insisted that it was squealing when they took it away. It was a boy and she could see its arms and legs moving, but they insisted it was dead.

"She was convinced that the nuns had taken him away and sent him to America for some rich couple who had no children of their own and could pay for him. She said the priests arranged the deals regularly and that she had been told by several of the girls who worked in the laundry that the same had happened them.

"She never got over that and she had to stay in the Nazareth House because her parents wouldn't take her back into the house on account of the shame - so they said. Everybody knew she had a baby, so they were fooling nobody but themselves. Kate never accepted the story about the baby being stillborn and she never divulged who the father was either, even to her closest friends. "Anyway they say that the whole thing got to her and she got increasingly more depressed about life in general. It definitely got to her head in the end, and one morning earlier this week, she was found hanging from a staircase with a sheet around her neck. The nuns tried to cover up the whole episode, but one of the girls saw her hanging there and told one of her friends. Derry being Derry, soon half the town knew what happened. The nuns still maintained it was an accident so

LION FOR A DAY

that she could have a proper funeral Mass and get buried in consecrated ground."

At the end of January, I reported to the barracks at Omagh and was told that I would be transferred to the Royal Irish Regiment and based at the Curragh in County Kildare, where I would be helping to train the new recruits.

The Curragh Camp was enormous and a great starting point for our almost daily marches along the flat plains of Kildare. We did as much as 12 miles some days to get the recruits into condition during their twelve-week training period. Discipline among us, the instructors, was fairly informal, and we could do fairly much what we wanted after the morning walks. This gave me time to write loads of letters to Gertie. The rest of my free time was given over to doing exercises in our physical training (PT) hall, and as usual, I only had a couple of beers at the weekend.

When I got a few days leave, I put on my civilian clothes and stayed in Dublin with my brother John, whose barbershop was thriving. I was even able to use my leave at Christmas for a quick trip to Rugby to visit Gertie, but with the world in such turmoil, we could not make any concrete plans for our future.

As wars went, mine was going quite well miles from the front, but that was to change dramatically on my return to the Curragh in early January 1918. We were told we were to be transferred to a new Royal Irish Regiment battalion and sent to France.

Recruitment had fallen to such low levels in Ireland that they had to round up everybody in uniform, even those not tall enough to be accepted in the regular army—the bantams, as they were known.

We landed in France in April but were held behind the lines supporting the troops ahead who were actually doing the fighting. In truth, my immediate impression was that the war had turned into a fight between two heavyweight boxers who had long since run out of energy but intermittently slugged away at each other only when they mustered sufficient energy to raise their fists.

It was clear that the British government feared an insurrection of the Irish regiments as these were broken up and spread across a number of divisions. To dilute the national identity further, British recruits were being sent to regiments that were formerly 100 per cent Irish. For instance, the Sixteenth, which returned to France in August, ceased to be an Irish formation, with one Welsh, two Scottish and five English battalions now integrated; the Fifth Irish Fusiliers was the only remaining battalion from Ireland.

The lack of any obvious plan to solidify the Irish regiments only strengthened the hand of the conspiracy theorists at home and reduced recruitment to a trickle in the southern part of the country. The growing sentiment was that, for Ireland, the war had become an irrelevancy and increasingly there was some serious heart-searching as to what exactly "Britishness" meant for inhabitants of the island.

LION FOR A DAY

Whilst German offences continued into August, even more alarming was the number of men now falling victim to a mysterious influenza bug, which came to be known as Spanish flu. The stretcher-bearers were taking away more men dead from the flu than from the conflict, though all I had was the sniffles for a week.

What the world did not know was that the illness had also taken grip of the Americans, Germans, and French, because the news was suppressed in the newspapers of the four countries. In neutral Spain, the papers were reporting the virulent and deadly nature of this strain of the influenza bug, including the grave illness of their king, Alfonso XIII.

These stories gave the incorrect impression that Spain was particularly severely affected. Thus, it became known as Spanish flu. The pandemic went on to infect 500 million worldwide, with anywhere between 10 and 20 per cent of that number dying of the virus. This was reflected in the number of men being hospitalised in the temporary hospitals and no doubt hastened the end of the conflict, with both sides rapidly running short of fighting men.

It was this depletion of numbers available to them that forced the Germans to sign an armistice on 11 November 1918 to end fighting on all fronts. It was not a surrender by the Germans and their allies but an acknowledgement of defeat and the acceptance of harsh conditions, such as withdrawing all forces to behind the Rhine, the surrender of all military hardware, and the release of Allied prisoners.

The conditions were not reciprocal, with the German prisoners failing to secure their freedom and the naval blockade of German ports continuing. Although the armistice ended the fighting on the Western Front, it did not come soon enough for me with my being back in hospital in September with a recurrence of neurasthenia, leading to me being shipped back to the Royal Irish Regiment's military hospital in Clonmel.

I got my discharge papers in nearby Cork in March 1919, earning two medals and a silver bar badge in recognition of the wound suffered in Gallipoli. I thought that crafty old jackal would have been proud of me.

CHAPTER 12

BACK HOME IN DERRY

*You will never be completely at home
again, because part of your heart will
always be elsewhere. That is the price
you pay for the richness of loving and
knowing people in more than one place.*

—Miriam Adeney

The Derry I returned to in March 1919 was a much different city to the one I had left some seven years earlier. The Catholic community was buoyant; Sinn Féin, the party that sought an independent and sovereign Irish nation, had won seventy-three seats in the General Election held at the start of that year.

Their representative, Eoin MacNeill, had taken the seat in Derry at the expense of the Unionist candidate, Alderman Robert Anderson. The moderate Irish Parliamentary Party, led by John Redmond, that had advocated Irishmen join the British Army in 1914, on the understanding that this would gain Ireland home rule at the conclusion of the war, suffered annihilation, losing sixty-two of the sixty-eight seats it had won four years previous.

The Sinn Féin deputies immediately convened their own parliament in the Mansion House in Dublin in January 1919 and claimed jurisdiction over the whole island of Ireland. The campaign against British rule in Ireland commenced the very same day with an ambush on a police patrol in Tipperary.

I had found lodgings with my sister Cathy, who squeezed me into a room at her house in Howard Street, and whilst politics was on everyone's lips, my paramount concern was to find gainful employment.

The war had boosted the economy in Derry, and with the boom had come jobs in the factories that had produced shirts and uniforms and goods for the war effort. That had all come to a standstill with the Armistice though, with wages lowered and output reduced, particularly in the shirt factories.

There had also been a revival of trade union activity in Derry earlier in the year which had been connected to the general strike in Belfast, and not for the first time, the Derry trades council failed to give effective leadership. Added to that, the sectarian nature of the city prevented effective cross-community collaboration, which would have been necessary for the working class to influence wages and working conditions.

The rift between workers of the two different creeds led to the formation of the Unionist Labour Association (ULA), founded by Edward Carson, which stressed the importance of Protestant jobs for Protestant workers. They argued that trade union support was equivalent to Republican activism and successfully influenced the authorities to cancel that year's May Day rally on the grounds that it would be hijacked by Sinn Fein.

The sectarian divide and the shrinking job market, as well as the return of hundreds of soldiers from the war all seeking employment, only served to exacerbate the situation. I quickly found that I was caught between two stools. Ex-soldiers were not welcomed in what few Catholic-owned businesses there were in the city, while the Protestant firms preferred to give their jobs to members of their own community, in line with the diktat of the ULA.

My first port of call in my job hunt had been the docks, where a friend from schoolboy days, John McCauley, was one of the people who had the authority to hire and fire. Men queued up early each morning, and the lucky ones chosen could expect a fair day's pay, by Derry standards. Unfortunately, engagements were on a casual basis with no such thing as any continuity of employment, much less sick pay, or holiday pay. McCauley, a tall, fair-haired man with a slight turn in one eye, always had a reputation for straight-talking and did not hold back on this occasion.

"Anton, it's like this," he said as he paused. Then he took in a deep breath before he continued. "I could give you a few hours work four or five days a week, but since you were a British soldier, that wouldn't go down well with a lot of the boys here. Surely, you could come in, but sooner or later, someone would let a load of coal drop on you. If you weren't killed instantly, you'd be crippled for the rest of your life." He paused again for a second before asking, "Aren't you related to Liam Hegarty from Westland Street?"

"He's a cousin of me Da's," I replied, without really thinking or wondering why he'd asked.

"Well, that might change things. Without asking too much of your business, where would you say you stood now *politically* with all this bother going on?" he said stressing the word politically and obviously taking great care to be as diplomatic as possible in what was a very sensitive area.

"I would say that I'm as Irish as the next man, maybe more so, given what I've seen in India and other places and how us Irish soldiers were treated towards the end of the war."

"Well, that might put a different complexion on it. I still don't think you'd be entirely safe working here but given you're a close friend of one of the top IRA leaders in Derry, I'll tell you what I'll do. I have a brother-in-law, James O'Neill, who works down in Biggar's shipyard. It's run by some Belfast company now, but we still call it Biggar's. I'll have a word with him.

"Give me until the weekend when I'll see him at Mass, and then you can call down next Monday morning and see him at the shipyard. But don't take the huff if there's nothing there for you. But I suspect they might be interested in a man with your—let's say experience, and not just for the job."

LION FOR A DAY

I made the short journey to Pennyburn dock the following Monday, and true to form, I asked for James O'Neill. What I had not told John McCauley was that O'Neill was also a relation of mine, on my mother's side, who had lived down the street in Nailors Row from us when I was a child.

I had not seen James O'Neill for ten years, but he was now a man of near 6 feet and looked a lot older than he actually was. He still had those bright blue eyes and a pleasant aspect. He looked me up and down, and wanting to be open with him, I told him about the gunshot wound to my hand and how I still suffered a little bit of immobility. He hesitated a moment, as if doing some calculation, and said, "Don't worry about that. You've got a job, sir. When can you start?"

"What about tomorrow morning?" I queried.

"OK, report here at 8 a.m. You finish at six and have an hour for lunch with two fifteen-minute breaks. Bring your own food. The men generally have a rota for making the tea."

I could not have more pleased as I walked up the Strand from the Pennyburn shipyard. When I got home, I scribbled out a letter to Gertie and went out and bought myself some second-hand working clothes in Canning's drapery shop in Waterloo Street.

I slept well that night, and I was pleased to note that my nightmares about rats and gas were only happening once in a while since my return home.

MALCOLM MCCAUSLAND

I turned up a quarter of an hour early the next morning to create a good impression. I was given a job as an apprentice shipbuilder and assigned to the team in the dry dock led by George Campbell, a Scot in his fifties, who I was to learn had come over from a small fishing port near Aberdeen called Arbroath. Although a Protestant, he had married a local Catholic girl and their children were now adults, with his two sons among the six hundred employees engaged in the shipyard.

With a job sorted, my attention switched to getting back to my fitness regime, and I started doing some walking in the evenings after work.

I was in the shipyard a few days later when one of the bosses called me to his office. Mr Hugh C. Beasant was one of the engineers and stood up to greet me when I entered his office, which had a view out over the Foyle.

"Thank you, Hegarty, for coming up." He barely lifted his eyes from the papers in front of him on the desk. Jumping to his feet and offering his hand, he continued. "I'll get straight to the point. I believe you're an accomplished cross-country runner."

"Well, I did do a bit of running in the army," I said a bit reticently, not knowing where the conversation was leading.

"A number of us are interested in forming a harrier club here in Londonderry. My own running background is in the Duncairn Nomads club in Belfast. In fact, my brother still runs for them and is quite good. Would you like to attend a meeting in the Gainsborough public house next Monday night with a view to starting a club? A runner of your experience would be worth his weight in gold to us at this embryonic stage."

I took myself along to the meeting and was surprised at the number who were there—at least thirty young men and a few more senior people whom I took to be followers of the sport. The enthusiasm to form a club was contagious, and very quickly we had agreed to affiliate City of Derry Harriers to the Irish Athletics Association.

Figure 4: Anton (left) with his friend Hugh Casey shortly after City of Derry Harriers were founded in 1919. Casey would become one of the top sprinters in Ulster. Photo: Richie Kelly collection.

MALCOLM MCCAUSLAND

It was the first occasion that I met Hugh Casey, who would become my companion to many sports meetings and would emerge as one of the top 220-yard specialists in the country.

We initiated weekly Saturday afternoon runs from a hut at Edanmount Park on the Glen Road, kindly made available to us by a local publican called Eddie Tinney. Generally, the hares went off fifteen minutes before the pack and led us to the old racecourse in Ballyarnett by a circuitous route, taking in some difficult obstacles, such as hawthorn hedges and high ditches, before returning via the Northland Road, a route of between 8 and 10 miles.

As was traditional in harrier clubs, we would all wait at a fixed point for the Run Home, a hard effort for the final mile or so back to the clubrooms. I would supplement this training with a long walk on a Sunday of as much as three hours, going out the Letterkenny Road, up the steep Braehead, and over into Donegal with a return by way of Sherriff's Mountain.

I knew my job in the shipyard came at a price, and I was always waiting for someone to call in my tab. It was only a few weeks before one of the workers that I did not know sidled up to me during one of our tea breaks.

"Mr McGlinchey would like a few words with you," he whispered, trying to look in all directions at one time to see if anyone was watching us. "You know who I mean?"

I had been long enough home to know that Commander James McGlinchey was the leader of the Irish Volunteers

LION FOR A DAY

who drilled each evening in Celtic Park. The Volunteers had started recruiting in Derry a few years earlier to combat the threat posed by the Protestant Ulster Volunteer Force. Initially, the organisation had met with opposition from both the moderate Nationalists of the Redmond persuasion and even the Catholic Church.

However, realising that they were fighting a losing battle against the volunteers' brand of Republicanism, which increasingly struck a chord with the ordinary people, both the Redmondites and the priests backed off—at least in public.

"Aye, of course," I replied. "Where and when?"

"Commandant McGlinchey says to knock at the door of McLaughlin's sewing machine shop in Waterloo Street tonight at nine o'clock, and don't be late."

I noticed that he had changed McGlinchey's title to commandant, but I duly knocked on the door of the sewing machine shop a few minutes ahead of the appointed time. A young woman beckoned me in as she glanced up and down Waterloo Street, a steep and narrow street that hugged the western wall of the city, to check if we were being watched by the police.

In a dimly lit backroom, a middle-aged man got up to greet me. I could see a tiredness in his eyes, and there was a faint smell of pipe tobacco from him. "Anton, I believe you're interested in helping us with the cause. We desperately need ammunition, but we need men like you even more. I've heard about your background. In fact, I knew your father well. Many a drink Sean and me had over the years, and many a horse I bought off him." He paused, and I got a smell of porter off his breath.

"I've a bunch of volunteers. Don't get me wrong. They're keen enough, but they wouldn't know one end of a Lee Enfield from the other." His tired green eyes stared into mine as if demanding a positive response.

I really didn't want to get involved, but they had got me a job, not easy in Derry, and as I wanted to keep it, I felt compelled to be compliant. I started to explain, stammering on the initial words. "I don't mind giving a bit of instruction, but I don't want to get involved in any fighting. I've been in some war or another for the past eight years, and being honest with you, it has taken its toll on me. I'll show your men how to take apart a rifle and put it together again, how to clean it and how to load it without looking, and most important of all, how to shoot straight."

"That's all we're looking for," he replied before going on to add, "You'll be worth your weight in gold to us if you can do that. You'll still need to be sworn in, but we can take care of that tonight. In fact, we have a special visitor coming who can do that for us."

McGlinchey was as good as his word, and I was not asked to be a member of the IRA, go out in operations, or get myself in any situation where I might be in conflict with the police. We went one Sunday to Ballyliffin beach in Donegal for a

LION FOR A DAY

sham fight against the Inishowen Brigade, and we had a few training days, again always on Sundays, at Ludden beach.

The volunteers, as McGlinchey had said, were totally untrained in the use of arms, but perhaps because they were so intent on playing a part in liberating Ireland from the "foreign oppressors," they learned quickly and in no time were as proficient in the use of a rifle as any British soldier.

The away days did not affect my training as I was generally able to get a long walk home from wherever we were. I thought it a good idea not to get spotted in the back of the lorries they used to convey the volunteers to and from these events.

Meanwhile, feeling that my fitness had returned and eager to test myself in competition, I decided to have a run out at the Christian Brothers Past Pupils sports at the Brandywell in mid-July. I saw this as preparation for the more serious Ballycastle Sports in County Antrim to be held the following week.

The overall standard was poor, and I started the afternoon with a second in the half-mile flat race, just failing to catch a clever young runner called Harry Armour, who had a 30-yard handicap on me. I had more than enough energy to win both the mile and the 3 miles, despite being on the scratch mark in both and conceding huge handicaps.

That set me up nicely for Ballycastle, where despite having little or no experience of this type of sports, I was able to win the handicap mile off a generous start, thanks to having no form known to the handicappers. I later finished runner-up in the half-mile, where I was caught for speed in the early part of the race but finished strongly.

This lack of basic speed was to be an enduring feature for me and brought back memories of my training with Barney Donaghey in Egypt when he would destroy me at any distance of 200 yards or less. Nevertheless, my successes in Ballycastle pleased Mr Beasant, who had become a solid supporter of mine to the point of having me moved to an easier job in the shipyard that did not require any lifting. All I had to do was ensure the shipwrights always had a full supply of nails, a full circle for a man born in Nailors Row. He encouraged me to enter the Celtic FC Sports in Glasgow, and the following day, I sent off an entry for the race. What I did not know was that Mr Beasant also sent off an entry for me.

I got Friday before the sports off work and went over on the cattle boat to Glasgow on Thursday night so that I could rest up until Sunday. I stayed with one of my cousins, Charlie McCafferty, and his family, who lived not far from Kelvingrove Park in the west of the city.

On arriving at Celtic Park, I noticed that I was listed twice on the programme. I was entered as Anton Hegarty from City of Derry and secondly as an individual with no club affiliation.

Obviously, this duplication had escaped the notice of the handicappers because they gave the City of Derry runner a start of 100 yards, while the other Anton Hegarty, entered as an individual, got a generous 140 yards. I should *perhaps*

LION FOR A DAY

have brought this to the attention of the officials, but I decided to capitalise on the generosity of the handicappers and collected the number which gave me the longer start.

There was a buzz about the meeting as the top British miler of the day, Albert Hill, was a confirmed starter and was rumoured to be going to attack the British record. Whilst betting was forbidden, at the risk of being banned for life from the sport, there were always bookmakers placed discreetly at these meetings, although it was against the amateur rules of the day.

Charlie was the first to notice them located behind one of the large stands, and he went off to reconnoitre. He came back saying that he could get 20/1 about me winning, while Hill was 3/1 despite having to run off scratch. We both dug deep into our pockets and came up with the princely sum of £2: one crisp pound note that I had brought over with me and the accumulated change of the both of us.

"You better win this, Anton. That's my wife's grocery money for the next week," he said. "And I'll not have a fag much less a drink."

I had never experienced nerves like it, even at the front in Gallipoli and France. Over 30,000 loud and vociferous spectators roaring on their favourites from all parts of Britain and Ireland. I was still naïve at the time to the process of warming up and merely jogged gently around the back of the stand for twenty minutes before doing some limbering exercises and a few desultory sprints over 40–50 yards. Meanwhile, I watched Hill run in the adjoining field

MALCOLM MCCAUSLAND

for the best part of an hour followed by some brisk sprints. I topped up my energy levels with my usual supply of raisins for energy and a couple of slugs of tap water in the changing rooms. I lined up on my mark alongside a runner from the famous Bellahouston Harriers, and we exchanged good luck salutations.

I was shaking like a leaf when the gun fired, but I remembered the advice Mr Beasant had given me before I left and did not go off like a hare. Nevertheless, I had gathered in most of those in front of me by the end of first two laps, with two to run, and I could hear no one coming behind.

I stole a glance over my shoulder at the sound of the bell for the final circuit and quickly reeled in and passed the remaining three in front. I was now at the front of the field with about 250 yards to run when I heard the roars rise from the crowd. I could not hear him but knew Hill was hunting me down. The adrenalin rushed through me and I tried to pick up the pace a little.

I knew I was tiring and stole another glance back going into the final bend to see the ominous figure of the Englishman, now only some 15 yards back and gaining ground rapidly. I tried to muster a sprint and ran the last straight like one of the terrified hares we used for coursing in Secunderabad. The straight seemed endless, but I finally broke the tape. I cannot describe the sweet relief it brought as all the tiredness and tension drained from my body. I had won. I had won the mile at the Celtic Sports, and I was little more than a novice.

LION FOR A DAY

There was a long deliberation by the officials before they gave me my prize: a Swiss-made gold watch. In the end, they accepted that the handicapping mistake had been theirs and that I had done nothing wrong.

The prize was appreciated but not as much as the money, with Charlie lifting £40 plus our own two back, which we split equally between us. We realised we might be marked men and were concerned about getting the money back to Charlie's home without being robbed. We hid the money as best we could and set off.

On the way out, we passed the changing rooms, where I bumped into Albert Hill. He was accompanied by his coach and recognised me immediately.

"I'm Hill," he said modestly as if I did not know him already. "I thought I had you caught with a furlong to run, but I tired and didn't gain an inch on you after that."

Slightly overawed, all I could say was a subdued "Thank you, Albert! Congratulations on your British record. I was sure you had me when I looked back on the last bend."

At this point, the elderly man I took to be his coach interrupted.

Figure 5: Sam Mussabini was an athletics coach who was years ahead of his time. Meeting him was to prove fortunate for Anton.

"That was some run, Hegarty. My name is Sam Mussabini. I'm a professional athletics coach at Polytechnic Harriers in London," he said. "That was a very impressive run from you. I'm surprised I've not seen or heard of you before."

I explained briefly that I'd been in the army and had only started running cross-country in India but that I had never raced on the track until this year and then only once at a sport in Ballycastle. He listened intently, but I could have been knocked down with a feather by what he said next.

"If you were to base yourself in London, I could make you an Olympic champion at next year's Olympic Games, but it would not be the mile, or more correctly 1,500-metre, that I'd enter you for there. You run uneconomically enough but you stride too long for your height. I could see you being more successful at 5,000-metre or 10,000-metre, but I think cross-country is your event.

LION FOR A DAY

"I would need to use a cine camera to analyse your running technique, but I'm certain you overstride a little, especially when you came under pressure in the later stages of the race like today. But we could correct that quite easily," he added thoughtfully.

"Thank you very much, but I've only settled back home in Derry after being away for nearly eight years and wouldn't want to go through all that moving again. Besides I'm almost 27 and have a fiancée, and we intend to get married sometime next year. That will probably end my career. But I'm flattered by the offer."

We shook hands, and Charlie and I headed off to make our way back to the west side of Glasgow. We thought we were being followed by a couple of thuggish-looking men, possibly tipped off, or more likely sent by the bookie who had to pay out £40 to us.

We walked as far as Gallowgate, where we went into a public house. As luck would have it, Charlie met two men that he knew drinking in one of the alcoves. Our two pursuers came in and took seats at the bar, where they could watch us from a discreet distance and still have the front door in view. Charlie whispered something to his two friends, and I saw him passing them a pound note.

"Take off your jacket and cap, Anton. I've a plan," he said in a low voice.

We both took off our jackets and caps and swapped them with Charlie's friends who had done the same.

MALCOLM MCCAUSLAND

"Boys, pull the caps down over your eyes, and I want yous to fly out of this alcove and straight out the front door, turn right back up Gallowgate, and don't stop until yous are at the gates of Tollcross Park about 2 miles away. I'll tell yous the craic when I see you at work tomorrow."

The two men followed the instructions to the letter, making a bolt for the door before heading up the busy Gallowgate in the direction from which we came. The two pursuers waited a moment or two before taking to their feet and going after them like a pair of greyhounds that had just got the scent of the hare. Meanwhile we quietly slipped out the back door, hailed a hackney cab, and were back in Charlie's within thirty minutes for a slap-up feed made by his good wife.

The next morning, after a good night's sleep aided by a couple of pints of the local beer, I picked up a copy of the *Glasgow Herald* to read accounts of the meeting. But my win in the mile was overshadowed by Albert Hill's record.

> *"Records at Parkhead. Evidently the officials at the Celtic Football Club expected that new records would be created in the half and one mile at Parkhead on Saturday, as the best times on the books of the Scottish Amateur Athletic Association for these distances were given in the programme. Expectation was fulfilled, Sgt Mason lowering the half-mile time, and AG Hill that of the mile. In one way Hill's performance was the more meritorious, as the mile was an open event and the English mile champion had a very large field to get through. In the circumstances*

he did remarkably well, in reducing by 1 2-5th seconds a record that has stood since 1894. The weather was favourable for fast running, and good times were registered throughout the afternoon—that of the open 100 yards for instance being recorded as 10 seconds, the 220 yards at 22 seconds, and the mile at 4 min 17 13 4-5th seconds. The mile was won from 145 yards and it is not surprising that Hill—who of course ran the full distance—failed to finish first.

The other record was made in the invitation half-mile, which had an entry of 14, although some of those, including Hill, did not turn out. Sergeant Mason had an allowance of 10 yards but in the champion's absence, he preferred to start from scratch, and justified his optimism by winning the race and beating Homer Baker's 1 min 55 4-5th sec by two fifths. Next to Mason's successful attempt on record, the feature of the event was the fine effort of S Small, who from 30 yards, ran a good race and was actually moving faster than the New Zealander at the finish ... None of the southern visitors entered for the half-mile, and most abstained from the furlong probably in view of the relay race towards the end of the programme. By running this event on handicap terms, the issue was made more open than it otherwise would have been; but before the start, Maryhill Harriers were not too confident that the 45 yards allowed them *would enable them to beat the Polytechnic, and the fear proved well founded.*

There were about 30,000 spectators and the entries included "several well-known English and Colonial runners." The relay was won by Poly Harriers in 3 Min 32 4-5th sec, with Maryhill second and a Celtic Select third. The team was Sgt Mason, JB Bell, MC Cook and Sgt Lindsay."

About a month after the meeting, Mr Beasant came down to where I worked in the shipyard. He said he had received a package for me in the post, addressed simply:

**MR ANTHONY HEGARTY,
C/O THE SECRETARY,
CITY OF DERRY HARRIERS,
LONDONDONDERRY, IRELAND."**

He handed it over to me, and as he seemed curious as to what it might contain, I decided to open it there and then. It took a few minutes to tear off the wrapping as it was well sealed, but eventually out popped a book: *The Complete Athletic Trainer* by S.A. Mussabini in collaboration with Charles Ranson. I searched farther inside the packaging to find a single sheet of paper.

Dear Mr. Hegarty,

Congratulations once again on your splendid victory in Glasgow.

If you follow the training in my book (enclosed), I should expect to see you in the cross-country event in Antwerp.

Meantime good luck in preparation and competition.

Yours Sincerely,

Scipio Africanus (Sam) Mussabini

Mr Beasant and I looked at each other dumbfounded as Mr Mussabini was regarded as one of the leading coaches in Britain, if not the world. He read the note, I read the note, and he read it again. We could not believe it.

"You've no excuse now, Anton. You have to go for it."

Late in the year, we had the general meeting of City of Derry Harriers at Conlon's Rooms in Foyle Street, where Mr Beasant, in his role as club secretary, listed the club's achievements in what was its inaugural year. He gave special mention to Hugh Casey, Sam Jack, and me on our performances. He said we were among the best in Ireland in our respective events.

He went on that our successes made a remarkable record for a club in its infancy, and he hoped it would be an incentive to other members to prepare to take part in the various sports meetings next season, assuring them that the club would give them every assistance towards that end.

He was also pleased to note that it was the intention of the club committee to send teams to represent the city at Ulster and All-Ireland championships the following year. He did not mention that I had bigger plans like going to the Olympic Games, which by now had been confirmed to take place in Antwerp the following August.

CHAPTER 13

THE ROAD TO THE OLYMPICS

Ambition is the path to success.
Persistence is the vehicle you arrive in.
—Bill Bradley

I began 1920 fired up and ready for what I hoped would be an outstanding twelve months, with the Olympics and marriage on the horizon.

I had followed the advice in Sam Mussabini's book to the letter, with long walks of between three and four hours on a Sunday and faster runs over 3 miles during the week. I also practised the running style he recommended—shorter stride and relaxed arms—concentrating on leg speed. It was all coming together, and nobody in the club could now match my pace for any more than maybe half a mile, meaning I was left to do most of the fast runs on my own.

When I was not working, I was training, and in the evenings, I would read newspapers and books. That cycle would be repeated the following day. Being frank, I had to admit to myself that I had yet to settle back into the place I had considered home and the place I yearned for when I was in India and the hellholes of war in Gallipoli and France.

Whilst I enjoyed raising a glass or two with mates in the army, I now found myself uncomfortable in public houses, which for the most part were regarded as either Catholic or Protestant establishments. At one time I had relied in a manner on drink to help me sleep and avoid the nightmares of mutilated cadavers, exploding shells, and worst of all rats—huge black rats that ran all over me. Now I found my running settled my mind, and after a day of work and training, I was only too pleased to hit the hay for a sound night's sleep.

In any case, although I had been accepted back into the community, thanks largely to the little bit of training I did for the Republicans, I still felt I got a cool reception from my Catholic peers, who did not know of my involvement when they learned I had been a British soldier for almost eight years.

If I made the walk to a bar on the other side of the Carlisle Bridge in the Protestant Waterside, there was the danger of being recognised as a Catholic from the Bogside, and even military service for "king and country" would not save me from a hiding or worse.

My mood had not been improved by Gertie having to cancel her trip across to Derry to meet my family, as the Paynes would not give her time off over the Christmas period. Instead, she hoped to come at Easter. In the meantime, the letters kept coming and going between us. We still had not

LION FOR A DAY

ruled out that both of us would settle in Derry, but it was becoming less likely as the months went on.

So with a solid base of training and an abstemious Christmas and New Year, I prepared for my first cross-country race since I had run the inter-regimental championships in India at the end of September 1914.

The club members met early at the railway station on 28 February for the first appearance of City of Derry Harriers at the Northern Cross-Country Championships in Belvoir Park, Belfast.

Mr Beasant was his usual efficient self, black notebook in hand and ticking us off on his list as we appeared. With the train set to go, only young Danny Doherty, who was to run in the junior race, was missing, but he came panting into the station as the guard blew his whistle for the last passengers to get on board. Doherty sprinted along the platform to our carriage and joined us, muttering something about his alarm not going off. "You'd be late for your own funeral," retorted Mr Beasant, who was a stickler for punctuality.

On arrival in Belfast, we walked to a nearby tea rooms in Great Victoria Street, where Mr Beasant had pre-ordered a light meal for us all comprising of soup and sandwiches. He said that this had been sponsored by a patron, but I suspect he was the patron and paid for it out of his own pocket. That was his nature.

Before the cars came to take us to the course in south Belfast, Mr Beasant said a few words about this being

205

an auspicious day for us all and asked everyone to do our best and remember that we were representing not just our club but our families and city. He said he wanted our blue singlet with a white sash to become a symbol of fair play and dedication in the years to come. I took the opportunity while the cars were arriving to nip to a grocer's shop to pick up a bag of raisins for energy.

The race could not have gone any better, despite my nervousness due to the fact that it had been such a long time since I had last raced. I was heartened to be surrounded by teammates in their new colours: royal blue vests with a white sash. With us all kitted out in the same uniform, I felt the same camaraderie I had enjoyed in the army—all in it together.

We knew this was an important race for us all, but especially for me as a lot was expected after my win in the mile over in Scotland. To a man they clapped me on the back or shook my hand to wish me well, and instead of this putting pressure on me, it calmed my nerves.

When the gun fired, I could feel the immediate release of tension and my diligent training kicked in. I felt like a well-oiled machine, everything in working order, flowing over the grass, almost floating on air. I found myself clear after the long starting straight. My legs felt so light, I seemed to go faster and faster as the race progressed, despite the testing hills and steep descents of Belvoir Park.

I could have run all day but was pleased to cross the finish line as the new Northern cross-country champion, the first one since before the war. Better still, I had broken the course record by a minute and the club had finished a respectable fifth in the team listings on our debut. A Belfast newspaper was fulsome in its praise of the event and my performance in particular.

"A really splendid race for the northern cross-country championship took place in Belvoir Park on Saturday afternoon, and it was favoured with the best of weather conditions. The venue proved quite an attraction in itself, for it would be difficult, if not, indeed, altogether impossible, to find a better within the whole limits of Ulster. With characteristic thoughtfulness and consideration, the park—which is beautifully undulating, and adorned in many parts by clumps of giant trees— was kindly placed at the disposal of the committee by the right honourable Sir James Johnston J.P., The present occupant, who, attending with some friends, manifested a deep interest in the contest. Trams, motor waggons, and cars carried a large crowd of spectators to the scene, and this was another distinctly encouraging feature on the side of success. No doubt was left in the mind of anyone who saw the arrangements, the admirable manner they were carried out, and the workmanlike way all went about their duties, that the officials from top to bottom of the list were sportsmen of the first water ...

Derry club travelled specially to participate in the race, and had every reason to be gratified over their reception. A. Hegarty who created a sensation at Glasgow Gaelic sports by his work in the mile, belonged to this team, and the fine record he again established in the Northern championships at Belvoir Park made him an outstanding figure. He led all the way, improving the distance every lap, and finished magnificently. It was at once recognised that he and Crowe who had won in the junior race at Bloomfield a fortnight ago, would make fine assets for Ireland in an international contest, and it is almost certain that before long both will have their chances in this respect. Martin and Kerr, ex-champions: Magill, winner of the victory inter-team shield; and McBride, the Ulster four mile champion, were also in the field …

Hegarty made a splendid finish, coming in strongly a good way in front of Martin. Topping romped in 100 yards behind the latter, and then followed at shorter or longer intervals—Gowdy, Crothers, McCann, and Jackson, of Willowfield, and McBride, North Belfast. The time was 34 minutes 53 seconds. This proved a new record, Hegarty improving on the former time for a somewhat shorter course, by a minute."

Naturally, spirits were high on the train home, and a few followers of the club, who had been advised of our success by telephone, turned up at the station to greet us on our

LION FOR A DAY

return later that night. Some of the boys were going out to celebrate, but I decided to turn in early and was out for my long walk after the early Mass the following morning.

Work and training continued as normal for the next couple of weeks before I was again boarding the train, this time on my own to Dublin for the Irish championships.

I was fortunate that I was able to stay with my brother John but found difficulty sleeping as one of his children was sick several times during the night, waking the whole house. I, along with Tim Crowe and Larry Cummins, who lived in England, were the favourites to lift the individual title, but I never felt the same feeling of running on air that I had enjoyed in Belfast. Nevertheless, I thought I ran well to finish second and lift the silver medal. I was even more pleased to be named on the Ireland team for the upcoming international cross-country to be held on the Belvoir course three weeks later. The report in the following day's Dublin paper summed up the race very well.

> *"Cross-Country Running*
>
> *The Senior Cross-Country Championship was held on Saturday over a course of eight miles, near Liffey Junction. It was satisfactory, after the lapse of many years, to find a representative entry for the event. Belfast sent its two crack combinations: the Ulsterville Harriers and the North Belfast Harriers. Another Northern club was City of Derry Harriers and Dublin was represented by the Southern champions,*

the Donore Harriers, and the Clonliffe Harriers. In addition there were four individual entries, the latter including T. Crowe, the winner of the Junior and Southern, so that the field consisted of fifty competitors. Many objections might be urged against individual entries being received to the championship of a sport that cannot be pursued individually, but, in view of the desirability of getting the best possible team for the coming international contest, the Cross-Country Association probably acted wisely in the matter. It certainly gave Crowe an opportunity of demonstrating his outstanding merit amongst Irish runners. He got amongst the leaders when the field settled down, and although for some little distance Hegarty of Derry and Cummins, of the Surrey A.C., kept him company, he had a substantial lead at the end of two miles, and continued to increase it to the end, winning by nearly a minute from Hegarty, without ever being pressed. Cummins had the misfortune to get a heavy fall in the early part of the race and cut his hip badly. Details: 1, T. Crowe, Clonliffe (Indiv.) 46:25; 2, A Hegarty, City of Derry (Indiv.) 47:19, 3 L.M. Cummins, Clonliffe (Indiv.) 47:56; 4, J.M. Martin, Ulsterville 48:10; 5, B.H. Bingham Clonliffe 48:32; 6, W.E. Murray (Indiv.) 48:35; 7, J.J. Cronin Donore 48:36; 8, A. M'Auley, Ulsterville 48:38; 9, W. Gowdy, North Belfast 48:55; 10, J. Pyper, do. 48:56; 11. F. McBride, do 49:27; 12. R. K. Robinson, do 50:20.

Teams:

1. *North Belfast Harriers - 51 (5 Gowdy, 6 Pyper, 7 McBride, 8 Robinson, 12 W. McClung, 13 R. Wilkinson)*

2. *Donore Harriers - 67 (3, 9,10,11,14,20)*

3. *Ulsterville Harriers - 77 (1,4,15,16, 18,23)*

4. *Clonliffe Harriers - 136 (2,22,26,27, 29,30)"*

I shared a carriage on the train back to Belfast, the first stage of my journey home, with the triumphant North Belfast Harriers, who had deposed Clonliffe, winners the last time the race was held in 1914.

They had further cause for celebration with Billy Gowdy being named on the international team, along with me and Ulsterville' s William Murray and John Beattie, who was living in England.

Aside from the selection of Murray and Beattie, the Ulsterville lads were a little disappointed with their third place after they had beaten North Belfast Harriers in the Northern just two weeks earlier. They had really believed they could bring the title back to east Belfast for the first time.

I did not arrive back in Derry until near midnight with the station almost deserted apart from the few of us who had just disembarked. As I walked home, I could hear sporadic gunfire from various parts of the city but mostly from the Diamond area. Tension had been high in the city for some time, but this did not concern me as I made my way quietly towards home and to bed.

I awoke tired the next day, only went to Mass at midday and decided against my usual long walk, preferring to go out and get a Dublin paper to see if they had a report of the race. The paper also reported that the Frenchman Joseph Guillemot, running as a guest, had won the English Cross-Country Championship from Charlie Clibbon of Birchfield Harriers and Warrington AC's Chris Vose. Scotsman Jimmy Wilson had finished fourth. I looked forward to locking horns with them in Belfast at the international.

I was pleased to receive a formal letter after a few days confirming my selection for the international, which was also making a return for the first time since before the war. I cut back on my training for the next couple of weeks, anticipating wearing the green Irish singlet for the first time and wanting to be fresh.

Mr Beasant had arranged some time off for me at the shipyard, and I left work at lunchtime on the Thursday before the race. On my way out, the foreman handed me an envelope with money to make up for the wages I would lose through my absence, as I had been allowed time off without pay. They had done a collection round the workers on our

LION FOR A DAY

team and the foreman said that they had all been more than willing to contribute.

I went home and packed my trusty canvas backpack. I knew I would be supplied with a green Ireland singlet and woollen jumper but was careful to pack a change of clothes, an embrocation oil, a pair of white shorts that we had to supply ourselves, and of course, a generous supply of raisins for energy.

Mr Beasant had called by the house a few nights earlier and presented me with a new pair of spiked shoes for the occasion. He said these were made of the finest leather available and they were as light as a feather and had been paid for by the club. I packed them carefully into a little cotton bag inside my backpack and was now relishing the opportunity to run on the international stage on what I considered to be almost my home course.

Later that evening, I made the short walk from the train station in Belfast to the appointed hotel. The receptionist checked my name against a list and gave me the key to a room on the third floor that looked across to the Harland & Wolff shipyards, where I could see that a large merchant ship *(MV Dorsetshire)* was ready for launch on the high seas.

I was still unpacking my few items when there was a gentle knock on the door. It was Larry Cummins. He had taken third place behind me in the Irish championships a couple of weeks earlier, but apart from exchanging pleasantries after the race, we had not spoken before this. I knew he lived in England because he was listed as Surrey AC on the programme in Dublin, but I was surprised to hear a strong southern accent.

We got into conversation and exchanged backgrounds. He said he lived in Cheltenham but had received inducement to join Surrey AC from a man called Ted Vowles, who had a factory in New Malden. Some of the English team, he said, were also members of the club as well, notably Percy Hodge, who had beaten Cummins into second place in the previous year's AAA Championships at Stamford Bridge in London. Cummins regretted that he could not run the English championship as he felt his club could have beaten Birchfield Harriers and retained the title they had won in 1914 with his help.

We had a team meeting on Friday night before the race. Tom Murphy, president of the Irish Cross-Country Association, and the honorary secretary, Frank Osborne, both addressed us. Murphy said we should feel honoured to wear the green singlet at such an important competition and it would be a day we would look back on with pride the rest of our lives.

He said that he hoped that Ireland would be able to field a cross-country team at an Olympics Games in the near future, although he was not confident that this would happen later that year in Antwerp.

Frank Osborne, who was also our team manager, spoke about the prestige of the event and how it was a compliment to the country that we should be hosting the competition for the first time in six years. He went on to say that he had unfortunately just received word from his Welsh counterpart

LION FOR A DAY

that Wales would not be travelling due to a number of their key runners falling ill at the last minute with the Spanish flu.

Much of the rest of the meeting was given over to arrangements for the following day. Then we all retired to our bedrooms to make our final preparations for the morrow and what promised to be a memorable day.

The next morning, after a good breakfast, we were transported out to south Belfast by cars. I was immediately struck by the number of spectators already present in the park and was pleasantly surprised to see that a party of around thirty followers had made the trip from Derry to support me. Later I would hear them yelling my name on every corner during the race, but in the meantime, I made a beeline for Mr Beasant, whom I had spotted some distance away. I joined him and we went off for a quiet little walk together. Not usually given to showing any emotions, I could see his eyes mist over when he spoke.

"Anton, you don't realise the honour you're bringing to us all, your family, your club, your city," he said, looking me directly in the eyes. "You're possibly the only positive thing to come out of Derry this year—or for some years. You've trained hard for today, and I know you will do well. Try to take in everything you can because you will have few days like it in your life."

In return, I thanked him for his unflagging support, but my mind was already focussed on the race and I did not want to get engaged in much conversation. We promised to talk again after it was over. I re-joined the rest of the team and we went through a perfunctory warm-up of some calisthenics and a few spurts of speed.

The four countries marched behind their national flags. The Scots had the saltire, we had St. Patrick's cross in red on a white background, the English a St. George's cross, with the French standing to attention under their tricolour of red, white, and blue. It gave occasion a real international atmosphere.

We all lined up for the start, and we were off. All eyes were on Joseph Guillemot, who had already won both the French and English championships that year. We were told that he usually dashed to the front from the gun and simply ran away from the opposition, but he must have been having an off day because he was not in front of me at the end of the first lap. Instead the Scot, Jimmy Wilson, was trying to impose himself on the field, while we, the Irish, were jockeying with the English for team honours. It remained that way for five of the six laps when, despite the vociferous home support, the English white vests moved away for a comfortable team win.

I thought for most of the race that I could make a top-six place but I tired at the start of the final lap, which I put down to three hard races and the travelling in the space of a month. I slipped back to twelfth at the finish line. Against all odds, it was Wilson who ran out a convincing winner to add the international crown to his Scottish title. England's Chris Vose and Wally Freeman occupied silver and bronze medal places. Larry Cummins had an outstanding run to be first Irishman home, in fifth, followed by Tim Crowe,

LION FOR A DAY

who was affected by a poisoned hand, in eighth, and John Moran in tenth. The mercurial Guillemot failed to show the form that won him French and English titles and withdrew from the race on the third lap. He was the only man who failed to finish.

My initial disappointment was dissipated somewhat when we were told that we had finished second behind the English, with the Scots and France tying in third. As Scotland's sixth scorer finished in front of his French counterpart, they would be taking home the bronze medals. I dreaded to think what stick Monsieur Guillemot would have to take from his French teammates after abandoning them in midrace, especially as they had come with hopes of winning the team title for the first time.

I managed to snatch a few words with Mr Beasant before all the competitors and officials were escorted off to Belvoir Park House, the home of Sir James Johnston and Lady Johnston, who had made available their lands once again for the event. Lady Johnston presented us with our glittering silver medals, and we were treated to a full buffet meal of cold meats and salad potatoes, followed by a substantial portion of apple tart with custard and ample non-alcoholic drinks.

Before we left, Mr Murphy, on behalf of the Irish Cross-Country Association, proposed a hearty vote of thanks to Sir James and Lady Johnston for the admirable manner in which they had performed the part of host and hostess and also for the great kindness they had shown to the international board in placing the grounds at their disposal.

MALCOLM MCCAUSLAND

Mr George Hume, vice president of the Scottish Cross-Country Association, seconded, and the vote was passed by acclamation. Sir James Johnson said in reply that both Lady Johnson and he were delighted to have that opportunity of meeting their guests. He went on to add that cross-country running was an excellent form of sport, clean and healthy, and he was always pleased to do anything to assist. We loudly applauded this sentiment and the gathering then broke into smaller groups before we were conveyed back to our hotel.

Whilst most of the runners and officials were staying another night, I packed my bag, and after making my hurried farewells, I was on the next train home to Derry with my precious medal safely housed in the inside pocket of my jacket.

The newspapers reported on the resounding success of the event and complimented the organisers on the manner it was put together.

England Successful at Belvoir Park

The largest attendance that has ever graced a cross-country fixture in this country was present at Belvoir park on Saturday, when the 13th annual international championship took place. The course, over which the race had been decided 10 years ago, is an ideal one, providing a real test for the competitors, and the Irish Cross-Country Association are deeply grateful to Sir James Johnston, *who very kindly placed it at their disposal. Considerable interest attached to the meeting by reason of the fact that Guillemot, the Frenchman, who had already carried off the English and French national championships, turned out for France, while the Irish champion Tim Crowe, one of the best runners who has ever worn the national colours, was among Ireland's representatives. Included in the English team were runners of proved worth in Vose, Clibborn, and Blewitt, and the hopes of Scotland rested on Wilson, who won the Scottish championship on the 6th March, and a week later ran fourth in the English championship at Windsor Great Park*

There has been no international contest since 1914, and on the 12 previous occasions on which the championship has been decided England has been successful in every instance in providing the winning team. Nine times has a representative of the winning team carried off the individual owners. France being credited with this distinction thrice in 1911, 1912, and 1913 through the agency of Jean Bouin, a brilliant cross-country performer, who fell in action during the war* it was regretted that owing to the serious illness of several of their runners the Welsh CCA were reluctantly compelled to withdraw their team on the eve of the race.

Contrary to expectations, Guillemot, did not play the part in the contest his earlier performances had indicated, and he retired in the third lap, being the only competitor who failed to finish. Crowe, too, did not realise the high hopes entertained of him. He was however, suffering from a poisoned hand, which must have had an adverse effect on his fitness. The individual winner turned up in James Wilson, Greenock Glenpark Harriers, who led from shortly after the start and won by 120 yards from C. Vose, Warrington AC. England won the team championship with 38 points, her runners packing very well and finishing five men in the first ten home. Ireland whose team had been running well together for five of the six circuits of the course, cut up badly in the last round, and only secured second place with 70 points. Scotland and France tied for third place, each scoring 114 points. The distance was nine miles 600 yards, the winner's time being 55 minutes, 6 seconds.

Results: 1 Jim Wilson Scotland 55:06, 2 Christopher Vose England 55:33, 3 Wally Freeman England 55:52, 4 Charles Clibbon England 56:26, 5 Larry Cummins Ireland 56:27, 6 Bobby Mills England 56:40, 7 Lucien Duquesne France 57:05, 8 Tim Crowe Ireland 57:11, 9 Percy Hodge England 57:15, 10 J. Moran Ireland 57:18, 11 Louis Bouchard France 57:25, 12 Anton Hegarty Ireland 57:30, 13 Louis Corlet France 57:31, 14 James Hatton England 57:35, 15 Alf Pepper England 57:37, 16 John Martin

Ireland 57:41, 17 Joe Blewitt England 57:43, 18 Angus Kerr Scotland 57:44, 19 J. Beattie Ireland 57:47, 20 Archie Craig Sr. Scotland 57:49, 21 René Vignaud France, 22 Dunky Wright Scotland, 23 A. Topping Ireland, 24 Bevy Bingham Ireland, 25 Joe Pratt England, 26 Alex Barrie Scotland, 27 John Strain Scotland, 28 J.J. Cronin Ireland, 29 Andrew Semple Scotland, 30 Joseph Servella France, 31 Albert Smith Scotland, 32 Amar Alim Arbidi France, 33 Danton Heuet France, 34 Albert Isola France; DNF - Joseph Guillemot France Teams: 1 England 38, 2 Ireland 70, 3 Scotland 114, 4 France 114."

CHAPTER 14

FRIENDS AND RIVALS

*Mind is everything. Muscles—just
pieces of rubber. All that I am,
I am because of my mind.*

—*Paavo Nurmi*

Every boy has a hero, and Paavo Nurmi was no different. Nurmi's hero was Juho Pietari "Hannes" Kolehmainen, who was one of the stars of the 1912 Summer Olympics in Stockholm, winning three gold medals. The most memorable of these was the 5,000-metre, in which he defeated Jean Bouin in what was regarded as one of the tightest battles ever over the distance.

Kolehmainen was from Kuopio, a town in the centre of Finland. He had two brothers, both of whom were international-class distance runners. Kolehmainen competed for a number of years in the United States, wearing on his singlet the Winged Fist of the Irish American Athletic Club. He was the first of a legendary group who became known as the "Flying Finns," winning European and Olympic medals.

LION FOR A DAY

More importantly, he was to influence a young man who was indisputably the greatest of all of the Flying Finns.

Paavo Johannes Nurmi, just 15 at the time, had been enthralled reading newspaper accounts of his hero Kolehmainen at the 1912 Olympic Games in Stockholm, just across the Gulf of Bothnia from his home in Turku. Kolehmainen had, in twelve days, captivated the hearts of the entire Finnish nation by winning the 5,000-metre, 10,000-metre, and both cross-country individual and team gold medals. He had opened by winning a heat of the 10,000-metre on the first day, before taking in the final the following evening. Two days later, he won his 5,000-metre heat and beat Jean Bouin in the final after the Frenchman had shown ahead on no less than eight occasions during the final lap. The Flying Finn completed his hat-trick of individual gold medals by winning the cross-country and leading his country to team victory.

He was one of two outstanding athletes at the Games, the other being American Jim Thorpe, winner of the pentathlon and the newly created decathlon. But Thorpe's gold medals were stripped by the International Olympic Committee in 1913, after the IOC had been advised that he had taken expense money for playing baseball prior to the 1912 Games, so violating the strict Olympic rules of amateurism. That disqualification would later be revoked, though sadly not in Thorpe's lifetime. Nurmi would fall foul of the self-same rules later in his career.

Meantime, the Finns were elated with Kolehmainen's successes, a boost to the national morale after years of oppression by Russia. Boys all over Finland took to the roads, wearing ordinary clothes and footwear, and they could be found in every town and village pounding out kilometre after kilometre, inspired by their new national hero.

However, when Kolehmainen changed from his bourgeois sports club to a workers' one, his boss fired him. And, like many Finns, with hungry times still prevailing in their country, he emigrated to the United States, where one of his brothers, Willis, was making a living as a professional runner. Kolehmainen wisely stayed amateur and made his living as a stonemason, marrying the daughter of a fellow Finn. He continued his training for the 1916 Olympics, relishing the return match with his rival Bouin. Alas, it was not to be as the Games in Berlin were cancelled following the outbreak of World War I.

Nurmi was born on 13 June 1897, the son of a reportedly frail ebony worker and his wife, who lived in a small house on the outskirts of Turku, a city on the south-west coast of Finland at the mouth of the Aura River. He joined a local athletics club at the age of 9, and there are records of times that Nurmi ran at that age right through until the end of his career.

Disaster struck the family when his father died, it seems not unexpectedly, leaving a widow and family of five, of which Paavo was the eldest. At 13, he had to leave school to assume the responsibility of providing for the family by taking a job as a delivery boy, pushing a hand truck up the steep slopes of the former Finnish capital. Nurmi was later to attribute the phenomenal strength in his lower back and

LION FOR A DAY

thighs to this work. Despite the toll of hard work during the day, Nurmi continued to pursue a running career in the evenings.

Like many other boys of his age, Kolehmainen's successes inspired him to even greater efforts than previous, running to exhaustion against the tram cars in what is a hilly city. He joined Turku's top athletics club, Turun Urheilutto, and was a familiar figure lapping the track in his everyday clothes. For a number of years, his athletics equipment consisted solely of a well-worn pair of plimsolls. His times at 17 still did not mark him out as anything special, but he continued with the grind, eschewing the company of clubmates, except for gymnastic sessions during the winter, with long runs on the roads near his home or on trails through local woods.

All outdoor athletics training normally came to an end in October as the harsh Arctic winter descended upon Turku, but in April, Nurmi would start anew with the desire to improve his times. Progress was slow as evidenced by his 5,000-metre times—15:57.5 in 1915; 5:52.8 in 1916; 15:47.4 in 1917; and 15:50.7 in 1918—but a letter he received changed his life.

After the declaration of the Finnish Republic in December 1917, in the wake of the Bolshevik Revolution earlier that year, trouble arose over the continued presence of a large Russian garrison in Finland. Disturbances in Helsinki led to its seizure by the Red Guards triggering a bitter war. Nurmi was called up and, as ordered, reported to the barracks at Pori, some 60 miles (96 kilometres) north of Turku.

He was surprised to find that, despite the ongoing hostilities, athletes were still valued in the Finnish military. He was entered for the Finnish Army March, a demanding event that required the participants to cover 15 kilometres (9.3 miles) in full uniform, with a rifle, ammunition, and a haversack containing 25 kilogrammes (4 stone) of sand.

The official starter joked before they set off that they could run, if they wished, and that is exactly what Nurmi did, arriving at the finish fifty-nine minutes later. Initially, he was suspected of having taken a short cut or cheated in some other manner, but when his time was found to be genuine, he was hailed as a star. With the confidence from that achievement, he ripped through his personal bests, improving the 5,000-metre time to 15:31.5 and becoming second-ranked in Finland in both the 3,000-metre (8:58.1) and 10,000-metre (32:56.0).

He put his metamorphosis down to the advice of one man: Hannes Kolehmainen. In letters to the aspiring young athlete in 1919, the three-time Olympic champion advised him to vary his speed and include frequent sprints, balanced by what he described as "shacking," which was the building up of stamina with long walks. The stubborn Nurmi was not normally receptive to advice, but coming from his hero, it was a different matter and he fell to his new regime of training with fresh zeal.

Instead of abandoning his training in October, he continued his long walks in the snow during the long Scandinavian winter of 1919–20, with hopes of fulfilling his dreams by running at the Olympics in Antwerp.

Figure 6: Paavo Nurmi leads the 1920 Finnish Olympic trials in Helsinki. (https://commons.wikimedia.org/wiki)

Kolehmainen was persuaded to come to the USA after the 1912 Olympics by the coach of the Irish-American Athletic Club, Lawson Robertson. He was an instant success, winning the American Athletic Union (AAU) 5-mile title that year, the following year, and again in 1915. Kolehmainen was a meticulous trainer and one of the first athletes to pay special attention to his diet. He was a devoted vegetarian but ate meat for its nutritional benefits later in his running career. Despite that, he realised at 30 he would be too old to compete with the same success on the track in Antwerp and switched his attention to the marathon. He ran the Boston Marathon in 1917, finishing fourth, and won the New York Marathon three years later in 2:47:49.4. That was the American Olympic trial, but the three Finns living in the United States also used the event as their own national qualifying race.

Bouin's defeat in Stockholm at the hands of Kolehmainen had been a national disappointment for the French, and they immediately looked forward to their champion avenging that defeat at the next Games to be held in Berlin.

Alexandre François Étienne Jean Bouin had been born on 21 December 1888, and prior to his silver medal in Stockholm, he also competed in the 1908 London Olympics. Apart from his legendary race against Kolehmainen, he was also remembered for setting three more world records: two in 1911 (3,000-metre and 10,000-metre) and one in 1913 (the one-hour run of 19,021 metres). He was small in stature (1.67 metres/70 kilogrammes) and famous not only for his running exploits but also for his training methods, which were far ahead of his time.

He also paid special attention to his daily hygiene and to the food he consumed. He was arguably the best-known French athlete to die during the war, falling on 29 September 1914, hit in the spine by shrapnel in the Meuse while he was the liaison messenger of the 163rd Regiment infantry.

As for the circumstances of his death, they remain a mystery; while some reported a glorious death charging the enemy lines to the cry of "Long live France!" others tell of him being struck by misdirected fire from his own French artillery. He is not forgotten. A stadium is named after him in Paris, the home of Stade Francais Rugby Union Club, and the Jean Bouin 10-kilometre race has taken place every year through the streets of Barcelona since 1920.

The French were soon to find an unlikely replacement for Bouin in Joseph Guillemot, who was born in Le Dorat, Haute-Viene, 31 miles (50 kilometres) north of Limoges. He suffered the rare condition of having his heart on the right side of his chest (situs inversus), and his lungs had been severely damaged by the effects of mustard gas during World War I. The physician who treated him was years ahead of his time by prescribing lots of long runs as a possible means of undoing the damage caused by the gas.

Guillemot was a small man at only 1.60-metre height and 54 kilogrammes, but despite his physical disadvantages, he won his regimental cross-country championships in 1918 and the French Military Championship the following year. He won both French and English cross-country championships in 1920, qualifying for the France team at the 1920 International Cross-Country Championships in Belfast.

Starting as favourite for the individual title, the mercurial Guillemot failed to finish, the only man in the field to do so. Later in the year he picked up his first French national championship title over 5,000 metres, which gained him selection for the Antwerp Olympics and set up the prospect of more epic France-Finland duels against Paavo Nurmi, who was the clear favourite in both of the distance races.

Across the channel in England, another athlete was beginning to emerge as a potential gold medallist in the middle-distance events. When discussing the 1-mile event, coach Sam

Mussabini said, "The great mile runner will be found to be quite a useful sprinter, a much more than average quarter-miler (440m), very little behind champion form at half a mile (800m) and as good as can be met at three-quarters of a mile (1200m). He is, moreover, capable of running 10 miles and more and be a champion of all time."

And that man was Albert Hill, who had won the 1910 English 4-mile title and was more than competent over longer distances. He did not compete in 1911 and 1912 and fought throughout the war years as a signaller in the Royal Flying Corps.

On returning home after the war, he met Sam Mussabini at Polytechnic Harriers and the coach encouraged him to tackle the shorter distances. He won the AAA 880-yard and mile in 1919 and equalled the British record for the latter distance late in the season at the Celtic Sports in Glasgow.

He was beaten in the AAA 880-yard at the 1920 AAA championships and was nearly not selected for the Antwerp Olympics as he was considered too old at 31 years of age.

Great Britain also had high hopes in the distance events for James (Jimmy) Wilson who was born in Windsor, Berkshire, on 2 October 1891. He and his brother John were twins and the youngest of the five children of Isabella and Robert Wilson, both Scots from near Aberdeen, where his father had built up a reputation for animal husbandry.

Robert Wilson obtained the job of herdsman at the Prince Consort's Shaw Farm in New Windsor and was responsible

LION FOR A DAY

for Queen Victoria's award-winning pure-bred cattle stock. The perks of this job included living at the Shaw Farm Lodge within the grounds of Windsor Castle. The estate workers' children attended Windsor Park Royal School, and as well as a basic education, they were also taught farming and gardening. It was an unusual environment in which to grow up, with royal contact particularly at Christmas when he would attend a huge party in the castle for all the estate workers' children and receive gifts from the monarchy. After leaving school, Jimmy did an apprenticeship with a local blacksmith, which was to prove significant when World War I broke out.

Wilson and his twin brother were inspired to take up running when they saw the start of the 1908 Olympic marathon in the Windsor Castle grounds, about a mile from their home. The gold medal in that race was eventually awarded to the runner-up, Johnny Hayes from the United States, whose parents were from Nenagh in County Tipperary.

Later, Hayes was a trainer to the US Olympic team in 1912 and would have been well-known to Hannes Kolehmainen, as both were members of the Irish-American Athletic Club. It is likely that Hayes played a role in bringing the Finn to the US after Kolehmainen's successes in Stockholm. The experience of seeing Olympic runners at such close quarters motivated the Wilson twins and soon afterwards they joined the local club: Slough Harriers.

Jimmy immediately showed promise, finishing thirteenth behind Hallamshire Harrier Ernie Glover in the 1913 English National Cross-Country Championships at Wolverhampton.

Later that year, Glover, who had competed for Great Britain in three events at the Stockholm Olympics, finished second behind Bouin in the International Cross-Country.

Wilson's performance at Wolverhampton earned him selection as a reserve on the England team for the International, but with no withdrawals, he did not get the opportunity to compete.

The next season was even better for Wilson, as he came third in the English National at Chesham Park behind AAA steeplechase champion Charlie Ruffell and Ireland's Frank O'Neill, an army man and a member of the Connaught Rangers. The course was considered one of the longest and toughest in the four-decade history of the event. He was named to represent England in the international, which was also held at Chesham Park, and justified the selectors' faith by finishing sixth, fourth counter, on the England team that ran out relatively comfortable winners from Scotland and a France selection that was missing Bouin.

England's Alfie Nichols was the winner of that 1914 championship. He was another of a number of Surrey AC athletes employed by Ted Vowles in his shirt factory, and it was his only appearance at the international, but he would play a crucial role for Great Britain in the cross-country event at the Antwerp Olympics.

Meantime, Jimmy Wilson would reappear at the international again when it resumed after the war, but not in an England vest.

Aware of his Scottish heritage, and perhaps persuaded by the influential George Wallach, who was also an Anglo Scot, Wilson was soon a member of Greenock Glenpark Harriers and eligible to wear the dark blue singlet of Scotland. He was quick to make the most of his Scottish eligibility and made his track debut north of the border in the Scottish championships held at Powderhall on 27 June 1914, when he outsprinted Wallach to win the 4-mile championship in 20:30.0.

A week after becoming Scottish champion, he finished fourth in the AAA 4-mile championship in 20:01.0, despite being spiked after leading for the opening 3 miles. This gained him selection for England in the inaugural triangular international against Ireland and Scotland at Hampden Park, but he declined the invitation in favour of competing for Scotland.

The Scot did not enlist for the war as his metalworking and fabricating skills made him eligible for exemption from conscription as an essential occupation. His twin brother, John, did join up and was sent to the front, where he died in 1916 after contracting peritonitis.

Through his contacts in Scotland, specifically Greenock, Jimmy Wilson was able to spend the duration of the war in Greenock, building ships and munitions essential to the war effort. After the armistice, he was quick to regain his fitness and opened 1920 with a comfortable victory in the Scottish Cross-Country Championships at Rouken Glen, taking the lead from the gun and building up a winning margin of around four hundred yards by the time he passed the finishing post.

He went back to his former hometown and Windsor Great Park the following weekend but was not allowed to compete as a team member of Slough AC as he had not made the three necessary qualifying appearances during the winter for them. Nevertheless, he was allowed to compete as an individual for Greenock Glenpark, finishing fourth in a race won by Guillemot.

His greatest triumph to date came the following month, when he represented Scotland at the International Cross-Country Championships in Belvoir Park, Belfast. Wilson adapted perfectly to the soft going, and in front of 3,000 spectators, he raced into an early lead that he was never to lose.

He won a hastily arranged AAA trial over 6.5 miles (10.4 kilometre) in Rugby for the Olympic cross-country event at the end of July and was named in the team a few days later, along with Wally Freeman, Larry Cummins, Anton Hegarty, Chris Vose, and Alfie Nichols. The reserves named were W.J. Monk and J. Halton. This meant that the selection included the winners of the last two International Cross-Country Championships—Wilson and Nichols—as well as the top three in 1920: Wilson, Vose, and Freeman.

Wally Freeman worked for the Enfield Cycle Company at Redditch and was a member of the famous Birchfield Harriers club. He had only taken up the sport on return from the war after serving with the Army Cyclist Corps in France. He won international honours in his first full season

LION FOR A DAY

in 1920, after finishing fourth in the English National. He was third in the International Cross-Country in Belfast, helping England to the team gold medals.

Chris Vose was another member of that winning English team and the most experienced. The Warrington athlete had competed at the International Cross-Country Championships from 1911 to 1913 and in 1920, during which time he won one individual silver and four team gold medals. Unlike many of his cross-country contemporaries, he did not excel on the track, but could also perform on the roads.

Eric Backman was the dark horse that Sweden hoped would deliver for them in Antwerp. Born in Vastergotland in south-west Sweden, Backman was younger than most of his rivals at 24 years of age. Despite being a heavy smoker and enjoying a drink, he would win eight Swedish titles in the 5,000-metre and 10,000-metre, as well as holding Swedish records for four distances: 5,000-metre, 10,000-metre, 5-mile, and one-hour run. He had the misfortune to be born in the same age as Nurmi; otherwise, he may have joined the hall of fame as one of the greatest distance runners of his epoch.

Anton Hegarty was not the only Irishman in the Great Britain selection, with Kinsale-born Larry Cummins also making the team. Cummins had left his native Cork early in the century and made his home in Cheltenham. He was affiliated to Surrey AC and, in Ireland, to Clonliffe Harriers. He had run the International Cross-Country earlier in the year, finishing fifth, defeating Irish champion Tim Crowe

MALCOLM MCCAUSLAND

and leading Ireland to team silver medals. He came from Kinsale in County Cork and with ambitions of becoming a top-class jockey had gone to work in stables in England when he was just 14. He grew too tall to be a successful race rider and got a job, first as a stable lad and then assisting the trainer.

It was during this time that he took to doing long walks and runs to keep his weight in check but found that he enjoyed walking and running better than riding out the horses. He was persuaded in 1910, when aged 20, to enter a cross-country race on the famous Cheltenham racecourse and found to his surprise that he finished third.

This is when he came to the attention of Ted Vowles, who was trying to put together a team at Surrey AC to rival the all-conquering Birchfield Harriers from Birmingham, who had dominated the English National Championship since its inception. He had succeeded when the London club triumphed for the first time in 1914, only for the championships to be discontinued until 1920, when Birchfield regained the team title.

Two other Irishmen were also set for the cross-country competition in Antwerp, after the USA selections were announced. Patrick (Patsy) J. Flynn was born in County Cork, the eldest child of farmers Patrick and Ellen Flynn. Under the guidance of local international athlete, Bob Hales, of the well-known Republican family, he began competing in 1912, and the following year, as a 19-year-old, he won the Irish Four-Miles Championship, which gained him selection for Ireland in the annual international match against Scotland in Celtic Park, Belfast. His win in the 4-mile helped Ireland defeat the Scots 7–4, after the two countries had tied with five victories and a shared event the previous year in Edinburgh, when Hales had won the mile.

Flynn emigrated to America in 1913 and soon found work as a shipping clerk. He joined the Paulist Athletic Club, which was a constituent of the Irish American Athletic Club. During this time, he lost out in a close finish to Kolehmainen in a memorable 5,000-metre race, when the Olympic champion set a new world record of 14:33:6.

Following America's entrance into the war, he put his athletics career on hold to enlist in the 165th Infantry Regiment in the spring of 1916. He received a purple heart after being shot in his left arm during an act of heroism. On his return from the war, he was persuaded to concentrate on the steeplechase and was selected for that event, as well as the cross-country.

Belfast-born Bob Crawford, at 21, was the youngest of the American squad and had lived at Auburn Street in his native city as a child, along with parents John and Elizabeth, before the family left for Frankenmuth, Michigan. He would have been looking forward to his trip to Europe after winning a place on the US team in the American trial.

CHAPTER 15

TROUBLE AND STRIFE

*On the dogmas of religion as distinguished
from moral principles, all mankind,
from the beginning of the world to
this day, have been quarrelling,
fighting, burning, and torturing one
another, for abstractions unintelligible
to themselves and to all others.*

—Thomas Jefferson

On arriving at the station in Derry, I could hear again the intermittent sound of gunfire in various parts of the city. Clashes between the two communities had been become increasingly more frequent and vicious in recent weeks. Sectarian clashes were now commonplace throughout the city, with frequent shootings, and it was quite easy to be in wrong place at the wrong time.

The year 1920 had started well for Nationalists, gaining control of Londonderry Corporation for the first time. To prevent another Sinn Féin landslide such as happened in

LION FOR A DAY

1918, the government had introduced the proportional representation system of voting, which had exposed the tenuous majority that the numerically inferior Protestant population had in the city. The Protestants tried to avert the shift in power by manipulating the ward boundaries, but even this failed, as the Nationalist councillors ended up outnumbering their Unionist counterparts by a narrow 21–20 majority.

This led to a local solicitor, Hugh C. O'Doherty, becoming the first ever Catholic mayor of Derry in modern times and the introduction of some little more than symbolic changes to the way the city conducted business, like the Union Jack no longer being flown over the Guildhall.

The corporation ceased to be represented at government functions but was equivocal about its dealings with the Dáil and continued to have links with the British local government board in Dublin.

What was more marked was the mood in the Catholic parts of the city, where a seemingly more buoyant and confident populace was emerging. After centuries of feeling like second-class citizens in Derry, Nationalists relished the prospect of taking control of Londonderry Corporation for the first time. Sinn Fein's earlier victory had only been symbolic because they would not be attending the British Parliament, but this was real power for the Catholic burghers of the city.

And while Sinn Féin's goal was aspirational in securing independence for Ireland, the new corporation was actually running its own affairs. Of course, the Protestants in Londonderry and the north of the Ireland were resistant even to a Parliament based in Dublin albeit accountable to Westminster. Increasingly, their first choice was partition of the island, with the northern part administered from a Parliament in Belfast. Unfortunately, the rise in Nationalist control only precipitated a backs-to-the-wall response from the Protestant community and led to a general rush in recruitment for the paramilitary Ulster Volunteer Force.

While reflecting on the political situation, I had made my way out of the station and just crossed the road from John Street into Carlisle Road, close to the Protestant Fountain Area. Looking up, I noticed in the gloom of the dim streetlight a group of ten to twelve men. I instantly recognised them as being UVF on account of the Union Jack insignias on the jackets of a few of them. They had handkerchiefs over the lower part of their faces so that they could not be identified, and they had now stepped out of the shadows to block my way.

A quick glance over my shoulder told me another group had come out of Wapping Lane and were cutting off any possibility of me turning and running. Besides, I had already run a hard 10-mile race that day and was not sure if my legs would carry me far at this point. Continuing on, I found myself looking down the barrel of a service revolver.

"What's your name, and where are you going?" said one of the men in a rough, raised voice.

LION FOR A DAY

I paused; I knew there were Protestants called Hegarty in the Waterside, and I might get away with that, but the name Anton, or even Anthony, would be a giveaway that I was a Catholic.

What is more, if I said I was going to Howard Street, they would be sure to know I was a Catholic and assumed to be a Sinn Féin supporter.

By this time, I was close enough to see that nearly all of them had revolvers peeping out from inside their jackets.

"Who's asking?" I had decided to brazen it out.

"The Ulster Volunteer Force. We're here to ensure Londonderry remains a British city. I'll not ask you again."

The man raised his revolver and pointed it at me. I was now looking down the barrel and could see it was a make used by the British army.

Before I could answer I heard "He's a Skin."

The authoritative voice came from the shadows of a doorway in the Tillie and Henderson shirt factory on the other side of the road. All eyes, including mine, turned in that direction. I could not make out who it was, nor did I recognise the voice, but it certainly carried some authority. Peering as hard as I could, I only saw a dark, indistinct figure standing in a doorway. He raised his hand to his forehead and saluted in military fashion.

MALCOLM MCCAUSLAND

I responded in similar fashion.

"Let him pass!" came the order from the shadows. The UVF men promptly stepped aside, and I was able to make my way home without further incident. I was never able to find out who my saviour was, but I was indebted to him.

An army acquaintance was not so fortunate a few weeks later. Young Bernard Doherty, whose family lived in Anne Street, was a 21-year-old Catholic who had only returned recently from France. He had suffered mustard gas poisoning but, by all accounts, was recovering well from the damage to his lungs.

Being only young, he was out one Sunday night for a walk with his mate Paddy Starrs when he decided that he wanted to see a lady friend. Starrs accompanied him the short distance to the Diamond, where they heard there was rioting in Carlisle Road. Starrs warned him that they should go no further, but Doherty did not heed the advice and went on in the direction of Ferryquay Gate, where he received a wound to the stomach.

As soon as he was hit, he ran down Newmarket Street but fell at the corner. He got up again and staggered on another bit before collapsing for a second time. He was immediately taken to the nearby house of William Simms but was pronounced dead by the doctor when he arrived a short time later. The inquest revealed that the poor man had suffered horrendous internal injuries with the bullet ricocheting around inside him, causing mortal damage to his vital organs.

LION FOR A DAY

Doherty did not realise that he had blundered into the middle of a minor scuffle that had being going on since the previous evening. It had started when a Sergeant Moroney, of the Royal Irish Constabulary, received a fatal shot to the lung in the area of the docks when in pursuit of a group of Republicans.

Hostilities were renewed on Sunday night. The city had remained calm up until 11 p.m., when two Sinn Féin groups converged at Carlisle Square. This triggered off rioting even more violent than the previous evening, before the Unionists retaliated with revolver fire, giving them the upper hand, and driving the Republicans back down John Street.

The opposing factions confronted each other on Bridge Street, shouting slogans such as "Up the Rebels!" by the Republicans and "No surrender!" from the Unionists. The half dozen police on duty withdrew to the safety of the nearby Diamond, leaving the factions to fight it out among themselves. It was at this point that Doherty had the misfortune of entering the wrong place at the wrong time.

His funeral was one of the largest ever seen in the city. I was one of the ex-soldiers who turned out to carry the coffin in relays to the cemetery. We—the ex-soldiers, the dockers, and other workers—marched four abreast behind the coffin, orchestrated by Sergeant Hugh O'Donnell, another man who had served Britain in the war and returned to his community.

It was not just Derry witnessing this internecine violence; it was also creeping into sport. There had been disturbances at Celtic Park when Derry Celtic had met Linfield, the emblematic Protestant team, on Boxing Day the previous year, but that paled in comparison with what happened at the replay of the Irish Cup semi-final between Belfast Celtic and Glentoran, held at Cliftonville's ground in north Belfast.

A group of Sinn Feiners in the crowd gathered around an Irish tricolour flag, singing "The Soldier's Song" and "A Nation Once Again" and a parody of a well-known Orange ballad, with the words changed to insult the king. When the referee dismissed Celtic's defender Barrett for a foul on Glentoran centre forward Gowdy with just ten minutes to go, all hell broke loose.

Resenting the decision, the Celtic fans congregated around the Sinn Féin flag and invaded the pitch with the object of attacking the referee. One of their number opened fire with a revolver on the opposing fans, wounding a police sergeant and three spectators.

The police were forced to make several baton charges to restore order. The man with the revolver was arrested, his name was given as George Goodman, and he was taken to the Central Police Office in Chichester Street, where serious charges were brought against him. A number of people were treated in the Great Victoria Hospital, the majority of whom had sustained baton wounds.

The upshot of it all was that the Belfast Celtic club was suspended, while Glentoran was disqualified from the competition for using an unlisted player. This handed the

LION FOR A DAY

trophy to Shelbourne, who were the winners of the other semi-final. But with the fans being denied a cup final, the Irish Football Association decided to arrange a match between Glentoran and Shelbourne for a set of gold medals. Glentoran defied the odds to win 3–1, aided by the fact that Shelbourne's influential full back McGlaughlin had to go off injured early in the match.

Further afield, Irish Republicanism was rearing its head, even in the British Army. I had witnessed signs of this in the final year of the war, when more and more Irish soldiers felt it was not *their* war. This disillusionment with the British war effort had been exacerbated by the feeling that Irish troops were being asked to do the least pleasant assignments or, more often, the most dangerous.

Since the Rising, it was also obvious that Irish regiments were being diluted by merging parts of them with British ones and keeping them out of Ireland, while British regiments were sent over to man the garrison in Ireland.

Consequently, it came as no surprise when I read in the newspapers that the Connaught Rangers had mutinied in India. Some men had "refused to do duty on the ground of the alleged wrongs inflicted on Ireland." The report went on to say that the situation was in hand and only a section of the regiment was affected. It seems that the trouble, according to Reuters, began at Jalandha, where half a battalion was stationed performing garrison duties.

A number of the Connaughts informed their commanding officer that they were no longer able to serve, with Reuters adding cynically they were quite prepared to draw their pay. It was pointed out that the mutineers had been respectful throughout and indicated their willingness to hand over their arms to any British troops sent to relieve them.

They were subsequently disarmed, and over two hundred were put under guard. Their places were taken by the Seaforths and the Welsh Regiment. Another company of Connaught Rangers was stationed at Solan on the Kalka-Simla railway where, Reuters reported, two emissaries were arrested. This precipitated a small number of the Connaught Rangers trying to rush the armoury. They were resisted by their comrades, resulting in two being killed and one wounded.

Fuller details soon emerged in the Dublin press in that a private Joseph Hawes had been home on leave in County Clare, where he had witnessed the beginning of the War of Independence and the banning of all public meetings and GAA games, including a hurling match prevented at bayonet point in Kilrush.

On his return to Jullundur, he spread the word among his colleagues to the following effect: "We'll soldier no more for England." The men's protest was passive at first: a sit-in. They volunteered to be locked up in the guardroom. But the mutiny spread quickly, and Hawes and his comrades were joined by four hundred others at Jullundur. When the colonel addressed the men and recounted all the battle honours of the regiment, Joseph Hawes replied, "All the honours on the colours of the Connaught Rangers are for

England. There is none for Ireland, but there is going to be one today, and it will be the greatest honour of them all."

The mutineers elected a committee, took over the barracks, and hauled down the Union Jack. The Irish tricolour was raised on the regimental quarter guard by Private Frank Geraghty of Castleblayney, County Monaghan, and also flew on every single barracks, where the Irish soldiers sang patriotic ballads.

Meanwhile, 200 miles away, another part of the regiment was based at the hill station of Solan. There, Private James Daly of Tyrellspass, County Westmeath, led the rebellion. He took a company of men to parade outside the officers' mess and informed the officers that the parade was a protest at British atrocities in Ireland. The men refused to obey the officers' orders and demanded the release of the two soldiers who had been arrested after bringing the news of the mutiny from Jullundur. Two men, Privates Patrick Smythe of Drogheda and Peter Sears of Neale, County Mayo, were killed trying to get hold of the company's magazine, while another, Private Egan, was wounded and survived despite getting a bullet through his lung. These shootings marked the end of the mutiny.

Seventy-five of the mutineers were rounded up and held in the harsh conditions at Dagshai Prison, resulting in the death of Private John Miranda from Liverpool. The mutineers were court-martialled and fourteen men were sentenced to death, with the remainder sentenced to prison terms of between ten and twenty years in prison; thirteen of the death sentences were later commuted to life imprisonment. The one death

MALCOLM MCCAUSLAND

sentence that remained was that of James Daly who was led out into the prison yard and executed by a firing squad. "It is all for Ireland. I am not afraid to die," he wrote in his last letter to his mother.

At home tension was raised even further in Derry in April with the arrival at the jail of several Republican prisoners. Rival groups of Nationalists and Unionists, who had gathered to watch the event, clashed, and it soon developed into a riot. The conflict was still going on when I passed the junction of Long Tower Street and Fountain Street, one of the usual flashpoints, on my way home from work. Shots were later fired into the Catholic Bogside and the police, with bayonets fixed, charged a group of Nationalists near the city centre.

I had still maintained hopes of Gertie being able to come over for a visit although these were extinguished by the deteriorating political situation. I reluctantly wrote saying that I did not see a future for us in this society and advised that she should start to look out for rooms in Rugby where we could start to make a life together far from the conflict that was engulfing my native city.

Despite the obvious distractions, my training continued relatively uninterrupted and I was keen to test my form. I ran at a low-key sports meeting organised on May Day by the trade unions for the workers of the city and district, using the day as a good quality training session.

There was a poor attendance, with the general opinion that the public had lost its taste for such events and it was in the balance whether it would be held again. After winning the mile, I turned out later to win the 2-mile steeplechase, picking up valuable prizes of a canteen of cutlery and a barometer for my efforts.

Two weeks later and still in May, there was a good turn-out for the Shipbuilders' Sports at the Brandywell, where I used the occasion once again as a glorified training session. This time I won the mile, the 3 miles in which I was off the scratch mark in a time of sixteen minutes and forty-seven seconds, as well as a second place in the handicap 880 yards. All told it was a decent afternoon's work by any standards and told me that my form was heading in the right direction.

Encouraged by this, I dipped into my savings to go to Dublin for the Irish Championships on Whit Monday. There had been much discussion about setting the date for the meeting, but they eventually opted for the Whit Monday bank holiday. The track was laid around the rugby pitch at Lansdowne Road, which was in excellent condition. I entered the mile and 4 miles but decided to concentrate on the former. I felt a lethargy warming up, which I put down to several nights of broken sleep and the ongoing troubles in Derry, which kept me awake during the night, with prolonged spells of rifle fire in the vicinity of the Fountain and Bishop Street areas of the city. I had also started to have the dreaded nightmares again, recalling events from Gallipoli and France.

I started the mile sluggishly and never seemed to find any energy at any point. I ended up a somewhat distant third behind Ted Rogers, who had come over from Liverpool for the event. The time was given as four minutes and thirty-five, meaning I had run about the same time as in Glasgow when you considered the handicap. The winner was unknown to me at that time, but I learned from one of the other runners that the previous year he had been third in the AAA 4-mile at Stamford Bridge and had finished runner-up in the Northern Counties Mile Championship.

Although born in Liverpool, Rogers had Irish qualifications and would go on later in the afternoon to win the 4-mile as well, easily outdistancing, amongst others, Tim Crowe, who ended up only third on this occasion. Aside from my personal disappointment, the press hailed the meeting a huge success with fine weather and a good turn-out. The correspondent did add that it was not up to the standard witnessed before the war. A well-known footballer named M.J. Stafford of Bohemians FC, who won both the 100 yards and 220, was deemed the star of the meeting, only just eclipsing Rogers.

I spent a few more days in Dublin before, with some reluctance, returning to Derry, which was descending further to a civil war footing. The election of a Catholic mayor and the ongoing War of Independence continued to heighten tension on the Unionist side, leading to more and more Protestants, including ex-soldiers, joining the Ulster Volunteer Force.

Gunfights were a regular occurrence, and at times, the dead lay in the street for several days simply because no one risked going near them for fear of being shot. Businesses were closed and shops were shuttered to prevent looting. I tried

LION FOR A DAY

to keep out of it and was relieved that I had not been asked for some time to go to any of the IRA's training camps. It was no longer safe to go out on the streets after dark without a revolver. Even at home, the evenings and nights were punctuated by gunfire, and I blamed that for the return of my nightmares.

I took another break from Derry to go to the Northern Branch Championships at Windsor Park and found myself in much better form than three weeks earlier in Dublin. In such good shape, in fact, that I ran both the mile and the 4-mile. I had a real ding-dong with Macauley of Ulsterville in the mile, with him getting the better of me by just 10 yards.

My time was given as four minutes and forty-three seconds, seven seconds behind Macauley, as I walked the last few yards after I realised that I was not going to beat him. Macauley went on to win the 880 yards before we met again in the 4-mile, by which time tiredness had overcome him and I was able to beat him by half a lap in a respectable twenty minutes and fifty-three one-fifth seconds.

Again, a footballer-cum-sprinter grabbed the headlines, with Cliftonville outside right J. Daly winning both the 100-yard championship and handicap. I thought my friend Barney Donaghey might have had something to say about the outcome of those races, had he survived.

Back home again, things continued to deteriorate into June, and late one evening at about 11 p.m. there was a frantic knocking on my front door. I was the only one in

MALCOLM MCCAUSLAND

the house with the courage to respond. I had a solid walking stick within reach when I opened the door slightly to peek through the gap, only to find the IRA commandant, Joseph McGlinchey, on my doorstep in a distressed condition.

"Anton, you'll have to come," he gasped. "The Protestants have St Columb's College under siege and they're going to kill everyone. My son, Jim, was shot dead by a sniper in Abercorn Road earlier this evening when he was taking down a Union Jack from a lamppost outside Long Tower Chapel. They took him to the hospital immediately, but it was too late. He died before either his mother or me could get there. Luckily, there was already a priest in the hospital visiting another patient and he was able to give him the last rites."

"Joe, you know my feelings. I've done my share of fighting and I've seen too many men killed already. I don't want to get involved."

"Anton, you may think you have done your share of fighting, but that was for Britain," said McGlinchey. "I'm asking you now to fight for your family, your friends, for Derry, and for an Ireland where we'll all be equal citizens. You can't say you're not involved in that!"

I had no answer and reluctantly grabbed a warm coat, bringing my cudgel with me. There were about half a dozen other men outside waiting on me, and McGlinchey led us through quiet alleyways until we were in Windmill Terrace, just outside the grounds of St Columb's College. These were

LION FOR A DAY

located on the fringes of the Catholic Bogside, but at the same time only a short walk from the Protestant Fountain.

St Columb's had been opened as a seminary but now educated boys from the Catholic middle class from the city and beyond. The president of the college, John McShane, had sent out an SOS to the Republicans for assistance, fearing they would all be killed.

By now, we could hear constant noise of rifle fire coming from the direction of Ferguson Street that led back towards the Protestant enclave of the Fountain. McGlinchey knocked on a wooden door, said a few indistinct words, and we were admitted. We passed by the remains of the old windmill, where a famous battle had been fought between the besieging Catholic forces of King James and the Protestant defenders of the city in 1689.

The Protestants had won that one, and I could not help but think how little some things had changed in the intervening two hundred-odd years. The two communities in Derry were still going at each other's throats.

"Take these men and get them armed," barked McGlinchey. "They're all ex-soldiers and will know how to handle a rifle."

With that, we were led towards the school, darting from the shelter of one tree to another, as the snipers' rifles continued to rain their fire on the main building. On passing through the now bullet-marked front door, we were greeted by the overall leader of the IRA in Derry, Patrick Shiels, and his number two, Michael Sheerin.

MALCOLM MCCAUSLAND

I had worked with Sheerin at the shipyard before he had been transferred to the Swan Hunter yard in Glasgow about nine months earlier. He had come back to the Pennyburn yard again at the start of the year, and the word at work was that he had taken over as officer commanding the Derry Brigade until Shiels's recent release from prison.

They led us through the building to what I took, from the aroma, to be a huge refectory, where the boarders in the college took their meals. Thankfully, all of the pupils had been given an early start to their summer holidays on account of the troubles and only the staff of approximately ten to twelve priests were left in the building. On entering the room, we could see that there were roughly two dozen Mauser rifles stacked against a wall, with an array of ammunition scattered across the huge dining table.

"Grab yourselves a rifle, boys, but go easy on the ammunition as it's in short supply. We're hoping that Peadar O'Donnell and his Donegal volunteers will smuggle us in some more when they get the chance. Meantime, would you each go up to one of the boarders' bedrooms on the third floor and take up position there? Only fire when you've a clear target because, as I said, we don't have ammunition to waste. We'll bring you tea and food when we can."

For the next two nights, we came under constant sniper fire and all we could do was fire back at where we had seen a gun flash or movement around the Bishop Street entrance to the grounds. It was obvious from the lack of targets presented to us that the assailants were professionals and ex-army. Probably I had served with them, shared a beer with them,

254

LION FOR A DAY

played football with them, and now we were trying to kill each other simply because we went to a different church on a Sunday.

I could not help but think how the horrible experiences we had endured during the war had hardened us, had made us compassionless, and made us believe that might is right without any empathy for the person on the other side of the sight on your rifle. This continued for two days, and then the Dorset Regiment took to the streets to enforce a curfew, though not before they had joined the UVF in sending a sustained final battery of fire into the building.

Fortunately, by now, the Donegal volunteers had arrived in numbers, creeping up through the quarry on the southern side of the college grounds and out of sight of our attackers. Many of them were ex-Connaught Rangers and ex-Skins discharged after the war, and we were able to give as good as we got. On the third night, with the curfew solidly in place and checkpoints set up throughout the city, we were able to retreat out the back gate of the college and slip away in twos and threes through the darkness of the narrow streets in the Bogside.

Whilst we all escaped unscathed from the college, the same could not be said of the innocent people in the street going about their daily business. Apart from Jim McGlinchey, killed while taking down a flag, Patrick Mallett had been shot dead nearby in Long Tower Street, whilst Thomas Farren was murdered in the same street two nights later.

The following day, James Doherty was shot dead in the same spot, just after leaving Farren's wake. Also among the dead were local residents Mrs Eliza Moore, Thomas McLoughlin, Mrs McLaughlin, another James Doherty, from Tyrconnell Street, and James McVeigh, who was killed by Protestants despite having three sons who had served in the war, including one who died in France.

A 12-year-old boy, George Caldwell, was also killed when a bullet from the direction of St Columb's College entered his cubicle in the Nazareth House. Despite being exhausted, I only slept fitfully but rose early and was on the first train to Belfast with all my worldly possessions in my khaki backpack. I did not wait to say goodbye to anyone. Is it better to live one hundred years as a jackal than one day as a lion?

CHAPTER 16

THE ANTWERP GAMES

"There is something in the Olympics, indefinable, springing from the soul, that must be preserved."

- Chris Brasher

Within a month of the assassination of Archduke Franz Ferdinand in 1914, Austria had declared war on Serbia, triggering a huge mobilisation of its military by Russia and its ally France.

Germany then declared war on Russia and delivered an ultimatum to Belgium. The Germans claimed that the French were advancing towards Belgium with plans to invade Germany, who intended to counter-attack across Belgian territory.

The Belgians knew that the German claims were untrue. In fact, the French government had told its army not to go into Belgium before a German invasion. The Germans requested that Belgium adopt a position of "benevolent neutrality" and went on to say that any resistance would be seen as an act of hostility.

The German stance ignored earlier assurances of respecting Belgium's permanent neutrality, but those promises now stood in the way of German military domination of Europe. In any case, they did not believe the Belgians would put up anything other than token resistance. However, they had not reckoned on the Belgians' sense of honour, much less their bravery or the role of the inspiring young King Albert I, who had come to the throne only after the early deaths of his cousin and elder brother.

King Albert was a devout Catholic who eschewed the trappings of state and was devoted to his duty. He was militarily trained and had surrounded himself with forward-looking advisors who were able to guide him prudently through the difficult years to come.

The defiant young king realised that if he yielded to German pressure, it would violate his country's neutrality, assist an attack on France, and also lead to permanent occupation of his kingdom and consequent loss of sovereignty. The Belgians chose to stand strong.

Their official response to the Germans stated that to allow Germany passage through their country would "sacrifice the honour of the nation and betray its duty to Europe." Albert immediately took command of his six infantry and one cavalry division and prepared to defend his country against Germany's thirty-four divisions, totalling 700,000 fighting men.

LION FOR A DAY

The Belgian army blew up bridges and railways as well as set other obstacles to slow the German advance. It delayed the Germans at Liege, the gateway to the Meuse and the way to France. When Liege eventually fell, the king withdrew to Brussels, then to Antwerp, before digging in on a small strip of territory in the north of the country.

The Germans were infuriated by the guerrilla tactics adopted and what they described as "perfidious street fighting so contrary to international law." Their reprisals saw the occupiers wreak cruel vengeance against the indigenous population, priests, and office holders almost from the first days of their arrival.

Masterful tactical retreats saw Albert retain his army to harass the German forces from the rear. It was German practice to line up the entire population of small towns in their centre, men along one side and women and children on the other, and proceed to shoot or bayonet them without mercy until the last had fallen.

It was not just the Belgian population that came under assault. National treasures were also sought out and devastated through sheer vindictiveness. In August 2014, hordes of Germans descended on the ancient university city of Leuven, where they burned and destroyed the irreplaceable and incomparable library of ancient manuscripts and gallery of priceless paintings. "We will teach them to respect Germany," an officer is reported to have told an American diplomatic official who came to inspect the damage. "For generations people will come here to see what we have done."

MALCOLM MCCAUSLAND

The German invasion brought Britain—one of the guarantors of Belgium's neutrality under the Treaty of 1839—into the war, but Albert was able to hold the Germans off long enough for Britain and France to make hurried preparations for the Battle of the Marne in September 1914. He continued to command the Belgian forces through the Siege of Antwerp and the Battle of the Yser as they were driven back to a last, tiny strip of Belgian land near the North Sea.

The Belgians dug in there, in trenches behind the River Yser, and collaborated with the armies of the *Triple Entente*—Russia, France, and Britain—for the next four years. During this period, King Albert fought alongside his troops and shared their dangers, while his wife, Queen Elisabeth, worked as a nurse at the front.

While he was on active duty, rumours spread on both sides of the lines that the German soldiers never fired upon him out of respect for him being the highest ranked commander in the field. Others said that the German troops feared the wrath of his cousin, the Kaiser, if he was harmed.

The king also allowed his 14-year-old son, Prince Leopold, to enlist in the Belgian Army as a private and fight in the ranks. Away from the front, Albert tried to act as peacemaker, seeking a resolution to the conflict by using the slogan "No victors, no vanquished," but neither side wanted anything other than an outright victory.

When hostilities did finally cease, he led the drive to oust the occupiers from his kingdom, and when successful, he

LION FOR A DAY

and Queen Elisabeth, as well as their children, re-entered Brussels to heroes' welcomes.

Four years of carnage had resulted in the deaths of an estimated nine million combatants as well as seven million civilians. Subsequent genocides and the 1918 influenza pandemic accounted for another 100 to 200 million deaths worldwide.

The war had also taken an awful toll on Belgium and its people, with 100,000 young men dead or seriously injured and countless civilian mortalities, a collapsed economy, industries that made Belgium's rich now defunct, a huge war debt, and a grave shortage of even the essentials in terms of food.

The plucky Belgians were undeterred and set back to restore their country to its former affluence. On the day the Armistice was signed, they immediately went back to work, relighting the furnace fires of Liege. Within three months, they had cleared the harbour of the Schelt in Antwerp for sea traffic.

As King Albert was turning his attention to economic renewal, he was approached by Baron de Coubertin with the offer to stage the revived Games in Antwerp the following year. Seven years earlier, a committee, including various office holders from the Beerschot Stadium, had made an application for the 1920 Games and continued to lobby during the war "a precious tribute to my brave homeland, which may be oppressed now but shall never be enslaved," said the king.

In many ways, the offer of the Games at such short notice was a poisoned chalice in that Belgium was only just rising from its knees. There was truly little money and the Games were scheduled to take place in little more than a year. Previous host cities, not recovering from war, had been given four or five years to organise.

But undeterred, the Belgians took it on and set about preparing the facilities for the various sports. The organisers improvised and made do with what they had at their disposal. The money promised by the Belgian Olympic Committee never materialised, making their task even harder. The Games were made part of a traditional festival that drew funds from national and provincial coffers, as well city governments and a variety of businesses.

The organisers continued to improvise, converting a 7-acre sports field called Champs de Beerschot, which had been the site of the World Fair in 1894, into a hastily remodelled 30,000-capacity stadium.

Swimming was to take place in a converted part of the city's ancient moat, with a wooden tower constructed for the diving events. Polo and yachting events were to take place at Ostend, a neighbouring city along the coast; equestrian events were to be accommodated at the Hoogboom Country Club; and boxing and wrestling were to be housed at the Great Room of Zoology at Antwerp Zoo.

Surprisingly, two of the most popular Belgian sports—soccer and cycling—were seemingly given scant regard. The cycling road race was held a week before the Games started

and the soccer matches were allocated to three venues—
Antwerp, Brussels, and Ghent—making it difficult for fans
to get to see all the events.

With the world still recovering from the war, many other
countries' national Olympic committees were not prepared,
either financially or logistically, to send teams to Antwerp.

The British Olympic Committee met at 42 Russell Square in
London on 23 July 1919, when Lord Downham of Fulham
accepted the chairmanship of the Council. It was decided to
accept the invitation of the Belgian Olympic Committee for
the seventh Olympiad to take part in the Olympic Games
in Antwerp.

A special Competitions Committee was appointed whose
first duty was to co-ordinate the "criticisms" of the various
governing bodies of sport on the tentative programme
proposed by the Belgian Olympic Committee, submitted
to the governing bodies of the country the previous May.

The Competitions Committee was instructed to draw up
a report to be sent to the Belgian Olympic Committee,
despite the definite programme for the Games not yet being
finalised. The finance committee was also instructed to draw
up estimates for the current year (September 1919) and
September 1920 and to formulate a scheme for securing the
necessary funds.

The debate merely reflected what had happened after
the 1912 Games, when it was realised, particularly in
comparison to the USA, that British athletics was amateur

MALCOLM MCCAUSLAND

and backward-looking, with the ethos of the amateur gentleman holding the sport back.

As a consequence, in February 1914, the British Olympic Council had appointed Walter Knox to take charge for the proposed Games in Germany two years later, having earlier offered the very same post to an Irish American, Tom Keane, who had politely declined the offer.

This showed that the British Olympic Council had decided to move away from the amateur approach adopted hitherto—Knox and Keane were both paid professionals— and compete on the same level as the Americans and other countries that were making rapid progress towards engaging full-time coaches and officials for their national teams.

World War I intervened, and when the 1916 Games were cancelled, Knox went back home to Canada, while the British slipped back into their amateur gentleman ways for the most part.

Knox reappeared at the Antwerp Games as head coach for Canada, while the British sport continued to be run by ex-public schoolboys, to whom professionalism was an anathema and training was held to be ungentlemanly.

Meanwhile, other countries were not so slow to embrace a more systematic approach to both the preparation and management of their teams.

Canada had been quick to snap up the services of Knox on his return from England. He had been an athlete himself,

LION FOR A DAY

winning national titles in five separate events—100 yards, pole vault, long jump, discus, and shot-put—at the 1907 Canadian Track Championships. His coaching skills transcended sprints, jumps, and throws and contributed to the success of Canadian athletes in Antwerp.

The greater problem for the British Olympic Committee was a lack of a reliable source of funding to send teams to the Olympic Games. Following the trend of Stockholm and Berlin, the money to cover the cost of the British team going to Antwerp had to be met by public subscription. The appeal was launched with a British Olympic Council statement in *The Times* on 31 January 1920, meaning that there was barely six months to raise the necessary £30,000 required.

The situation was not helped by the state of the nation's finances immediately after a long and costly war, and many charities competing for whatever spare cash the general public could afford to donate.

Lord Downham wrote the request personally for the newspaper and appealed to the nation's sense of identity, pointing out the revived Games were not just a "great athletic gathering" but also to "leaven the world with the true spirit of sport." He ended by stating that "they are all amateurs" and "men who can be relied on to uphold the national prestige." This was to counter the popular argument that the money would be used to create a team of "professionals."

King George V was one of the first to respond to the appeal, donating £100, but progress was slow in comparison to the appeals for the 1912 and 1916 Games. The *Athletics News*

MALCOLM MCCAUSLAND

believed the British Olympic Committee were not doing enough to promote the appeal, pointing out that apart from the letter to the newspaper, nothing else had been done.

It was reported that in May, four months after the appeal, only £1,600 had been gathered, leaving just two months for the remainder of the targeted £30,000 to be raised. In the end, the team took off for Antwerp with the British Olympic Committee hugely carrying forward debts associated with the Games.

Across the Atlantic, finding a form of transport to carry the United States team to Antwerp was a problem, exacerbated by civilians being prohibited from using military transport. Members of the American Olympic Committee appeared before the House of Representatives' Committee on Military Affairs in Washington in May 1920 to seek a relaxation of the rule.

According to a statement by Gustavus T. Kirby, president of the Olympic Committee, commercial steamship travel conditions were such that it would be doubtful if a really representative team could be sent to Belgium unless government support was forthcoming.

Kirby was a rich and powerful man with influential connections, and it was no surprise when he managed to achieve a joint resolution of Congress that allowed civilian team members to travel on board a military vessel. The speedy *Northern Pacific* was earmarked for the journey, which normally took eight days. However, he may have regretted what he wished for when the team turned up at the end of July to find that the allocated vessel had been taken into dry dock for repairs and had to be replaced by the much slower *Princess Matoika*.

The ship started life as the *Princess Alice* and was owned by the north German Lloyd line but became a trophy of war when seized by the Americans in Manila Harbour. The German crew tried to scuttle the vessel, but the Americans soon had her repaired and seaworthy again. They rechristened her and had her plying the route between America's east coast and Europe, ferrying cargos of hemp and pig tin to aid the war effort.

Then she was used to bring home soldiers, some living, some suffering from the flu epidemic, and many others wounded or dying. What the expectant officials and athletes waiting to board the ship for Europe did not realise was that its latest cargo had been the cadavers of American soldiers who had lost their life in the last days of the conflict. These had been waiting almost two years for repatriation.

The *Princess Matoika* had not sailed past the Statue of Liberty before all on board realised that she was filthy and rat infested, and the stink of death permeated the whole hold area beneath the waterline, where 108 of the male athletes were housed. And because the ship took the southern route to avoid icebergs, the journey would take an extra three days, eleven in total, whilst the unexpected hot weather only amplified the smell of death on board.

The "imprisoned" passengers grew angrier as the *Princess Matoika* made its way across the Atlantic at a snail's pace.

Star swimmer Norman Ross and sprinter Charley Paddock were among those to voice their complaints, and when they were not being seasick or working out on the cork track, they held secret meetings to vent their displeasure.

This displeasure grew more acute when they heard that Antwerp would not be providing the level of accommodation and meals to which they were accustomed. War had not affected the food supply in America in the same way it had done in Europe. They issued a statement to a number of different agencies, including the secretary of war, complaining of the "unbearable" conditions that they considered "entirely unsuitable for housing the country's best athletes."

They were quick to attach the blame to the American Olympic Committee, who they accused of "laxity and gross inefficiency" bordering on "gross negligence." The statement and subsequent incidents only served to blight the image of the American athletes, who many considered to be overcome by their own sense of importance. Their lack of sensitivity as to what Europe had suffered and the incredible job the Belgians had done to even put on the Games, especially after suffering such privations as inflicted on them by the Germans, only cemented the image of the spoiled brat American.

The discontent did not end when the *Princess Matoika* eventually docked in Antwerp on 8 August. Although arriving in the morning, it had to wait for a change of tide to enter the estuary and did not tie up at the quay until sunset. This meant the athletes had been on board for thirteen

LION FOR A DAY

days. Their hopes of spending the night on terra firma were then dashed when they were told that there was not enough transportation to get them to their accommodation before dark.

Things got no better. The next morning, army trucks turned up to take them to lodgings, where they found that the majority of the male athletes were to stay in a schoolhouse rather than, as they had expected, a comfortable hotel. They were going to have to sleep in narrow beds on mattresses stuffed with straw, and there were no warm showers. They were then served lunch without butter, milk, or sugar, all items in scarce supply at the time, but after protests from the athletes, they were fed from then on by the American Army of Occupation, whose supplies came in directly from the USA. Many then complained they could not sleep on account of the snoring of colleagues.

Finally, the whole saga came to a head when world hop, step, and jump record holder, Dan Ahearn (Ahearne), moved to a hotel without permission of the team's officials, thus violating the 10 p.m. curfew. Ahearn had set the world record in 1909 before bettering it two years later and again in 1915. He won eight American titles in the event as well two Canadian, but by 1920, he was past his best. He had left Ireland some years before with his family, including brother Timothy—Olympic champion in 1908 at the hop, step, and jump.

He rented a room in a tavern in protest against his sleeping quarters. For this, he was immediately removed from the American Olympic team. In response, two hundred of that team signed a petition demanding better accommodation and that Ahearn be reinstated immediately or the entire two hundred would withdraw en masse from their respective events. Eventually, the officials relented and the man from the small Limerick village of Athea was restored to the team without sanction.

Despite various attempts over the years and the apparent sympathy of Baron de Coubertin, Ireland was still not yet a member of the International Olympic Committee. The previous year, the British delegation on the IOC had sounded out the possibility of the four home countries each being represented individually and in team competitions, such as the soccer and rugby tournaments.

The IOC had considered this but eventually rejected the notion as they felt it could lead to all sorts of complications. In the end, a Great Britain team was entered in the soccer, but no agreement could be reached on the rugby selection, where the individual countries' nationality was deeply ingrained in the sport.

Nevertheless, it came as a surprise when a telegram from Brussels was received to the effect that the Irish athletes had refused to compete at the Olympic Games under the British flag. They wrote to the executive that they were willing to enter the series of events only if allowed to do so as members of an independent nation. The committee corresponded with the British and decided that the Irish could not be admitted on the footing demanded.

LION FOR A DAY

This might explain why there was extraordinarily little interest from the Irish press in covering the Games. No newspaper sent a correspondent to Belgium and all relied on agency reports to update their readers on what was happening. Their reports were usually filed deep into the sports pages, with the Nationalist press much more interested in concurrent Gaelic games.

Added to this, in 1920, Ireland was very much in the grip of a bloody War of Independence being waged against the occupying British forces. As had been evident at earlier Games, there was a desire for a separate Ireland team, with isolated protests, particularly from Irish athletes representing Great Britain.

In 1906, Peter O'Connor and two other athletes were sent to the Intercalated Games in Athens by the Irish Amateur Athletic Association and the Gaelic Athletic Association to represent Ireland. They were given green blazers and caps with gold shamrocks and also given an Irish flag (a golden harp on a green background). However, the rules were changed at the last minute, in that only athletes nominated by National Olympic Committees were eligible. Ireland did not have an Olympic Committee, and the British Olympic Council claimed the three. On registering for the Games, O'Connor and his fellow athletes found that they were listed as members of the Great Britain, not Ireland, team. It would be four more years before an Irish team would compete in its own right—at the 1924 Paris Games.

A total of twenty-nine nations responded to the invitation to send a team to the Antwerp Games—one more than in

1912. Germany, Austria, Hungary, Bulgaria, and Ottoman Empire were not invited, given their respective roles in the recent hostilities. Estonia was the only newly created European state to take part, while Czechoslovakia took the place of Bohemia, which had sent athletes prior to World War I as part of the Austrian Empire.

Poland was involved in Polish-Soviet War and therefore was unable to form an Olympic team. Russia was also not invited as part of its political embargo by the west. Argentina, the Kingdom of Serbs, Croats, and Slovenes, Brazil, and Monaco competed as nations at the Olympic Games for the first time. New Zealand, previously part of a combined team with Australia in 1908 and 1912, competed on its own for the first time.

Figure 7: The opening ceremony at the 1920 Olympics in Antwerp (https://upload.wikimedia.org/wikipedia/commons)

All the preparations and disputes were set aside for at least an hour when the opening ceremony took place on 14 August. This was far removed from the spectacular that is now *de rigueur* on these occasions. Instead it consisted of an emotional elegy for the athletes slain during World War I, including France's Jean Bouin and British duo George Hutson—who had finished third in that memorable 5,000-metre race in

LION FOR A DAY

Stockholm—and Wyndham Halswelle—the 1908 Olympic 400-metre champion.

The memorial service in Antwerp Cathedral was conducted by Cardinal Mercier and concluded with the "Te Deum" echoing around the walls of the ancient Gothic cathedral. The cardinal was less than reconciliatory in his tone, claiming that athleticism, used in the past as a form of training for military objectives, should now become training for peace.

The Antwerp Games espoused that message of peace and was the first to introduce an athletes' oath and releasing doves of peace. It also saw the introduction of what is now possibly the world's most recognisable emblem: the Olympic flag with five rings representing the five continents at the time.

CHAPTER 17

THE GAMES BEGIN

**The most important thing in the
Olympic Games is not winning but
taking part; the essential thing in life
is not conquering but fighting well.**

—Pierre de Coubertin

Lap after lap, circuit after circuit, the pair drew farther away from the other fourteen runners in the 1920 Olympic Games 5,000-metre final. Every pair of eyes in the Beerschot Stadium was fixed on the inscrutable Finn, cutting out the pace like a metronome, and the cocky little Frenchman dogging his every step.

The more it went on, the more it became a two-man race— the latest Flying Finn, toughened by the premature loss of his father and a spartan training regime, going head-to-head against a man who nearly died in a mustard gas attack Both had overcome adversity to make themselves stronger, unyielding, and uncompromising. Never give up, and never give in. But there could only be one winner.

LION FOR A DAY

The pace quickened again as the bell sounded for the last lap. The little man continued to stalk his prey. Past the covered stand on the back straight they flew, then around the final bend. The assassin held his nerve. As sudden as a snake bite, the little French cockerel struck, and he was away.

The Finn reacted, but he knew he had been outthought, outmanoeuvred, and on this unique occasion outrun. The gold medal was Joseph Guillemot's, and France's revenge for Jean Bouin's defeat in Stockholm had been exacted.

High up in the stands, Hannes Kolehmainen bowed his head and made for the exit. The defeat would change Paavo Nurmi's racing tactics for the rest of his career, and it would be years before he lost another important race. But it was a lesson hard earned for the taciturn athlete from Turku.

"Can you believe that?" said Jimmy Wilson in his southern English accent with a hint of hard Glaswegian coming through in some words.

"I bloody can't," said the betting man Larry Cummins incredulously. "I would have put the house on Nurmi. We'll not be able to stick that little French shit after this. He's hard enough to bear at the best of times."

"You mean *if* you had a house. You live in a stable with horses," I teased him, alluding to the fact that he was a jockey living in the yard with the horses.

"Well, you know what I mean, you smart alec Derryman. Anyway, don't all of you live in a bog or a Bogside or something?" Cummins laughed heartily at his own joke.

"I'm glad I decided not to run that 5,000," said Wilson, getting back to business. "Let's hope it's taken the edge off the both of them with the heats of the 10,000 in two days."

"Besides, you did Bertie Irwin a favour pulling out and getting him called up to replace you. Otherwise, he would've come here for nothing and not got a run at all. His mates at Clonliffe Harriers will be delighted for him," I reminded.

We stayed on to watch Albert Hill demolish the field in the 800-metre. He had lain in wait until the final straight when he came with an almighty sprint to overtake the American Earl Eby and South Africa's Bevel Rudd, who had beaten him at the AAA Championships earlier in the year.

It was Hill's third race in as many days, and he had another four to go before the week was out. But the intensive racing programme did not seem to be taking anything out of the 31-year-old, who had fought all through the war years.

He had been moulded into a running machine but also a master tactician by Sam Mussabini, for that matter in the manner of Nurmi. They were the professionals and we were the amateurs, and then, of course, there were the gentlemen!

The three of us—Jimmy Wilson, Larry Cummins, and me—had become almost inseparable since arriving a week earlier in Antwerp. We had got to know each other when we ran the trial for the British cross-country team in Rugby the previous month.

Wilson had won that, as he had done the international earlier in the year in Belfast, while Larry and I had been delighted to grab our places on the six-man team by taking third and fourth place respectively.

We had cemented the friendship with a few pints that night in the Raglan Arms, not far from Rugby School, where the two were staying. The Raglan would become my local in the years after Antwerp. In fact I would go to court to speak in support of the innkeeper having his licence renewed.

The morning after our celebration, we promised to meet up again at the Olympics before heading off in separate directions. My selection letter arrived a few days later by registered mail and I began my countdown to becoming the first Olympian from Derry.

On arrival in Antwerp, we had been transported to what appeared to be a local school converted into living accommodation for the Great Britain men's team. The officials had been allocated more comfortable lodgings in one of the few hotels close to the city centre to have been spared significant damage when Antwerp had been besieged by the Germans during the war.

The women on the team shared a large mansion some distance away from us. Camp beds with comfortable straw had been put into the classrooms and gymnasium, ten to each of the small classrooms, while the large gym housed fifty, arranged in neat rows of five.

Drawing on my experience in the army, I ensured that the three of us got beds as far away from the door as possible, and although it would mean a longer walk to the communal toilet, we would not be disturbed by latecomers at night. The "toffs," as Jimmy described the gentlemen on the team, were abhorred at the prospect of occupying shared accommodation, particularly with working men, as they would have described the three of us.

They made representations to the management to be moved, but despite offering to pay for their lodgings in local hostelries themselves, the request was denied—something they continued to moan about when they gathered in small groups for the duration of their stay.

These "toffs" also had a peculiar attitude to training in that they thought it was "very un-English." On our first morning, the three of us got up early and were heading to the grounds of Royal Antwerp FC, where some of the games of the football tournament were being held. We were told that we could use the facility when no match was being played that day.

On our way out, we disturbed one of the them, who complained bitterly and declared us "cheats" by resorting to underhand practices such as actually preparing for our events by "training."

We were joined at the last minute by Percy Hodge, who was a clubmate of Larry's at Surrey AC and was AAA steeplechase champion. Jimmy said he had seen that race but could scarcely believe his eyes when Hodge had to stop after losing a shoe, giving away 100 yards on the opposition, but starting up again, overhauling the leaders, and going on to win by 75 yards.

I also remembered that, although a track runner, he had finished ahead of me in the cross-country championships at Belfast. We were only too glad to have his company, and he would join us a couple more times prior to his event.

On the second day, we got access to the Beerschot Stadium and were able to train on the track where the Games' running events would be held.

"It's like Largs," said Jimmy, referring to a sandy beach not far from Glasgow, where he trained some weekends. "In fact, I'd rather have Largs than this surface. It would be firmer," he added.

We noticed Sam Mussabini was there supervising the training of his two athletes: Albert Hill and a young sprinter called Harold Abrahams. On spotting us, Mr Mussabini came over to greet us, and for me he had a special message.

"Good to see you here, Hegarty. You obviously followed the advice in my book. I was pleased to see you made the team after that trial in Rugby. I believe things have been rough recently in your neck of the woods back in Ireland."

"Yes, sir, thank you, Mr Mussabini," I replied, addressing him like I would have an officer in the army. Mr Mussabini had the same air of authority without the pips on his shoulders, and I would never have ventured to have called him Sam. I could see why athletes were so keen to work with him and why Polytechnic Harriers paid him a handsome salary for his coaching skills.

"Yes, Mr Mussabini, I followed it religiously, and I shortened my stride as you advised. It's made a big difference, and I'm very thankful to you for the advice. I wasn't expecting to hear from you. It was kind of you to send the book, which is now almost my Bible."

He smiled and bade us a brief farewell as he turned on his heel to return to the other side of the track, where he proceeded to put Abrahams through some sort of running-on-the-spot drill.

Hill, whom I had met in Glasgow, seemed to be practising the final 120 yards or so of his races. He came over later to have a brief conversation and seemed the most cordial of fellows. He told us that he intended running both the 800-metre and 1,500-metre as well as helping out in the 3,000-metre team race.

He had also been asked to make himself available for the latter but did not see this as a target and indicated he would be merely "running for the flag," as he described it. He said that he had seen some previews of the Games in the British press in which he had been referred to as "Albert over the

LION FOR A DAY

Hill" and said he wanted to ram that down the throats of the journalists who had written it.

Percy Groves had us wondering why he had brought a tray and an empty bottle with him. After a few laps, he went off to the changing rooms and came back with the bottle filled with water. He then showed us how he could hurdle the barriers with the bottle on the tray and still not spill any of the water. Incredible!

It was that evening that we heard that there was supposed to be a revolt by Irish athletes, in that they were refusing to represent Great Britain in Antwerp and wanted to compete under an Irish flag. The first person to tell us about it was one of the American team, who approached the three of us in the street when we were out for a little stroll to loosen out our legs before bedtime.

He said he had heard our accents, meaning that of Larry and me, and went on to say there had been a report in one of the newspapers in the United States that the Irish men on the British team were in revolt, refusing to compete for the Union Jack.

It only took a few words from him for us to realise he was Irish and he went on to introduce himself as Pat Flynn from Cork. He said there was quite a number of native-born Irishmen on the American team, while quite a few of the remainder seemed to be Irish parentage.

In regard to the revolt in the British team, Larry and I could not understand from where the story had emanated

281

to give rise to the report in America. We were only aware of six Irish in the British contingent; Larry and I were in the cross-country team and could not represent Ireland as there was no Irish team. Besides, we knew what we had signed up for when we ran the trial in Rugby.

Similarly, Noel Purcell from Dublin, who was in the water polo squad, could not form his own one-man team for Ireland. The high jumper Tim Carroll had represented Britain in the Stockholm Olympics, so obviously he had no difficulty with that; and Bertie Irwin and Hedges Worthington-Eyres were both from Anglo-Irish families. We could only conclude that the whole story was a bit of a fabrication.

It was on one of our days training in the park where the cross-country course had been marked out that we met two Indian runners. Having served in India, I naturally went over to talk to them when they had completed their training run. They told me that their names were Phadeppa Chaugule and Sadashir Datar. Both were running the marathon on the final day of the athletics programme.

Chaugule was the more experienced and had turned to running after suffering an injury in his first-choice sport: wrestling. I had greeted them in what little language I had learned during my service in Secunderabad. Chaugule had a good command of English, while his companion did not seem to have much understanding and never attempted to say anything, other than exchanging words in his own native tongue with Chaugule while we were having our conversation.

He asked me where I came from in England, and of course, I had to explain that I was from Ireland. He enquired how I knew some Indian words, and I told him about my time in India as a British soldier. I thought I noticed a dampening in his friendliness after that, but he did tell me with some pride that they were the first indigenous Indians to represent the country at an Olympic Games.

When the athletics programme started, we went to the stadium most days. On Thursday, we were there to support Jimmy in his semi-final of the 10,000-metre. It was cold and rainy, with very few spectators bothering to turn up. The track was softer than ever, with the runners leaving a spray of grit behind them. That did not affect Jimmy as he adopted his usual tactics and hit the front on the first lap before drawing steadily away from the field in the course of the next twenty-four circuits.

Nurmi finished almost half a minute behind him, content to do just enough to qualify in second place. I thought that Jimmy should have done the same and preserved his energy for the final the next day.

Guillemot was equally reckless in the second semi-final, running almost a minute faster than Jimmy as he handed out a spanking to the highly rated Swede Eric Backman. It seems that the Frenchman had not endeared himself to the hosts the day before by taking an hour to get changed, while King Albert waited to present him with his medal.

We stayed on to watch Albert Hill turn in another masterful performance in winning the 1,500-metre, again with a

MALCOLM MCCAUSLAND

strong finish along the home straight. He had looked out of it for most of the race, but in a masterful display of tactics, he had moved through on the final lap to win his second gold medal. He was assisted by the selfless pacemaking of our team captain, Philip Noel-Baker, who ran despite a broken bone in his foot and was rewarded with the silver medal.

Jimmy Wilson returned to the track on Friday afternoon for the 10,000-metre final and adopted his usual tactic of leading from the gun. The race had been due to start at 5.30 p.m. but had been brought forward to 1.45 p.m. Nobody seemed to have told Guillemot of the change of time until the last minute as he had eaten a substantial lunch before being informed. The race was similar to the 5,000-metre, except that it was Jimmy who was setting out a fast pace that carried him clear of everyone except Guillemot, with Nurmi and Italy's Augusto Maccario running together in close order just behind the Frenchman.

Five laps to go, Guillemot made a break, which Jimmy and Nurmi were able to cover, though not Maccario, who fell off the pace. For the next four circuits, the lead swung back and forth between Guillemot and Jimmy, with Nurmi drafting in their slipstream and poised to attack.

When the bell rang, Nurmi came alive and hit the front for the first time, utilising his superior speed to win comfortably. Guillemot staggered over the finishing line in second and promptly vomited over Nurmi, no doubt on account of eating a huge lunch too close to the race.

LION FOR A DAY

Jimmy was happy enough with his bronze medal, the first ever by a British athlete in the event. He admitted that the pair who beat him were simply in a different class and again pointed out that they were full-time professionals, whereas he had to fit his training in around ten-hour days as a welder.

Percy Hodge was at his sparkling best in the 3,000-metre steeplechase final that followed. It was held on the grass just on the inside of the cinder track and was soft after all the rain in the preceding days and the considerable footfall of the officials and photographers. Hodge had overcome the underfoot conditions to set an Olympic record in winning his heat, but he went even faster in the final, setting another Olympic record.

Italy's Ernesto Ambrosini led the first lap, but Percy then took over and soon ruined the race as a contest by quickly opening up a huge lead that increased to about 100 metres at the tape.

I was delighted for Pat Flynn, who came through strongly in the later stages to grab the silver medal. Larry said he was sorry he did not do the event as he thought he could have been at least third. He had become disillusioned with the steeplechase after finishing runner-up to Percy in the 1919 AAA championships. Percy had beaten him by such a distance that he thought he had no future, but from watching Percy in Antwerp, he had come to realise that he was exceptional and maybe Larry was not so bad after all. Certainly, he had finished closer to Hodge than either of the two medallists in Antwerp.

285

MALCOLM MCCAUSLAND

I had been looking forward to the marathon all week, and I was down early on Sunday morning to see the start. Jimmy decided to stay at our accommodation to give his legs a rest, while Larry thought he would get in a little bit of training in the park, where we would be running the following day. For some reason or another, he decided to give himself a 3-mile time trial "to open up the pipes," even though our race was less than twenty-four hours away.

I had heard so much about Hannes Kolehmainen and was looking forward to seeing the legend in action. My first impression when I saw him limbering up was that he looked older, frailer, and smaller than I had imagined. But obviously, underneath the frail exterior, he was as tough as teak. The field of thirty-five did two laps of the stadium before embarking on an out-and-back course that took them out through the suburbs and stone roads to the village of Runspi, where they turned for home again. Weather conditions were ideal with a cool breeze and the occasional light rain shower.

Reports of their progress were fed back to the stadium at irregular intervals, and we were informed that the South African Gitsham, who had been second eight years before in Stockholm, was cutting out the pace after going to the front around the 10-kilometre mark.

Kolehmainen was dogging the Springbok's every stride until the unfortunate Gitsham sustained a leg injury causing him to slow. Just before halfway, Estonia's Juri Lossman struck the front, before Kolehmainen decided to take charge around the 27-kilometre mark. The Finn piled on the pace but never

LION FOR A DAY

managed to shake off his younger and stronger adversary, who covered his every burst. Kolehmainen eventually finished very tired in 2:32:35.8, a new world and Olympic record, despite the distance being 42.75 kilometres—550 metres longer than the standard distance.

Lossman was just thirteen seconds back but could not close the distance. Nurmi was one of a huge crowd of Finns waiting to welcome the victor at the finish line and who insisted the exhausted Kolehmainen run a victory lap. Nurmi just stood there staring at Kolehmainen, eyes wide open like a schoolboy eyeing his hero for the first time. It was the only time in that week that he showed any human emotion.

India's Chaugule finished nineteenth in a respectable time of 2:50:45.4. Sadashir Datar was brought back in an ambulance with his feet cut and blistered, his canvas sandals totally unsuitable for the harsh, newly laid Belgian roads.

The following day was the last of the athletics and it was our turn. We were back in the Olympic Stadium for the cross-country race, with only a sparse crowd present. The race followed the usual format of being both an individual contest and a team competition, with separate sets of medals awarded for each.

The British team started with its full complement of six, of which I was probably ranked fourth, meaning that I might not get a medal, even if we won, as only the first three for each team counted in the adding up the score.

In all, forty-eight runners faced the starter, with the course supposedly set at a distance of 10,000 metres, starting and finishing in the stadium. We had warmed up in the park, where the bulk of the course was marked out, and found that the going was going to be softish, which would have suited all three of us.

Jimmy was still complaining that his legs were still tired after two 10,000-metre races, in which he had done more than his share of the pacemaking, during the week.

The seemingly indefatigable Nurmi, who had appeared almost human at the conclusion of the marathon, had regained his game face. Despite running his fifth race in seven days, he looked remarkably fresh as he jogged around while awaiting the call to the start line.

I caught sight of Mr Mussabini standing at the rail next to the track with the tail of my eye, and he beckoned me towards him with a subtle nod of the head. I went over to the fence and leaned towards him to listen. As I did, I caught a whiff of French cologne and a vaguely familiar smell of cigarettes.

"Hegarty, this is ideal for you," he said, barely raising his voice as I moved closer to listen. "Soft going and you're well rested, and it's only your first race of the week. Everyone here, apart from that cunning young fox Nurmi, is going to go off too fast given the conditions. Keep your powder dry, lad, and work the second half of the race as if your life depended on it. You'll find them all coming back to you."

LION FOR A DAY

Figure 8: Joseph Guillemot leads the field out of the stadium followed by Wally Freeman GBR, Jimmy Wilson in sixth. Anton is partially obscured in 11th behind Alf Nichols. Nurmi is back in the pack beside Chris Vose GBR. Pat Flynn is the leading US runner in 7th. Photo: Bibliothèque nationale de France

Just then the call went out to get to the start line. I nodded, unable to even mutter a reply on account of my nerves. Mr Mussabini was right. It did go off like a mile race, with Guillemot leading the cavalry charge followed by my teammate Wally Freeman—a cross-country specialist—and Guillemot's compatriot Gaston Heuet.

We made our way out of the stadium and on to the street, with our spiked shoes now starting to make a clattering noise on the cobbles. We crossed the dual carriageway with the tramline in the middle and then onto the other side straight into the park, where our spiked shoes were at home in the soft grass once again.

MALCOLM MCCAUSLAND

It was only here, after about a kilometre, that I looked up to see the leaders were about 100 yards ahead of me and that I was probably in the second half of the field.

Mr Mussabini's words came back to me, and I did not panic as Nurmi came past me. I slipped into his slipstream for a about half a mile as we moved through the field, but he was too strong and I had to let him go on. On the second lap of our three in the park, I went past Wally and Alfred Nichols both of whom were slipping back, probably victims of overambitious starts.

Leaving the park to make our way back to the stadium, an official was counting as we went by him. *"Neuf, dix, onze,"* I heard. My French wasn't good but I knew I was eleventh, as best I could make out. I thought of our club runs around Ballyarnett and the race for home at the end of it. I pictured myself back on the steep climbs of Lowry's Lane heading towards our hut on the Glen Road.

I passed Guillemot standing in the middle of the dual carriageway; he had gone over on his ankle crossing the tramline. I was now tenth. Two Swedes, running shoulder to shoulder, were my next victims. I was eighth with the main gates to the stadium now in sight.

I overtook Pat Flynn, who grunted some words of encouragement as I went by. I was seventh. A fading Heuet and a Belgian slipped back as I moved to fifth as we entered the track. I could now see Jimmy was the only Briton in front of me, but before I could fix a bead on him, I heard the footfall of someone behind. I gave it all I had along the

LION FOR A DAY

final straight on the track to get home in fifth ahead of the fast-finishing runner behind me, who turned out to be the Finn Koskenniemi.

Up front, Nurmi had claimed his second individual gold of the Games, only passing Backman metres from the finish line, much to the Swede's chagrin. Backman was still complaining about Nurmi's tactics when I finished.

With Jimmy fourth, myself in fifth, and Alfred Nichols holding down twelfth, we were almost certain of a team medal, and we were delighted when it was confirmed to be silver behind the seemingly unbeatable Finns, with the Swedes in third.

Pat Flynn was twelfth, Wally Freeman faded to twenty-second after being in the leading group out of the stadium, while poor Larry had a nightmare of a race and struggled home in twenty-sixth, probably not helped by the time trial the previous day. Finishing out of the scoring three meant no team medal for him.

Young Bob Crawford, who had been born in Belfast before his parents emigrated to the USA, found the going tough and was fortieth of the forty-two finishers.

Mr Mussabini came over to offer his congratulations. "Well run, Hegarty. I like an athlete who can take advice," he said. "In fact, if it had been the correct distance, 10 kilometres instead of 8, I think you might have taken an individual medal."

In the heat of battle, I had not realised that the race was 2 kilometres less than I had anticipated. I thanked Mr Mussabini for all his assistance and encouragement."

"A pleasure, young man," he replied. "You were truly a lion today."

As he turned and went off, he lit one of his little, dark cigarettes. The aroma of the tobacco immediately took me to a place and time I had almost forgotten, a place and time I had buried in the recesses of my memory: Gallipoli and the waft of cigarette smoke coming over on the evening air from the Turkish trenches.

I had to be a cheetah to survive there, but today in Antwerp I was a lion. Mr Mussabini said so!

CHAPTER 18

LIVE HAPPILY EVER AFTER

A book may be compared to your neighbour:
if it be good, it cannot last too long; if
bad, you cannot get rid of it too early.

— Rupert Brooke

There was no official welcome or anything to greet Anton when he got back to Rugby. That did bother him when he saw Gertie waiting at the end of the platform, wrapped up well against a cold wind that heralded the oncoming autumn. "No bugles. No drums," she said. "Just me." And that was all he wanted or expected.

Two months later, they were gathered at St Matthews Church of England, where they married almost six years after they had first met by chance at the Middletons' house.

Gertie's sister and brother-in-law were the witnesses, and they went back to the Raglan Inn for a little reception afterwards. Nobody came over from Derry for the occasion. They may have still been smarting from Anton's unannounced departure earlier in the year, or maybe they just did not like him getting married in a Protestant church.

The year following the Olympics, Anton came over to the Irish Cross-Country Championships but failed to finish, citing stomach problems. Nevertheless, given he was an Olympic silver medallist, the Irish selectors included him in the team for the International, to be held on that year at Caerleon in Wales. His best form deserted him once again as he finished back in twenty-eighth and didn't make the Irish scoring six. Wally Freeman, who had only finished twenty-second in Antwerp, was the individual winner, with Chris Vose fourth, Tim Crowe sixth, and Larry Cummins seventh.

Later in the year, Anton and Gertie were able to make their first trip together to Derry in June 1921. During their stay, he took up the challenge to race against a fast-trotting pony, owned by Peter McLernon of Donaghmore, County Tyrone, during the agricultural show at the Brandywell. Anton was to run sixteen laps (4 miles), while the pony's distance was twenty laps (5 miles). Despite failing by half a lap, he was given a standing ovation by the large crowd.

He continued to run competitively until well into his 30s, finishing twentieth in the 1926 English National, but never recaptured the form he showed in Antwerp. During this time, he also played football, captaining his team to the Rugby & District Division Two title in 1923.

After his retirement from athletics, he became involved in the organisation of British Thomson-Houston Athletics

Club (now Rugby & Northampton AC) and qualified as a football referee.

He and Gertie had three children: Henry John, Alec David, and Margaret Izabelle. Their grandchildren still live in the Rugby area.

CHAPTER 19

THE TRAGIC EVENING

The boast of heraldry, the pomp of pow'r,
And all that beauty, all that
wealth e'er gave,
Awaits alike th' inevitable hour.

—*Thomas Gray, "Elegy in a Country Churchyard"*

On 9 August 1944, on the Western Front, the Canadian Second Corps continued attacking along the Caen-Falaise Road, while the American forces were under fire from the Germans at Mortain. The US Fifteenth Corps had turned north from Le Mans, aiming for Argentan and eventually a junction with the Canadian advance southward between Argentan and Falaise. Allied fight-bombers were active throughout the day.

A few days earlier, following a tip-off from a Dutch informer, the Gestapo had searched a warehouse in a sealed-off area of Amsterdam. There, they found the young diarist Anne Frank and her family, who had been hiding for over two years in rooms at the office building of her father, Otto

Frank. The family was transported to concentration camps. Anne and her sister Margot eventually ended up in the notorious Bergen-Belsen, where they both died of typhus.

In the quiet Midlands town of Rugby, the Normandy front probably seemed a long way away from the daily tedium of wartime Britain. Leslie Ernest Radmall, an only son, had just married Marjorie Stoppard, the eldest daughter of Mr and Mrs Vernon Stoppard in nearby Northampton. Mrs Lockyer had been ordered to pay eight shillings and sixpence (approximately 43 pence) costs after her dog had bitten her neighbour Mrs Eaton. It seems that Mrs Lockyer's dog was a serial offender in that she had received a caution twelve months earlier from the local constabulary after a similar incident.

The strict wartime regulations were also being enforced zealously by the local police, and Frederick Dye was summoned for displaying an unscreened light at 12.30 a.m. In his defence, Dye said he must have inadvertently hit the switch when carrying his baby upstairs and did not notice the light was on because it was still daylight. He was fined £2, a hefty amount at the time.

There was much commotion at the military establishments around Rugby, with nightly bombing raids on German forces in France being carried out from local air force bases. Canadian and American forces were based in the area, bolstering the British war effort, although their presence was not always to the pleasing of the populace in Rugby.

A number of Canadians had recently been in court for breaking windows in the town centre after a night on the

MALCOLM MCCAUSLAND

town, while the Americans were frequently in altercations with the younger local males. There was a heavier security presence in place, with the king and queen expected to visit the Canadian Air Force squadron based at a local airbase.

Company Sergeant Major Frank Taylor was making his way home from meeting with an eminent orthopaedic surgeon at Harley Street in London. The train back to Birmingham New Street had been delayed, meaning he was now in a rush to get home while there was still light and before the blackout at 10.30 p.m.

The diagnosis he had been given was not what he had hoped for, and the prognosis was no better. Although only 28, it seemed that the cartilage in his left knee was beyond repair. Although he had played for England against Scotland in a wartime unofficial international just a month earlier, it looked like his career as a footballer may be soon over.

He had difficulty turning on the pitch, and frequently his knee locked in just ordinary circumstances like descending the stairs at home. He had come down from his native Yorkshire to play for the mighty Wolverhampton Wanderers at just 16, following in the footsteps of his brother Jack, who was a first team regular.

Frank had made his debut the following year, when Jack was transferred to Norwich City, taking his place as full back. He was in the Wolves team that lost 1–4 to Portsmouth at Wembley in the 1939 FA Cup Final, but it now looked like his playing career could be at a premature end. Only the hope of getting a job somewhere in management lifted the dark cloud that had been hanging over him since he heard the bad news earlier that day.

Figure 9: Oliver Street in Rugby as it is today. Anton would have descended this street and been found prostrate in the middle of the road approximately where the right-turn arrow is painted today. Photo: MMcC

He had by now reached Rugby, and there was still enough light to get him the short distance to his home in Tower Road. Turning off the Newbold Road, he headed down Oliver Street to avoid the town centre and almost immediately spotted a figure lying prostrate in the middle of the road. Two men were attending him. One was cradling the injured man's head in his lap, while the other in khaki was now flagging him down.

Braking urgently, Taylor quickly assessed the situation and had the still motionless body put in the back of the car before driving him to the nearby hospital of St Cross. The medical staff quickly took ownership of the injured man and rushed him through on a stretcher for treatment.

Taylor made the short journey onwards to his home, where he related the events of the day to his wife. The concern with her husband's sporting career overshadowed the injured man in the street, and they discussed what the future might hold for them without football and the end of the war now possibly in sight.

It had not been the best of days for them, but it was even worse for Gertie Turland, who was watching by her front door at Union Street, waiting and wondering what had happened to her husband.

He had gone out on his bicycle at 8.15 p.m., but it was now 11 p.m. and he was usually home by 10 p.m. at the latest. It was then that a police constable came around the corner on foot.

"Mrs Hegarty?" he asked.

"I'm sorry. I've bad news for you." He hesitated.

"What sort of bad news?" Gertie interjected before the young policemen could finish what he was saying.

"There's been an accident. Your husband is in the hospital. It appears that he fell off his bike, but we're still making enquiries. He was still unconscious the last I heard."

Gertie grabbed a cardigan. She told her sons, John and Alec, and their younger sister, Maggie, what had happened. John volunteered to go to the hospital, and they both set off on foot to make the ten-minute journey down the Barby Road to the hospital.

It was Friday and Frank Taylor was not working until the afternoon. They had slept late, and he picked up the *Rugby Advertiser* newspaper, which had come through the letterbox, as he passed the front door. He had not given any thought to the accident he had come across almost two days earlier, but opening the paper, as his wife poured him a cup of tea, his attention immediately fell on a story on the front page.

> *"Dying Man in Road*
> *Oliver Street Discovery*
>
> *51-years old Rugby milling engineer, Anthony Hegarty, 52 Union Street, was found lying injured near his bicycle in Oliver Street, Rugby, about 150 yards from the junction with Newbold Road, opposite the footpath leading into Round's allotments, at 10:15 p.m. on Wednesday night, and died in the Hospital of St Cross yesterday morning. He was admitted suffering from head injuries and concussion.*
>
> *Rugby police are anxious to trace the military vehicle which conveyed the injured man to hospital, and also a civilian who is believed to have found Hegarty in the street. They would welcome any information which can be given concerning the accident."*

MALCOLM MCCAUSLAND

After breakfast, Taylor reported to the police station, where he made a statement and signed a number of autographs for the sons of a number of the policemen. He was asked to attend the inquest the following morning.

The police officers said that they all desired a prompt return to normality, which included Saturday afternoon football. Although most were Aston Villa fans, they had asked for autographs for their sons and wished Taylor a speedy return to action for the mighty Wolves. He mentioned nothing about the prognosis and merely thanked them for their kind wishes.

He recalled what Karl Marx had said about religion being the "opium of the masses," but he thought it could have equally been applied to football, which drew huge crowds every weekend. Football in Britain had long been the escape for the urban working class from the mundane existence of long hours, poor working conditions, and low pay.

Taylor was given time off from duty the next day to be present at the inquest, where the coroner, Dr H.S. Tibbits, was presiding. The newly widowed Gertie Hegarty was the first to give evidence, outlining how she had become anxious when her husband did not return by his normal time.

She said, on being informed of his being in St Cross's, that she and her son John had rushed to her unconscious husband's side, where she had remained until he was declared dead at 9.30 a.m. on Thursday morning.

Police War Reserve Drinkwater said he had made enquiries about the circumstances of the accident. He read from his notebook, "On arriving at the scene I found a pool of blood almost in the exact centre of the road and 147 yards from the junction with Newbold Road.

"Hegarty's bike was standing up against the fence, having been moved there by the time I arrived. There were a few scratches on it and the saddle had been knocked a little out of position.

"A possible cause of the accident may have been the very fierce front brake. I traced Hegarty's movements that evening from leaving his home to the Co-Operative Club on Bilton Road. He had gone on from there at about 9 p.m., before visiting the Avon Mill Inn, which he left at about 10 p.m.

"He had walked up the steep incline of Newbold Road before mounting his bike to cycle down Oliver Street and onwards toward home. I have been unable to find anyone who had actually witnessed the accident, but I observed the gradient on Oliver Street was steep where the fall had occurred and any sharp touch of the front brakes could have precipitated a nasty accident."

Charles William Hoy of 14 Newbold Road also testified that he had been standing at the door of his house when Anton went by pushing his bike and talking to a woman. Hoy said that he did not know the woman but Anton and her were engaged in casual conversation. Hoy reckoned this was about ten o'clock and he recalled that he had greeted Hegarty as he knew him and he had replied, "Goodnight, Bill." That could have been his final words as he then mounted his bicycle and turned down Oliver Street. Hoy

MALCOLM MCCAUSLAND

added that Hegarty had appeared "perfectly normal" and that there had been no traffic about at the time.

Mrs Norah Edith Wilson of 80 Oliver Street said that around 10.25 p.m. she was in the house and heard the crash of someone falling off a bicycle in the street outside. She had looked out through the window but could not see anything, possibly on account of her view of the dip in the road being obscured by a tree outside her house.

Seeing nothing, she had thought no more about it until about five minutes later when she heard the voice of a man shouting to someone to come and give him a hand and then a man calling for a car to stop. She could not recall any other traffic in the road at that time.

Mrs Alice M. Atkins, 3 Seabroke Avenue, gave evidence that on the way down Oliver Street, she saw a dark object in the middle of the road which, at first, she thought to be a dog. On closer inspection, she discovered it was an injured man and two men attending him. One of the men was in khaki, the other holding the injured man's head. He was lying across the road with his head facing the allotments. She continued to point out that others began to arrive soon afterwards, and it was her who found the pair of glasses close to the body of the injured man.

Company Sergeant Major Taylor repeated what he had told the police. That he had come upon the man in the middle of the road with someone attending to him. They had put the body in the back of his car, and he and the other man had taken him to St Cross's Hospital.

LION FOR A DAY

They had parted company when the medical staff took charge and he had gone on home. He said he did not know the other man or where he was from and had never seen him before or after the accident. Taylor confirmed that he had seen no other traffic on the road before arriving at the scene of the accident.

This was borne out by George William Miller of "Frankton," Grange Estate, Newbold-on-Avon, who had been cycling along Oliver Street towards Newbold Road at about 10.30 p.m. when he saw several people attending to an injured man. No vehicles had passed him in either direction, and he only learned details of the accident from a young lady present at the scene when he arrived. What his testimony added to the evidence was unclear.

Dr F.M. Hall, the resident medical officer at the Hospital of St Cross, gave details of the dead man's injuries. Reading from his notes, he said, "Hegarty had a fractured skull and died of cerebral compression due to laceration of the brain, and haemorrhage, due to the fracture of the base of the skull. The injury is consistent with a fall on to his head from a bicycle."

The coroner summarised proceedings when all the evidence had been adduced and testimonies taken. "Nobody actually saw Hegarty fall from his bicycle but from the evidence it is perfectly clear to me that there were no other vehicles in Oliver Street at the time, and the possibility that he might have been knocked down can be ruled out.

"Hegarty might have had to apply his brake, or some minor trouble might have occurred, such as a speed wobble, but I am satisfied that Hegarty fell from his machine and that no other vehicle or person could be blamed for the accident."

Many people close to Anton were unhappy with the outcome of the inquest. They asked why the first two people on the scene, the unnamed man and soldier, had not been summoned to give evidence. They also wondered why WPR Drinkwater had seemingly made no effort to interview them at the scene of the accident. They dismissed the theory about the front brake as they knew Anton always kept his bike in tip-top running order. Besides, an injury on the back of the head, as Anton had suffered, was not consistent with someone going over the handlebars of a bike through braking too rashly.

Their dissatisfaction was heightened with rumours emanating from several residents of Oliver Street saying that a lorry had descended the street at a high speed shortly before Anton had been discovered in the middle of the road by the passer-by.

Others further down Oliver Street had seen a lorry with Canadian airmen heading in great haste towards Church Lawford runway around that time, adding that an increasing volume of military traffic was using the route to avoid the town centre.

These rumours only surfaced after the inquest, and when a few of Anton's workmates brought them to the attention of the police, enquiries were initiated. The police quickly established that indeed Canadian Air Force crews did frequently use Oliver Street but that particular night only one crew had been involved in the bombing operation over France. Unfortunately, they had not been able to interview the airmen in question as they had failed to return from the mission, presumed shot down over Brittany.

This did nothing to allay the fear of Anton's family and friends that the inquest had only been perfunctory at best, a "whitewash" at best. They pointed to other fatalities in the Rugby area, where cyclists had been killed in the previous few weeks in similar circumstances. In the first of these, Walter Fountain of 17 Worcester Street had decided to go fishing in the canal near the Avon Mill Inn, which Anton had visited on what was to prove to be his final evening.

Cycling down Newbold Road, he had seen a lorry with a trailer in tow approaching from behind. As the road narrowed to go under the railway bridge at this point, he pulled into the side to allow it to pass but was still struck by the trailer and ended up thrown on the grass verge.

His wife was sent for and she arrived promptly to hear directly from Mr Fountain what had happened. His account was corroborated by John Thomas Watson, who lived farther up Newbold Road, who also pointed out that the trailer was veering slightly from side to side when it passed him.

Mr Fountain died the next morning at the Hospital of St Cross during an operation necessitated by the accident. He had a broken pelvis and internal injuries.

Bernard John Watson of the Rectory, Churchover, was passing and stopped. When he heard Mr Fountain's account

MALCOLM MCCAUSLAND

of what had happened, he set off in pursuit of the lorry that had failed to stop. Mr Watson caught the vehicle and got it to pull into the side of the road.

He told the driver what had happened and advised him to report the accident at Lutterworth, about 7 miles from the scene of the accident. In the meantime, the police had issued a description of the lorry, and it was stopped some time later at Barby, in the complete opposite direction to Lutterworth out of Rugby.

In court, the driver, Sidney Walter Lewis of 72 Leicester Road in Syston, gave evidence that he was unaware of his vehicle striking Mr Fountain. He said he would have reported the accident at Lutterworth but passed through when he realised the police station was not on the main road.

He did not explain why he was proceeding in the opposite direction when detained by the police. He said it was his intention to report it in Leicester, over 20 miles from the Newbold Road where the accident occurred. His explanations were accepted by the coroner, Dr H.S. Tibbits, who had also conducted Anton's inquest. He returned a verdict of accidental death.

Dr Tibbits was also the coroner at the inquest into the death of Edward Woosey, a 51-year-old Liverpool grocery store manager who was killed on Watling Street near Rugby. Mr Woosey was visiting his in-laws at Lilbourne and was out cycling with his 13-year-old son, Eric, who testified that they met two American forces lorries on a bend. The first of these slowed up and passed them without incident, but the second did not appear to reduce speed and went into a slide, the rear of the vehicle hitting his father.

Mrs Woosey had gone ahead of her husband and son to Rugby, where they were to rendezvous with friends. She was informed of the accident and went immediately to the hospital, where she found her husband only semi-conscious and unable to tell her anything of the accident. He died at 7.30 p.m. as the consequence of a crushing injury to the right of his chest and a punctured lung. He also had a broken right arm.

Charles Edward Smith of the United States Army was the driver of the second lorry. He said he had seen his colleague braking as he approached the bend and, seeing the cyclists, had tried to get as far as possible over to his left-hand side. He had struck the kerb, setting the lorry into a skid eventually he was able to rectify. He did not realise that he had struck anyone until he got out of the vehicle. Dr Tibbits pointed out that there had been an almost identical accident on the same part of the road but found Mr Woosey's death to be accidental.

This did nothing to assuage the grief of Anton's family, and the absence of any obituary in the *Rugby Advertiser* rankled with them, especially given that he was a decorated soldier and an Olympic medallist.

He had also played a significant role in local sport after he retired as a trainer of the British Thomson-Houston Athletics Club, an athletics official, and a football referee. It seemed he was being forgotten already.

Figure 10: The unkempt grave of Anton and his wife Beatrice (Gertie) in the grounds of St. Marie's RC Church, Rugby (October 2019) - Photo: MMcC

EPILOGUE

Philip John Noel-Baker, Baron Noel-Baker: The British team captain and flagbearer at the opening ceremony changed his name by deed poll in 1921, having married Irene Noel at the start of World War I. He went on to be a successful British politician, diplomat, academic, and renowned campaigner for disarmament.

Noel-Baker is the only person to have won an Olympic medal and received a Nobel Prize. He was a Labour MP from 1929 to 1931 and from 1936 to 1970, serving in several ministerial offices and the cabinet. He died on 8 October 1992 at the age 92.

Hugh Charles Beasant: He returned to his native Belfast after the shipyard in Derry closed in 1920, died on 20 November 1928 (aged 38), and was buried from his father's home at 28, Allworthy Avenue.

Timothy Crowe: Continued in athletics and finished sixth in the 1921 Polytechnic Marathon, despite going off course and running at least a mile extra. An outstanding Irish step dancer and musician, he also accompanied the Tipperary hurling team to America in 1926 in the role of trainer.

The horse Tipperary Tim that won the 1928 English Grand National was said to be named after him. Even in advanced years, he was known to cycle to Dublin, a round trip of over 220 miles (360 kilometres), for an All-Ireland final. He died on 11 November 1962, aged 79. A cup is presented annually in his name to the first Tipperary finisher in the Dundrum 10-kilometre road race.

Laurence Michael "Larry" Cummins: His career as an athlete continued long after the Olympics. He ran in the International Cross-Country three more times—1921, 1922, and 1927—and was the first Irishman home, in fifth place, in 1921. He later became a stud manager and owned and bred many greyhounds, including Kinsale, named after his hometown in Ireland.

He also became a boxing judge in 1938 and two years later was appointed a referee. He was chairman of St Gregory's Boxing Club in Cheltenham and served on the committee of the Gloucester County AAA in the 1930s before becoming chairman in 1945. Also, as a journalist, he contributed sports articles to the *Gloucestershire Echo*. He died in Cheltenham on 16 March 1954, aged 64.

Patrick (Patsy) Flynn: He continued to run following his return from Antwerp but appears to have retired from competitive running after 1925. He married Florence in 1924, and they lived in the Upper West Side, Manhattan, in close proximity to US Customs, where he worked as a customs clerk. At the age of 47, he applied for service in World War II, but his application was refused. Patsy Flynn died on 5 January 1969 at the age of 74.

Joseph Guillemot: The Frenchman remained in the sport after the 1920 Olympics. He won three titles in the International Cross-Country Championships: one individual title in 1922 and two with the French team in 1922 and 1926. He won the French 5,000-metre title on three occasions but missed the 1924 Olympics due to disagreements with the French Athletics Union. His career ended in 1926 after the France-Sweden match. He was a heavy smoker, a pack a day, and died of lung cancer on 9 March 1975, aged 75.

Albert George Hill: There was no celebration for Hill on his return from Antwerp. He went immediately back to work as a ticket collector at Tooting underground station in London. Hill had one more year as an athlete after the Olympics, running one of his best races ever to win the 1921 AAA mile title, breaking the British mile record in the process. He then turned his attention to coaching, becoming Sam Mussabini's assistant at Polytechnic Harriers. He would later coach and mentor with Sydney Wooderson, Britain's star middle-distance runner of the 1930s, who set world 880-yard and mile records.

He moved to Canada shortly after World War II with his wife and daughter and died there on 8 January 1969, aged 79. No British athlete would emulate his Olympic 800-metre/1,500-metre double until Kelly Holmes achieved it at Athens in 2004.

Percy Hodges: The Guernsey native continued to win AAA steeplechase titles until 1923. No record has been found of his involvement in the sport after that. He died on 27 December 1967, one day after his seventy-seventh birthday.

Herbert Carmichael (Bertie) Irwin: The Clonliffe Harrier was only named as a reserve for the Great Britain team in Antwerp but was allowed to run in the 5,000-metre when Jimmy Wilson withdrew from the event to concentrate on the 10,000-metre and cross-country races.

He served in the Royal Naval Air Service (later to become the RAF) in World War I. He was the captain of the *R101* airship, which crashed in France on 5 October 1930 during its maiden journey to India. He was one of the forty-eight out of the fifty-four on board who died. A cup in his memory was presented to Clonliffe Harriers in 1932 and is still awarded annually to the club's cross-country champion.

Hannes Kolehmainen: He continued to compete after Antwerp but mostly at longer distances, setting several world records. Despite taking out American citizenship in 1921, he returned to Finland shortly afterwards. Kolehmainen ran no marathons between 1920 and 1924 but convinced the Finnish selectors to include him in their team for Paris in 1924, although he did not finish the race. He ran one more marathon in 1928 when he entered the Finnish Olympic trial but again failed to finish. It was his last competition. He worked in various jobs back in Finland, and along with Paavo Nurmi, lit the cauldron at the 1952 Olympics. He died in Helsinki in 1966 aged 76. He is remembered to this day as Smiling Hannes, the first of the Flying Finns.

Keith Murdoch: After exposing the shambles of the military offensive in Gallipoli, Murdoch remained for a while in London working as a journalist. However, he returned to Australia in January 1921 to assume the role of editor at the *Melbourne Herald,* focusing on political controversy. Later he became managing director of the company. He married debutante Elisabeth Joy Greene in 1927 and they had three children together, including Rupert (born 1931), who would become a world-renowned media magnate.

Scipio Africanus (Sam) Mussabini: A coach years ahead of his time. He was one of the principal characters portrayed in the film *Chariots of Fire* (1981) as coach of Harold Abrahams, who won the 100-metre. He is depicted as having to watch the Games from the attic in a nearby building as he was reputedly not allowed entry to the stadium as he was a professional. In 1998, the Mussabini Medal was introduced to mark his contribution to coaching. He died on 12 March 1927, aged 59.

Alfred Hubert Nichols: Little is known of the career of Alfred Nichols after his twelfth place in Antwerp. He died on 1 May 1952, aged 61.

Paavo Johannes Nurmi: The Flying Finn returned to the Olympic stage in Paris in 1924, winning a record five gold medals in the athletics events. He came back again to Amsterdam in 1928, despite suffering from rheumatism and having Achilles tendon problems in the interim. That did not prevent him adding another gold and two silver medals to his already impressive Olympic collection. He had plans to run the marathon at the 1932 Los Angeles Games but was barred from amateur competition for taking what were considered excessive expenses during various tours.

He set multiple world records from 1,500 metres to 20 kilometres. He went on to be a successful businessman in his own country. He made a brief reappearance at the Olympics when he entered the stadium with the flame at the 1952 Games in Helsinki before handing it over to Hannes Kolehmainen. He died on 2 October 1973 at the age of 76. A track and field meeting, the Paavo Nurmi Games, is held annually in Turku to celebrate the life of the most famous of The Flying Finns.

Frank Taylor: He was forced to retire from playing football in 1944. In June 1948, he was appointed manager of Scarborough, before becoming Frank Buckley's assistant at Hull City and holding down a similar role at Leeds United. He took over from long-serving manager Bob

McGrory as Stoke City manager in 1952. He remained in charge at the Victoria Ground until, after a disastrous 1959–60 season, when Stoke City finished seventeenth, he was sacked. Taylor vowed never to work in football again and died in 1970, aged 54.

Chris Vose: There was no medal for Vose in Antwerp as he was not among the three scoring Britons. He went to the International Cross-Country in 1921 and finished fourth, helping England to another team victory. He died in Warrington on 12 August 1970, aged 83. A 7.5-mile road race was initiated in his honour in 1961 but was discontinued a few years ago as increased traffic made the traditional route of the race unsafe.

James (Jimmy) Wilson: After the 1920 Olympics, Jimmy Wilson found a job as mechanical engineer at the Neasden Power Station in London. He semi-retired from running but resumed competing in 1923, when he joined Surrey Athletic Club. Jimmy helped Surrey AC to victory in the inaugural ten-stage London to Brighton relay race in 1924 and represented Scotland in the International Cross-Country that year and again in 1925. A lifelong bachelor, he died in 1973, aged 81.

BIBLIOGRAPHY

Acorns and Oak Leaves – Charles Gallagher 8898

A History of Ulster – Jonathan Bardon (1992)

A Shorter Illustrated History of Ulster – Jonathan Bardon (1996)

Empire – Jeremy Paxman (2012)

Forging the Border – Okan Ozseker (2019)

Gallipoli – Alan Moorehead (1956)

Gold, Silver and Green – Kevin McCarthy (2010)

History of NI Marathon Running – John T Glover

India – John Keay (2000)

Inglorious Empire – Shashi Tharoor (2018)

Irish Championship Athletics 1873-1914 – Tony O'Donoghue

Old Soldier Sahib – Frank Richards

Sahib -Richard Holmes (2005)

Siege City – Brian Lacy (1990)

The Politics of Irish Athletics 1850-1990 – Padraig Griffin (1990)

The Field of Bones – Philip Orr (2006)

The Somme - Sam Sutcliffe (2016)

Lightning Source UK Ltd.
Milton Keynes UK
UKHW011842051020
371066UK00001B/56